On Art, Labor, and Religion

On Art, Labor, and Religion

Ellen Gates Starr

Edited with an introduction by
Mary Jo Deegan and **Ana-Maria Wahl**

Transaction Publishers
New Brunswick (U.S.A.) and London (U.K.)

Library of Congress Catalog Number: 2002073211
ISBN: 0-7658-0143-4
Printed in Canada

Library of Congress Cataloging-in-Publication Data

Starr, Ellen Gates
    On art, labor, and religion / Ellen Gates Starr ; edited with an introduction
by Mary Jo Deegan and Ana-Maria Wahl.
        p. cm.
    Includes bibliographical references and index.
    ISBN 0-7658-0143-4 (alk. paper)
    1. Starr, Ellen Gates—Political and social views.   2. Women social
reformers—United States—Biography.   3. Labor movement—Illinois—Chicago—History.   4. Hull House (Chicago, Ill.)—History.   5. Arts and crafts
movement—Illinois—Chicago—History.   6. Christian life—Catholic authors. I. Deegan, Mary Jo, 1946- II. Wahl, Ana-Maria. III. Title.

HQ1413.S674 A3 2002
361.92--dc21
[B]   2002073211

Contents

Part 3: Religion

List of Charts and Tables

Preface

Ellen Gates Starr is delightfully unique and a long-neglected, important figure in Chicago, the nation, and around the world. Many people helped recover her work. Robert J. Hohl, M.L.S. of St. Mary's College, Cushwa-Leighton Library, generously shared the resources of his library and personal papers on Eliza Allen Starr, and his support is greatly appreciated. Similarly, Smith College Archives, Sophia Smith Collection, Kathleen Nutter; Rockford College Archives; the University of Illinois at Chicago, University Library, Department of Special Collections, Jane Addams Memorial Collection, Mary Ann Bamberger; and the University of Notre Dame, Archives, Hezburgh Library, Eliza Allen Starr Papers. Our thanks to the good people at Transaction Publishers; especially Irving Louis Horowitz, colleague extraordinaire and President of Transaction Publishers, and Laurence Mintz, our extremely helpful and patient editor. Lori Ratzlaff aided in the preparation of the manuscript and designed the charts. Michael R. Hill has been invaluable as an archival researcher and photographer, hunting up manuscripts and scanning them into the computer, as well as supporting this project. Steven Gunkel also provided much appreciated intellectual support and editorial assistance.

Introduction
Ellen Gates Starr and Her Journey toward Social Justice and Beauty

Chicago was tumultuous and exciting in 1889: Immigration, industrialization, urbanization, and politics created a vortex of change. This lively chaos called out for reform and celebration, and two women, Ellen Gates Starr and Jane Addams, responded to this challenge by founding the social settlement Hull-House (Addams 1910; see chapters 2, 3, 4, and 20 here). Addams has become world famous as a Nobel Laureate,[1] but Starr remains virtually unknown. In this anthology Starr's writings and biography are introduced for the first time as a contribution to national and international sociological thought and practice.

Although Addams is perhaps the most famous woman in American history and a major figure in American sociology (Deegan 1988), Starr was a remarkable figure in her own right. In addition to co-founding the now famous Hull-House, Starr actively brought the British Arts and Crafts movement to Chicago through extensive and intensive relations with this group of artisans, theorists, socialists, and proto-sociologists. Her professional connection with them began in 1888 when she visited the social settlement Toynbee Hall in London (Addams 1910) and met Charles Ashbee (1894, 1901), a leading artist and social theorist of this movement. In 1891 Starr returned to England for more study and to meet with representatives of this group, especially T.C. Horsfall of Manchester, England (see chapters 1 and 5 here); and in 1898 she studied in England for fifteen months under the tutelage of T.J. Cobdon-Sanderson, then the greatest bookbinder in the world (see chapter 6 here), and a leading figure in the British Association of Arts and Crafts (BAAC).

Starr soon gained renown as one of the greatest female bookbinders in the world (see chapters 6-11), a major occupation for women in the arts at that time (D. Davis 1900; Way 1897, 1898). She founded a number of important art societies, often based on her connection with the BAAC, as well. Thus in 1894 she established the Chicago Public School Art Society (CPSAS) modeled on Horsfall's work, and in 1897 she founded the Chicago Arts and Crafts Society (CACS). This latter group emerged from the ideals and practices of the BAAC (Addams 1895a) and became one of the most important of such

1

groups in the United States (Darling 1977). Starr linked this work to her commitment to Fabian sociology, socialism and the establishment of women's labor unions. She was particularly active in the Women's Bookbinders' Union (WBU) and the Women's Trade Union League both nationally (NWTUL) and in Chicago (CWTUL). During this process, she befriended powerful labor leaders: Catherine Breshovsky, the "Little Mother" of Russia; Mary Kenney [O'Sullivan] [Kenney (O'Sullivan 1990)], first of the WBU and later of the Amalgamated Garment Workers of America (AGWA); and Sidney Hillman (Matthew 1952), President of the AGWA. She also worked with Charles Zueblin, the Chicago and Fabian sociologist (Deegan 1988); Rho Fisk Zueblin (1902a, 1903a, 1904), his wife and popularizer of the Arts and Crafts movement; and Vida Scudder (1937), Fabian socialist, social settlement leader, and religious figure.

Although Starr supported women's labor unions by the early 1890s, she became a more visible socialist and advocate of striking workers after 1910. In 1915 and 1916, in particular, Starr gained national notoriety and became popularly known as Chicago's "Angel of the Strikers" (e.g., "One Dead, Three Hurt," 1915) due to her vociferous defense of young female garment workers (see chapters 12 to 19 here). Starr was arrested on several occasions in 1915 and 1916 and her trials made headlines in Chicago newspapers. As she gained public support, her appearance on the picket line helped secure greater safety for many strikers.

Finally, Starr was a deeply religious woman who restlessly struggled with the meaning of her life from at least 1877, during her one year in college, until her conversion to Roman Catholicism in 1920 when she left Hull-House to journey down a more private path to God. In 1928 she entered the Benedictine religious order and remained there until her death in 1940 (see chapters 21-24 here).

Through her writings and praxis, Starr connected her life at Hull-House with the arts, socialism, and religion. In addition, her essays make a distinct contribution to our knowledge about early sociology and the social settlement. Between 1889 and 1920 Starr's life revolved around the social settlement and she made her major organizational and intellectual contributions during these years. We begin this introduction with Starr's biography and her work at Hull-House. Next, we discuss the intellectual and political underpinnings of her settlement work and writing, specifically the importance of the arts and crafts movement and labor struggles. Finally, we briefly analyze her writings after 1920 which revolved around Roman Catholicism and prayer.

The Journey Begins (1859-1877)

Ellen Gates Starr was born on 19 March 1859 into a modest farm family in "downstate" or southern Illinois, at Laona. Her father Caleb Allen Starr and her mother Susan Gates were descended from eminent families in New England (see chapters 21 and 22 here), but they scrambled for a living on what was then the western frontier.[2] They had four children, and Ellen became especially close to her sister Mary (see Mary Balisdell correspondence in the "Starr Papers," Sophia Smith Collection, Smith College). They raised their children in a very loosely structured Unitarianism that left Ellen spiritually dissatisfied. She attended a one-room schoolhouse as a child and learned home crafts from her grandmother. Her father was a member of the Grange, a co-operative farmer's political and economic alliance, and he taught her about democracy, equality, and neighborliness (Bosch 1993, 77).

The Allen branch of the family settled in Deerfield, Massachusetts in the mid-1800s and two of Ellen's cousins gained fame here as handicraft workers, echoing their cousin's interests in Chicago (Boris 1986).

Eliza Allen Starr (1824-1901)

In many ways, Ellen's aunt, Eliza Allen (E.A.) Starr, figures more prominently in Ellen's biography than her parents do (see chapter 21 here). E.A. Starr was a leader in the arts in Chicago where she helped to found the world-renown Art Institute of Chicago (AIC) (Horowitz 1989). She also created the Art Department at St. Mary's College, the "sister" institution to the then male-only University of Notre Dame, in South Bend Indiana. E.A. Starr was a well-known literary figure, as well, and wrote several books of poetry, lives of the saints, and essays on liturgy (see Byrne 1971). She was surrounded by a network of scholars and powerful friends in Chicago (see her published correspondence in McGovern 1935).

E.A. Starr's greatest influence on her niece was her deeply religious life and youthful conversion to Roman Catholicism. She became a major figure in this denomination in an era when women had strictly limited roles in the church, a singular achievement for any woman but particularly for one outside the religious life. E.A. Starr (1893), for example, was one of a handful of women who addressed the Roman Catholic Congress at the World's Columbian Exhibition in 1893. (She was also honored on this occasion with a Gold Medal for her teaching of art.) Here, she summarized women's erudition in the Church for almost 2000 years, a topic still popular with feminists today. In 1885 she received the Laetare medal conferred by the University of Notre Dame, and Pope Leo XIII later awarded her with a cameo medallion for her literary works. E.A. Starr was a strong emotional, intellectual, and familial model for her niece.

Boarding School Ideals and Friendships
at Rockford College Seminary (1877)

With help from her aunt, Starr was admitted to Rockford Seminary in 1877. Starr's parents could afford to send her to college for only one year, however, and she turned this into a rich experience. Here she befriended Addams (1910) who eloquently described this pioneer academy for women as a time of "boarding school ideals and friendships" where intense ties and values were developed. This epitomizes Starr's life-changing year.

Teaching School, Developing Friendships, and European Travel (1878-1889)

After Starr left Rockford Seminary, she and Addams continued a deeply philosophical exploration of themselves and the meaning of life. Starr was searching restlessly for religious meaning while Addams was rejecting this path but uncertain about the alternate ways to be fully alive and involved in society beyond her "family claim" (Addams 1893, 1910).

Starr began teaching at Miss Kirkland's School for Girls in 1879, an educational setting for elite young women in Chicago. Starr offered instruction in English literature here and made important contacts with Chicago's philanthropic and cultural elites. In 1884 she joined a "low" Episcopal church, and a few years later she encountered the Reverend James O.S. Huntington and joined a "high" Episcopal church. Starr then entered the Anglican Order of the Holy Cross, a lay religious group founded by Huntington that stressed daily prayer and an active commitment to others. Starr and Huntington developed a prodigious correspondence and a deep friendship that supported her religious quest, commitment to arts and crafts, and deep alliance with the poor and working class.[3]

During these years Starr avidly read the aesthetic and social theories of Thomas Carlyle, John Ruskin, and William Morris. These men became central figures in the BAAC and in Starr's work prior to 1920. Their unified commitment to work, art, and community inspired her for decades and led to one of the most active American expressions of the Arts and Crafts movement. Starr explored these interests and her spiritual quests with Addams in numerous letters between 1878 and 1887.

Starr taught at Miss Kirkland's for a decade until she set out on her groundbreaking tour of Europe in 1888, accompanied and funded by her wealthier friend, Addams.

Starr's First Conversion Experience (1888-1889): Toynbee Hall and Arts and Crafts

Both Starr and Addams had highly emotional, life-changing experiences on their European tour. Addams' conversion experience became famous through her eloquent autobiography. Starr's equally profound conversion experience on this same trip remains virtually unknown and highlights their similarities and differences: Addams became a pacifist while Starr became more passionately religious and committed to arts and crafts. Driven by these distinct yet complementary conversion experiences, both were inspired while in Europe to found Hull-House.

Addams' conversion occurred when she witnessed a bullfight in Spain. At first she reveled in its pageantry and drama but later she recoiled in horror at her heightened response to blood and death. This experience became the turning point that led Addams to found Hull-House: "Nothing less than the moral reaction following the experience at a bullfight had been able to reveal to me that so far from following in the wake of a chariot of philanthropic fire, I had been tied to the tail of the veriest ox-cart of self-seeking" (Addams 1910, 86). Her European adventure had initially appeared to be a conduit to a wider world, but after the bullfight her travel seemed wasteful and self-indulgent. The next day she began to plan with Starr how to turn her insight into a concrete program of action.

Starr's life-changing event occurred after the two friends visited Toynbee Hall in 1888 and 1889. This was an experiment in social justice sponsored by the Church of England and Oxford University and located in a poor district of London. Toynbee Hall articulated and led religiously inspired, radical activities in support of unionized labor. Addams and Starr modeled their social settlement, Hull-House, after Toynbee Hall but for Addams this soon became a secular center for teeming life, urban change, and democracy. She thrived in battles over labor legislation, intellectual debate, and the "subjective and objective necessity" (Addams 1893) for her work. Addams (1932, 123-41) was most impressed by its head, Canon Samuel Barnett, but she reflected that "In those early years at Hull-House, we were, however, in no danger of losing ourselves in mazes of speculation or mysticism" (Addams 1910, 116). Addams' description of Toynbee Hall and Hull-House starkly contrasts with Starr's ideal social settlement.

Starr envisioned social settlement work as a religious act that sought for harmony through art, community, and labor. Addams, however, quickly directed Hull-House down her brilliant but very different path. Starr offers a thorough statement of her religiously based ideas in 1896 (see chapter 20 here), only four years after Addams (1893) formulated her ground-shaking appraisal of her subjective and objective needs as a good neighbor.

Starr's visit to Toynbee Hall was equally as important as Addams' was, but they were drawn to different people and ideas there. Thus Canon Barnett impressed Addams and Charles Ashbee impressed Starr. Ashbee sponsored a workshop at Toynbee Hall following the model advocated by John Ruskin, who had helped create the original settlement (R. Zueblin 1902a, b), and William Morris. Ashbee became an important figure in the BAAC which was grounded in the naturalistic and idealistic work and writings of Ruskin and Morris, the works that Addams and Starr had been reading since their college days together. Ashbee impressed both women, but especially Starr.

In addition, Addams and Starr contacted other artists in the BAAC, and their social movement deeply affected both women. These aesthetic and social theorists in Britain stressed the need for a unitary life of meaningful work that was aesthetically expressive and in harmony with nature and the community. Ashbee was a major figure in the BAAC for decades, and in 1900 he lived at Hull-House when he lectured and taught in Chicago for a few weeks. In addition to speeches and demonstrations at Hull House, Ashbee presented several lectures at the AIC and significantly shaped the arts and crafts movement in that institution (Darling 1977).

Starr's Life at Hull-House and the Fabians:
Sociology, Socialism, and Urban Politics

The two friends also learned about the work of Charles Booth on this English journey. He was preparing then the multi-volume *The Life and Labour of the People of London* (beginning with publications in 1891 and continuing until 1902). Booth profoundly influenced their work, too, and they modeled their sociological classic *Hull-House Maps and Papers* (1895) on Booth's project (discussed in more detail later).

Simultaneously they met people who became significant leaders in the Fabian movement. This movement was committed to empiricism, systematic data collection, and political and popular interpretation of their findings. Some Fabians became sociologists, others playwrights, others politicians, and still others were part of the earlier arts and crafts movement. Morris was one of the people to substantially link both the arts and crafts movement and the Fabian sociologists (Goldman 1999; Harris 1999) who believed in the efficacy of social scientific data to influence social justice and the nation state. Patrick Geddes (1972; C. Zueblin 1899), the Scottish sociologist, was another person who merged both the arts and Fabian sociology. Geddes was considerably younger than Ruskin and Morris, however, so Geddes' influence on sociology and the Fabians continued until his death in 1932. Geddes' far-ranging intellect and leadership did not characterize all Fabian sociologists, however. Thus many Fabian sociologists, such as Beatrice and Sydney Webb, were not closely aligned with this earlier, aesthetic social movement and emphasized social policy and the statistical documentation of social issues.[4] Between 1889 and 1910, Starr became aligned more and more with the BAAC and their particular view of Fabian sociology and Addams became aligned more and more with the Fabian sociologists who stressed empirical social science and the welfare state.

These British alliances mimicked the compatibility yet differences between the two social movements that were echoed in the lives of Starr and Addams. This was not a dichotomous choice, but it reflected different emphases within one approach (e.g., see articles on the BAAC in the Fabian-controlled London Sociological Society between 1906 and 1911, especially those by J.A. Hobson, the Webbs, and Geddes). The frequent visits between Fabian sociologists and Hull House residents from 1892 to 1915 are noted in Chart 1.

Other Fabians, moreover, were less identified with sociology, but strongly embedded in the arts, especially the noted literary figures H.G. Wells and George Bernard Shaw. Addams and other Hull-House residents were drawn to the theater and often performed and staged Fabian plays written by both artists (see schedules in *Hull-House Yearbook, 1907-1935*). These performances were intrinsic to their major role in the Little Theater movement. Hull House became the national leader in "sociological theater" that was based in communities and celebrated cultural pluralism. They specialized in producing plays that promoted political action and ideas (MacKay 1917, 115-19). Fabian politicians and labor leaders, allied with the Fabian movement in sociology and the arts, also frequented Hull-House. Their ideas on urban policy, politics, and the welfare state influenced Addams and Starr as well as Charles Zueblin (e.g., 1902, 1905). These leaders and their association with Hull-House are noted in Chart 2.

After Starr's London visits in 1888 and 1889, she devoted her life to the arts and crafts movement until approximately 1916. Addams, meanwhile, saw this as only one of many interesting social practices. Starr's conversion experience at Toynbee Hall inspired her to live the ideas of Morris and Ruskin at Hull-House. For Starr, this also involved daily prayer and good deeds. Thus Starr combined the arts and practices espoused by Ruskin and Morris and their followers with the daily religious commitments developed for religious, Episcopalian women by Huntington. She was also influenced by sociology's unique development in Chicago after 1892, a topic we return to later in this introduction. Here, we continue her biographical account.

During the first years at Hull-House, Starr tried to support herself through paid lectures, tutoring, and her art work, but this generated insufficient funds for her full-time dedication to the neighborhood, laborers, union organizing, and her craft. Mary Wilmarth, whose husband was president of Chicago's Stock Exchange and owned the property on which the Congress Hotel was built, paid Starr an income to free her from financial constraints. Wilmarth's great wealth, therefore, enabled Starr to work full-time on her own interests and for the benefit of others.[5]

A sign of Starr's financial difficulties was her unusual dress, which also revealed a deeper uniqueness that set her apart from Addams in addition to other women.

Starr's Presentation of Self

Women's dress and demeanor are vital to their social acceptance, and, in the Victorian era, women's presentation of self and a moral *persona* were

Chart 1
Visits Between Fabian Sociologists and Hull-House

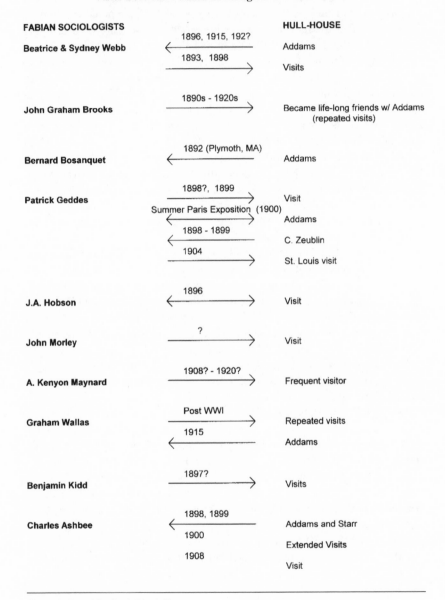

FABIAN SOCIOLOGISTS   HULL-HOUSE

                                1896, 1915, 192?
Beatrice & Sydney Webb   ←—————————————   Addams
                                1893, 1898
                          —————————————→   Visits

                                1890s - 1920s
John Graham Brooks   —————————————→   Became life-long friends w/ Addams
                                                          (repeated visits)

                                1892 (Plymoth, MA)
Bernard Bosanquet   ←—————————————   Addams

                                1898?, 1899
Patrick Geddes   —————————————→   Visit
                          Summer Paris Exposition (1900)
                          ←—————————————   Addams
                                1898 - 1899
                          ←—————————————   C. Zeublin
                                1904
                          —————————————→   St. Louis visit

                                1896
J.A. Hobson   ←—————————————→   Visit

                                ?
John Morley   —————————————→   Visit

                                1908? - 1920?
A. Kenyon Maynard   —————————————→   Frequent visitor

                                Post WWI
Graham Wallas   —————————————→   Repeated visits
                                1915
                          ←—————————————   Addams

                                1897?
Benjamin Kidd   —————————————→   Visits

                                1898, 1899
Charles Ashbee   ←—————————————   Addams and Starr
                                1900
                                                      Extended Visits
                                1908
                                                      Visit

Chart designed by Lori Ratzlaff

Chart 2
Visits Between Bristish and Canadian Fabians and Hull-House Residents

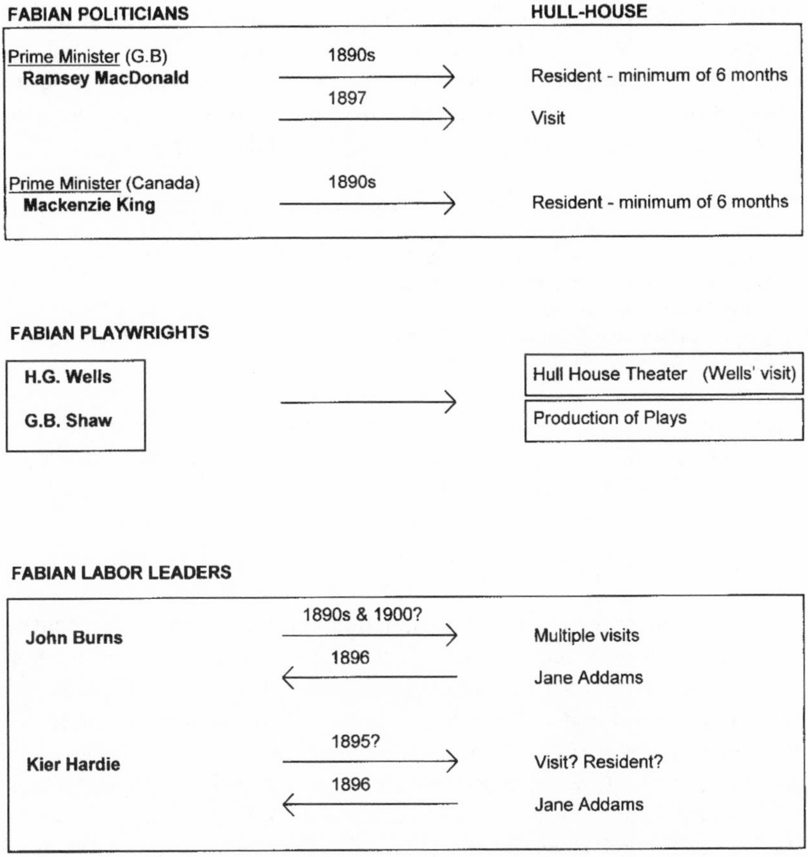

FABIAN POLITICIANS   **HULL-HOUSE**

Prime Minister (G.B)   1890s
 Ramsey MacDonald   ────────────→   Resident - minimum of 6 months
                                       1897
                             ────────────→   Visit

Prime Minister (Canada)   1890s
 Mackenzie King   ────────────→   Resident - minimum of 6 months

FABIAN PLAYWRIGHTS

H.G. Wells   Hull House Theater   (Wells' visit)
                             ────────────→
G.B. Shaw   Production of Plays

FABIAN LABOR LEADERS

                                 1890s & 1900?
John Burns   ────────────→   Multiple visits
                                      1896
                             ←────────────   Jane Addams

                                     1895?
Kier Hardie   ────────────→   Visit? Resident?
                                      1896
                             ←────────────   Jane Addams

Chart designed by Lori Ratzlaff

defined strictly (Gilman 2002; Goffman 1959). Addams, for example, cared little for fashion but she followed its dictates and was personally attractive (see Tolstoy's disgust with her compromises to dress acceptably; Addams 1910, 267-68). By these social standards, Starr's dress was eccentric. For example, Starr dressed only in lavender for a period, a color symbolically associated with mourning and the women's movement at this time, but we are unsure if these were the meanings Starr intended to display. Gioia Diliberto (1999, 167) found her style of clothing distinctly odd and noted,

> For years she wore a fraying raincoat that had belonged to an elderly machinist who frequented Hull-House events. The man, a bachelor named Mr. Dodge, left all his possessions and $3,000 to Ellen when he died—a token of his gratitude for Ellen's help in finding him suitable chess partners.
> Wearing "Mr. Dodge," as Ellen referred to her raincoat, and a small hat with a purple veil streaming out behind her, she strode purposefully through the neighborhood, shocking many with her outspokenness.

Although we understand that such presentations of a female self are subject to gossip and ridicule (Gilman 2002), we find Starr's dress amusing—artistic if you will, and not unattractive.

Starr's Life-Long Friendship with Mary Kenney

Many of the female residents at Hull-House, but especially Starr, consistently approached the problems of the disenfranchised laborer through union activities. In fact, the first female union leader to come to Hull-House was Mary Kenney. Intimidated at first by these college-educated and middle-class women, and particularly by Starr's forbidding demeanor, Kenney soon felt at ease with them and called on them to help organize female laborers. Kenney began the Women's Bookbinding Union (WBU) before she came to Hull-House around 1890, but it grew quickly as a result of the activism of Addams and Starr. They introduced her to British labor sympathizers, offered rooms for their meetings, distributed circulares, and ultimately provided her with a home at the Jane Club. This was a co-operative apartment house sponsored by Hull-House that provided inexpensive lodging for working-class women. Kenney helped establish the club after Addams' paid its first month's rent. Addams and Starr were also members of the residents' club which met weekly to discuss worker's rights.

A host of other women's labor unions organized at Hull-House at this time, too: the Shirt Makers' Union, the Men and Women's Cloak Maker's Union, the Cab Driver's Union, representatives of the Retail Clerk Workers, strike committees for garment workers, and the Clothing Cutters (Kenney [O'Sullivan] 1990, 22). The women in these groups formed alliances with women residents at Hull-House and in women's clubs; engaged in "consciousness raising" (before this term was coined); and organized strikes and protests. One of the most important of these unions was the National Women's Trade Union League (NWTUL). Their strongest branch was in Chicago where they published their national organ, *Life and Labor*.

Kenney left Chicago in 1893 and became an organizer for the AGWA and for the American Federation of Labor (AFL). She soon married Jack O'Sullivan, another labor organizer, and moved to Boston. Both Starr and Addams connected their Chicago experiences with the working class to their earlier roots in English social experiments.

Starr's Life at Hull-House and the Chicago School of Sociology (1892-1920)

The early years at Hull-House were lively and controversial. Anarchists, Marxists, socialists, unionists, and leading social theorists congregated there. As noted above, many of these visitors were Fabian sociologists from England, but the most direct sociological influence came from the University of Chicago and its eminent faculty. Thus the sociologists John Dewey, George Herbert Mead, and W.I. Thomas, among others, were frequent visitors, lecturers and close friends of Addams (Deegan 1988, 1999). Chicago pragmatism was born through their collegial contacts and intellectual exchanges; a dense community that Deegan calls the "world of Chicago pragmatism" flourished including family, friends, social reform, and students (1999, xiii-xxxi). They combined scientific and objective observation with ethical and moral values to generate a just and liberated society based on democracy and education. Addams and Starr shared these assumptions and they were directly linked through the organizations outlined in Chart 3.

These men's interpersonal relations with Starr are less clearly documented than their ties with Addams. Thus Mina Carson (1990) merely notes that Dewey respected Starr. His work in progressive education supported the Arts and Crafts movement in terms of art in the classroom and manual training (see also Dewey and Tufts 1908, 41-42, 45-46), and he was influential in the founding of the Labor Museum at Hull-House (Deegan 1988, 249-53, 282-85, 294). He supported social settlements in general and Hull-House in particular (Deegan 1999). Nonetheless, Dewey was personally and intellectually closer to Addams. Starr developed a similar relationship with Mead. Starr and Mead both fought on behalf of the striking garment workers in 1910 (Deegan 1988, 115-16, 292-93) and again in 1915. In fact, Mead co-authored a pamphlet, a *Brief History of the Clothing Strike in Chicago*, with one of the city's prosecutors and Hull-Hull residents, Harold Ickes (Ickes, Mead, and Tucker 1915). Here the authors summarized the linkages between the different garment workers' strikes and the manufacturers' failure to meet the workers' just demands. Despite Mead's support of the workers, his interactions with Starr

Chart 3
The Hull-House—University of Chicago Sociologists' Connections with the Arts and Crafts Movement

HULL-HOUSE   **UNIVERSITY OF CHICAGO**

CHARLES ZUEBLIN

Hull-House Resident (1890? - 1892) Visited his close friend, Geddes, in Scottland Founded Northwestern University Settlement (1892) Hull-House Maps & Papers (1895) CACS (1897 - 1908) Visited Geddes in Scottland (1898 - 1899) Municipal Museum (1908) Fabian Sociologists Park, Playground & Ecology Activist	University of Chicago Extension Department of Sociology (1892 - 1908)

GEORGE H. MEAD

Hull-House Frequent Visitor (1894 - 1931) Garment Workers Strikes (1910, 1915) Fabian Sociologists (1918) Labor Museum, 1900? Visited Wallas at Hull House Municipal Museum (1908)	University of Chicago Department of Philosophy, Pedagogy, Psychology (Sociologist) (1894 - 1931)

JOHN DEWEY

Hull-House Visitor (1894 - 1935) Hull-House Trustee (1896 - 1904) Labor Museum (1900 - 1904)	University of Chicago Department of Philosophy, Pedagogy Psychology (Sociologist) (1894 - 1904)

GEORGE E. VINCENT

Hull-House Visitor (1890s? - 1908) CACS (1897 - 1908?) Minicipal Museum (1908)	University of Chicago Department of Sociology (1894 - 1911)

Chart designed by Lori Ratzlaff

Chart 4
The Hull-House Labor Museum & The University of Chicago Laboratory Schools Connections

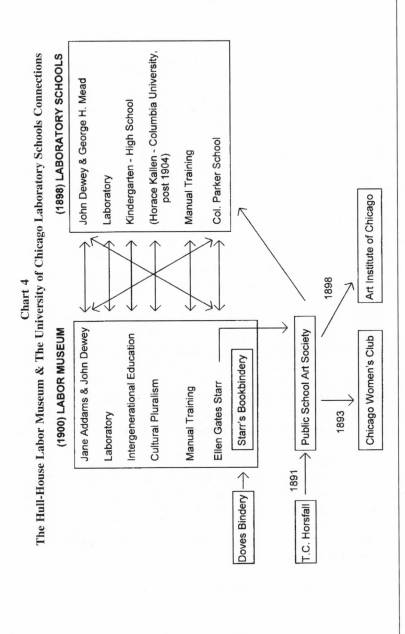

(1898) LABORATORY SCHOOLS

- John Dewey & George H. Mead
- Laboratory
- Kindergarten - High School
- (Horace Kallen - Columbia University, post 1904)
- Manual Training
- Col. Parker School

(1900) LABOR MUSEUM

- Jane Addams & John Dewey
- Laboratory
- Intergenerational Education
- Cultural Pluralism
- Manual Training
- Ellen Gates Starr

Starr's Bookbindery

Doves Bindery →

T.C. Horsfall → 1891 → Public School Art Society

Public School Art Society → 1898 → Art Institute of Chicago

Public School Art Society → 1893 → Chicago Women's Club

Chart designed by Lori Ratzlaff

during these violent labor confrontations remain undocumented. Starr, more-over, was the only sociologist in this group whose theory merged with Angli-can-Catholic beliefs between 1889 and 1920 (Boonin-Vail 1993).[6]

Other Chicago sociologists, notably Charles Henderson, George Vincent, and Charles Zueblin, were members of the CACS (see *The Chicago Arts and Crafts Society*. Catalogue, Exhibit, AIC, March 23-April 15, 1898. Pp. 119-21). This connection is discussed more fully below. Here we emphasize Starr's complex relationship with Charles Zueblin and his wife Rho Fisk Zueblin. Although their interpersonal relationships are also unknown, their organiza-tional ties were vital and multifaceted. Charles Zueblin (1899, 1902, 1905) was an active Fabian sociologist and joined the Extension Department in sociology at the University of Chicago in 1892. Before this, he was a resident at Hull-House and in 1892 he founded Northwestern University Settlement. He attended the first meetings of the CACS and remained active until he left Chicago around 1908 after he was forced to resign his position at the Univer-sity of Chicago (Deegan 1988, 177-78).

Both Zueblins were friends of Patrick Geddes and visited his social settle-ment, the Outlook Tower, in Scotland (C.Zueblin 1899). Rho Fiske Zueblin wrote an exciting series of articles on the Arts and Crafts movement for the *Chautauquan*, the major publication for the group of that name. This adult education movement was founded by Bishop John Vincent, the father of the Chicago sociologist, George Vincent (Deegan 1988, 92-98) and both the father and the son also supported the work of Ruskin and Morris (the support of arts and crafts at Chautauqua is discussed later in more detail). Charles Zueblin's writings on urban planning are ground-breaking and he initiated or followed changes in the modern city. He was politically astute and vocal, a characteristic leading to his forced resignation at the university and leaving Chicago for employment elsewhere. No extensive scholarship on his life exists,[7] and his interpersonal relationship with Starr remains undocumented. Organizationally and intellectually, both Zueblins worked side by side with her.

Zueblin (1895, 91-114) wrote a chapter on the Jewish ghetto in Chicago for *Hull-House Maps and Papers*, and this book's importance to Chicago sociology is explored in the next section. *Hull-House Maps and Papers* intel-lectually unites this alliance and once again brings in Addams.

Hull-House Maps and Papers (1895): Connecting Sociology at Hull-House, the University of Chicago, and in England

Both Addams and Starr were major sociologists with overlapping yet dis-tinct interests and ideas. Addams was a titan with a sweeping mind, personal charisma, and world leadership. She is one of the most important female sociologists who has ever lived. From 1890 to 1935, she was a leader for dozens of women in sociology, although after 1920 most of these women were forced out[8] of sociology and into other fields such as social work, home economics, applied psychology, pedagogy, higher education (especially deans of women), and anthropology. Although Starr was also a major sociologist, unlike Addams she was a strong-minded, dedicated socialist and bookbinder. Religious, ethical, and mystical questions also plagued her and she searched for answers until 1920 when she found a resolution to her drive for a meaningful and satisfying life by converting to Roman Catholicism and removing herself from the profane world. Thus many women in sociology left the field in 1920, but Starr's entry into the convent was a unique and dramatic termination of her ties to sociology.

Between 1892 and 1920 Hull-House became the institutional anchor for women's gender-segregated work in sociology. It served as a liaison with the most important male sociological center during this era, the University of Chicago. Addams' and Starr's ideas and praxis of feminist pragmatism guided their work and that of most women in the profession (Deegan 1978, 1987, 1988, 1991, 1995, 1996a, b, 1997, 1999; Deegan and Rynbrandt 2000).[9] During this time, Hull-House and Addams gained a national and international reputation as a radical, innovative, and successful institution. Oriented towards social change, it articulated an American dream, particularly adapted to bright, educated, Anglo women who wanted a new role in life and society. They found this new work by allying themselves with people of different ethnicities, races, classes, educational training, or family backgrounds. Starr was integral to this project for the first decade, but became increasingly estranged from its goals, personnel, and secular approach until she left the social settlement in 1920.

Hull-House residents published the groundbreaking sociological text, *Hull-House Maps and Papers*, in 1895, based on Booth's earlier volumes. *Hull-House Maps and Papers* predated and established the interests of the early Chicago male sociologists (except for Zueblin who was part of the process) and helped set the agenda for what became known as the Chicago school of sociology (Deegan 1988, 55-69). Starr's analysis of "Art and Labor" (see chapter 4 here) is a vital statement of feminist pragmatist's action and thought. In other words, she seamlessly connected art and work, as did Ruskin and Morris. Unlike them, she employed a more democratic and urban model in response to her life in Chicago.

The Appendix (see chapter 2 here) to the volume described life at Hull-House; named people, clubs, and activities; and depicted some of the buildings. This was based on a pamphlet published in 1893, *Hull-House: A Social Settlement* and co-authored by Starr and Addams (see annotation of pamphlet title page, Addams papers). This seminal pamphlet became the model for their later in-house publications, the *Hull-House Bulletin (1897-1910)* and the *Hull-House Yearbook (1913-1935)*.

Between 1892 and 1920, Starr developed and deepened her commitment to the arts and crafts movement and the ideas of Ruskin, Morris, Addams, the Fabians, and Chicago sociologists. These ideas greatly shaped her work and writing during this period, as discussed further below. In 1920, however, Starr's world turned topsy-turvy as she made a drastic break with her Hull-House network and life. Starr had grown increasingly suspicious about the impact of her work and ideas. After thirty-one years of unceasing labor in an organization that was praised world wide, Starr was restless and disappointed. Capitalism and its exploitation of labor flourished and her hand-bound and acclaimed book-bindings were too expensive for the poor to buy or enjoy. She weighed the pros and cons of Protestant beliefs against those of Roman Catholics and took the plunge: she became a Roman Catholic (see chapter 22 here). At sixty years of age, Starr, an elderly woman by 1920 standards, had a new conversion experience and threw off her old life to embrace a new one.

Conversion to Roman Catholicism and Life in a Convent (1920-1940)

As Max Weber (1976/1920) so persuasively explained, Roman Catholics are "other worldly" while Protestants are "this worldly." Starr became as most "other worldly" as possible for a woman in the Roman Catholic church in direct opposition to the "this worldly" commitment of Hull-House. Prayer, not good deeds or the Protestant ethic, became Starr's chosen path for harmony and community. Withdrawal from the world, not engagement, soothed her soul.

Paralysis and Taking the Veil

Although Starr visited Hull-House occasionally between 1920 and 1928, these trips virtually stopped in 1928 when she had surgery on her spine and paraplegia resulted. This same year she entered the novitiate to prepare for her final vows to enter the convent. During the next decade, her writings concentrated on religious rituals and her personal journey, and last major conversion experience, to Roman Catholicism. In 1935 Starr became an Oblate of the Third Order of St. Benedict. This religious community dedicates itself to a life of prayer, silence, and retreat from everyday life. The community has strict rules limiting social contacts with each other and with the world outside their walls. Thus Starr joined one of the most restrictive religious communities in the world, renouncing worldly activities that defined Hull-House in favor of prayer and seclusion.

Addams' Death

Addams died on 21 May 1935 and her death was mourned world wide. The Hull-House courtyard filled with thousands of mourners, and eulogies to her were published in numerous periodicals (see Linn 1935, 422-28). On 4 June 1935, Starr attended a memorial meeting for Addams that was held at the Chicago Commons (Amberg 1976, 194). Starr serenely accepted Addams' passing in a way that many other friends, and even strangers, did not.

Starr's Death

On 10 February 1940, Starr died and was buried in a secluded cemetery set aside for the dedicated sisters she had joined late in life. Unlike Addams' death, which was an international event, Starr quietly slipped away.

In the remainder of this introduction, we present more of the intellectual and historical context for interpreting and analyzing Starr's ideas and practices between 1889 and 1920.

Starr and the Arts and Crafts Movement in England and Chicago

Starr established a number of innovative organizations that shaped both Chicago and the nation. Hull-House was the first notable effort, but Starr also shone in the art world and labor struggles. She was a genius at seeing what needed to be done. She was charismatic in an irascible and challenging manner, and she brought the British experiments in art and labor to America.

The Chicago Public School Art Society: British Arts and Crafts and American Education

On 8 February 1893, Starr addressed the Chicago Woman's Club (CWC) on the work done by T.C. Horsfall in England. Horsfall was part of the BAAC and promoted art as part of children's education, stressing the interconnectedness of the mind and body. Following her visit with him in 1891, Starr argued that the CWC should start similar efforts in Chicago. A committee of the Art and Literature Department in the CWC promptly investigated this idea, assessed its costs, and visited a public school, the Polk Street School.

On 22 March they enthusiastically reported on their findings and voted to support a school with donations of pictures and money. In October they voted to place art in the Jones School, and in January, 1894 each member was asked for a financial contribution. By March, $79 had been raised, and they had recruited the Education Department of the CWC to join in their effort. As a result of this success, they formed the Chicago Public School Art Society (CPSAS) on 19 April 1894. Starr was elected its first president (Frank and Jerome 1916, 131-32), and she held this position until 1897. This group spread their work throughout the Chicago public schools and soon other women's groups and cities followed their lead. The society shared John Dewey's (e.g., 1899) goal of making the public school a source of good citizenship including a sharp appreciation of beauty and the public good. It was so successful that the work of the CPSAS continues now, over a century later.

Starr, therefore, combined this British idea with the American public school and the Chicago pragmatists' emphasis on citizenship and education. Starr added the belief that "The soul of man cannot live by the three R's alone" (see chapter 5 here). For Starr, art served the spirit and God: "It is a legitimate object to entertain and recreate the mind, but care must be taken to recreate it, indeed, into a more faithful image of its Source" (see chapter 1 here). Starr saw no contradiction between this religious goal and public education, unlike Addams and the Chicago pragmatists who endorsed the separation of church and state in schools. Again, Starr's position represents one that continues in contemporary debates on religion and education.

A bizarre twist of fate shows how important these women's work in the CPSAS was and how vital it is to remember and honor it. The *Chicago Tribune* reported on the "Discovery of $20 million worth of art lying around" in Chicago public schools (4 July 1999). This art had been bureaucratically forgotten and sometimes lost and abused. When it was "rediscovered," the newspaper reported that "Officials believe the art was acquired over decades through donations or outright purchases by individual schools or the board." Nowhere in this article or in the official memory was it recalled that a significant source of this collection was possibly if not probably the CPSCA.[10]

This group, with Starr as its leader and Addams (e.g., 1895a) as a powerful supporter, organized the Chicago women's clubs throughout the city (and later the suburbs) to "encourage the appreciation of true works of art and the ideals they suggest." In addition, they organized exhibits at the AIC in 1905, 1907, 1908, and 1910 and they had a sophisticated understanding of art, aesthetics, and public education.

The Butler Art Gallery (1891)

The first addition to the old Hull mansion was the Butler Art Gallery, modeled after the Whitechapel Art Gallery associated with Toynbee Hall (Sherman 1981, 47). Fund-raising was organized primarily by Starr who used her contacts from the Kirkland School for Girls and through her Aunt Eliza to attract donations for the project. In 1896 a third story was added to the gallery and Starr moved her studio and apartment here. For a short time, between 1899 and 1900, Starr's bookbindery was found here, too.

The Creative Beginnings of the CACS (1896-1897)

In addition to art exhibits sponsored by the CPSAS and at the Butler art gallery, Starr organized an "Easter Art Exhibit" in 1897 displaying work done by Hull-House residents and friends. This art work was intellectually connected to young female workers who had formed with Starr's help at Hull-House in 1896 a union called the Dorcas League. In October 1897, the group (now reformulated as the Dorcas Federal Labor Union) was reading works by Ruskin and Morris ("The Dorcas Federal Labor Union," 1897, 4). They met twice a month, with one meeting open to friendly allies of the laboring women. Thus, this urban group of laborers connected work and art, adopting the BAAC model.[11]

These two events, organizing the league and the Easter art exhibit, established the groundwork for Starr's formally co-founding the Chicago Arts and Crafts Society (CACS) on 22 October 1897 at Hull-House. This group rivaled the other major American arts and crafts society in Boston, but the latter group has been the focus of extensive scholarly analysis. The first major contemporary celebration of the CACS was published only in 1977 in Sharon Darling's book on *Chicago Metalsmiths* (1977). Her documentation of the scope and excellence of the group astounded many people (see also Darling 1984).

The connection between the BAAC and Chicago artisans and craftsman was explicit in the first meeting of the CACS. Two Hull-House residents were major leaders, Starr and George Mortimer Rendel Twose, a teacher at the Chicago Manual School ("Chicago Arts and Crafts Society," 1898). This school ultimately combined with Dewey and Mead's Laboratory Schools at the University of Chicago (Deegan 1999), and Twose continued his work there after the merger. He also sponsored metal workshops at Hull-House for the next ten to fifteen years. A third major member was the Chicago sociologist and former Hull-House resident Charles Zueblin. He and his wife Rho (R. Zueblin 1903a-g, 1904) were active leaders in the CACS for the next decade.

The first year's schedule of the CACS included:

Names	Topics
Henry D. Lloyd	William Morris
Mrs. Yale-Wynne	Silver Work (with poem)
Conference opened by [Jane Addams]	
Jane Addams	The Artisan and the Factory
Mrs. [Mary Kenney] O'Sullivan	The Artisan and the Factory
Mrs. W.H. Noyes	The Japanese Artisan

The first speaker, Henry Demarest Lloyd, edited the *Chicago Tribune* and was one of Addams' (1932, 39-48) dearest friends. Mary Kenney was one of Starr's closest friends, as noted above. Clearly the connection between art and the machine was important to this urban group from its beginnings, and it became an explosive issue through the voice of Frank Lloyd Wright.

The CACS and Frank Lloyd Wright (1897-1899)

Frank Lloyd Wright (1889-1959), the founder of the Chicago Prairie School of Architecture, was originally deeply involved in life at Hull-House. He had moved to Chicago in 1889, the year Hull-House opened, and his mother was a volunteer at the social settlement and even cared for Florence Kelley's children for a time (Bryan and Davis 1990, 85). Another tie was through Wright's maternal uncle, Jenkin Lloyd Jones. Jones offered courses at the settlement and was a very good friend of Addams (1918).

Wright was involved initially in the CACS, but this was a short-lived yet fruitful connection.[12] In 1899 he presented a speech[13] at the CACS denouncing it as outmoded: an impossible, passé movement ("Chicago Art and Craft Society" 1900). The Machine, not humans, was the source of future arts and craft. The Machine was flexible, inexpensive, a mass producer, and capable of spare, modern lines. It was the democratic source of beautiful commodities. The old Morris model was for the wealthy, a small market that could not and did not serve the common person.

Ironically, Starr was deeply democratic and a neighbor of the poor, but she defended the CACS against Wright's accurate criticisms. Wright, one of the most brilliant, arrogant, and self-centered men of the century, usually served wealthy clients, did not mass produce his architecturally designed masterpieces, but nonetheless attacked the CACS as elitist. His flamboyant, and not very accurate, account is worth citing in detail.

> I read the paper, protestant and yet affirmative—"The Art and Craft of the Machine." Next day there was an editorial in the *Chicago Tribune* commenting upon the fact that an artist had said the first word for the use of the machine as an artist's tool. Jane Addams herself must have written it, I suspect. She sympathized with me, as did Julia Lathrop.
>
> But my novel thesis was overwhelmed by Professors [Charles] Zueblin and [Oscar Lovell] Triggs[14] and the architects and handicraftsmen present that evening. The Society went "handicraft" and was soon defunct. (Wright 1943, 132)

Unlike Wright, we do not suspect that the editorial was written by Addams, but she probably wanted Wright to continue with the CACS. Wright also misrepresents the goals of the CACS that were always embedded in handicraft and did not change (but were clarified) after he left the group. The workers who supported the CACS, moreover, were very familiar with factories and industrial exploitation; more familiar than Wright was. Finally, the CACS did not soon become defunct after Wright withdrew, but rather flourished and made a major mark on American arts and crafts (Darling 1977, 1984).

Wright did, however, have some commitment to the mass housing he advocated in this pivotal speech. Thus in the 1950s, over a half century later, he did produce his $5,000.00 Usonian House to serve the middle-class, but these homes controlled space, objects, and storage so rigidly that they became impractical homes for the middle class. Only the elite who could afford to modify them could endure Wright's controlling vision. But they were initially relatively inexpensive and a part of Wright's dream of affordable, beautiful housing that he praised in 1899.

Hull-House, of course, continued to serve the poor and did not collect profits from its neighbors in the half century after Wright's speech that called the CACS to task. Wright was correct in saying that this movement would not catch on with the masses but with the elite who had the money, time, and training to enjoy handmade, beautiful objects.[15] Wright's views still rankled Starr in 1907 when she continued to criticize them in an article defending handicrafts (see chapter 7 here).

The CACS and House Beautiful and The Craftsman

The CACS became a major influence in American art through their production of beautiful objects, including Starr's acclaimed bookbinding. This work had a national influence through two popular journals aligned with the arts and crafts movements in both England and America: *House Beautiful* and *The Craftsman*. The former magazine was allied with the Chicago architecture movement in which Wright played a major role. The magazine continued to write about both Wright and the CACS despite their differences after 1900. The latter magazine, edited by the great artisan and craftsman Gustav Stickley, also supported the CACS and popularized their leaders and objects. Triggs (e.g., 1903), another important member of the CACS, frequently published his work in *The Craftsman*, too. The extensive coverage of the arts and crafts movements in both England and America is noted in only a few particularly relevant articles cited in Table 1 here.

The CACS also popularized their work through exhibits at the AIC and other groups.

The CACS and the AIC (1898)

From March 23-April 15, 1898 the CACS and the Chicago Architectural Club co-sponsored an exhibit at the AIC. It was a smashing success, drawing 17,000 visitors. The exhibition catalogue for this event also listed the CACS membership, and Table 2 lists those allies of Hull-House and the University of Chicago who helped shape sociology and were also active in the CACS. This network dramatically documents the ties between arts and crafts and sociology in England and Chicago.

The CACS (1900)

Wright's speech and disassociation from the group created waves within the fledgling organization, but other political forces may have also troubled

Table 1
Articles in *House Beautiful* and *The Craftsman* on the BAAC or the CACS between 1897 and 1905.

McCauley, M. "Municipal Art in Chicago." *Craftsman* 9 (December 1905): 321-40.

Nordhoff, Evelyn Hunter. "The Doves Bindery." *House Beautiful* 4 (June 1898): 21-28.

Preston, Emily. "Cobdon-Sanderson and the Doves Bindery." *The Craftsman* 2 (April 1902): 21-32.

Rice, Walter. "Miss Starr's Bookbinding." *House Beautiful* 12 (June 1902): 11-14.

Twose, George M.R. "The Coffee-Room at Hull House." *House Beautiful* 7 (January 1900): 107-9.

Way, W. Irving. "Women and Bookbinding." *House Beautiful* 1 (February 1897): 57-63.

_____. "Women and Bookbinding Again." *House Beautiful* 3 (February 1898): 76-81.

Table 2
Allies of Hull-House, women's trade unions, and the University of Chicago who helped shape sociology and were members of the CACS in 1898.[16]

Names	Hull-House	Women's trade unions or Chicago Architects*	U. of Chicago Sociology
Addams, Jane	x	x	x
American, Sadie	x		
Anderson, Mary	x	x	
Bartlett, Caroline	x	x	x
Culver, Helen	x		
Lloyd, Henry	x		
Lloyd, Bessie	x		
Perkins, Dwight	x	x*	
Perkins, Mrs. Dwight	x		
Pond, Irving K.	x	x*	
Pond, Allan	x	x*	
Smith, Mrs.	x		
Smith, Mary	x		
Starr, Ellen	x	x	x
Triggs, Oscar	x		
Twose, George	x	x*	
Vincent, George	x	x	
Vincent, Mrs. G.	x		
Young, Ella Flagg	x	x	x
Zueblin, Charles	x	x	x
Zueblin, Rho Fisk	x	x	x

Source: *The Chicago Arts and Crafts Society*. Catalogue, Exhibit. Art Institute of Chicago, March 23-April 15, 1898.

the waters. Thus in the Autumn 1900 *Hull-House Bulletin*, a public statement was issued that the group had redefined their constitution, noting the presence of two types of members: individuals who produced arts and crafts (like Wright, Starr, and Twose) and other members who were part of a society with a public commitment to the arts and crafts movement (like Charles and Rho Fisk Zueblin). Hull-House and the CACS intended to be a meeting ground for producers and their allies ("Chicago Arts and Crafts Society" 1900).

The group also heard a lecture by Miss Harmer on the general history of spinning. This was accompanied by distaff and wheel and by singing provided by Signora Anuninziata—typical activities sponsored by the Labor Museum (discussed more later).

The forthcoming lecture schedule included a visit by Ashbee on 23 November, addresses by Zonia Baber of the Chicago Institute (a forerunner to the Chicago School of Civics and Philanthropy and sponsored by the Department of Sociology between 1904 and 1920, Deegan 1978), and by Charles Zueblin. An exhibition was also planned for 27 November until 7 December, and it was scheduled for installation at the Woman's Temple. Starr's books were displayed there, among other objects ("Miss Starr's Book-Bindery" 1900).

Starr's Book-Bindery (1899)

Another major aspect of Starr's work in arts and crafts was her labor as a bookbinder. After Starr traveled to London in 1898 for fifteen months to study the craft with Cobdon-Sanderson, she returned to Chicago and opened a studio at Hull-House. Here she prepared her own volumes, trained three apprentices at any given time, and established an arts and crafts "business and school" that flourished until approximately 1919. This latter group was called a "guild," following the BAAC model, and provided a summer workshop for Hull-House residents and neighbors in 1900 ("Miss Starr's Book-Bindery" 1900).

In chapters 6 to 11 here Starr describes the "Hull-House Bookbindery" (1900, chapter 6) and her craft: "The Renaissance of Handicraft" (1902, chapter 7); "The Handicraft of Bookbinding [Article I]" (1915, chapter 8); "The Handicraft of Bookbinding (Article II)" (1916, chapter 9); "Bookbinding (Third Article and Article 4)" (1916, chapters 10 and 11).[17] Starr's technical writing on bookbinding is that of a master artisan. Few such step-by-step guides remain and this detailed information is indispensable to understand both her work and teaching in this subject. Starr's book-bindery was part of her apartment in 1899, but it soon moved into the Labor Museum, our next topic.

The Labor Museum (1900)

The Labor Museum was an important, popular extension of the BAAC which supported Ruskin's position on local museums done on a small scale.

Addams and Starr, with the support of John Dewey, adapted this approach to fit a more democratic, neighborhood-based institution that connected native-born Americans and immigrants. This served a twofold goal to interpret the Old World skills of the immigrants to the native-born Americans and to the children of immigrants born in the New World. This latter aim connected different generations in immigrant families that were socially distressed and culturally strained by their relocation from Europe to Chicago. The Labor Museum directly linked Dewey's pragmatism and approach to adult and vocational education with Addams' feminist values and settlement philosophy and Starr's socialism and bookbinding. Unsurprisingly, it was a huge success.[18]

It began, according to Addams, when she observed an Italian woman weaving on a street in Chicago. She was struck immediately by the isolation of this labor from its Old World context. Addams then turned to John Dewey, her friend and a Hull-House trustee at that time, to try to bring this early form of industry to Chicago so that immigrants and their children would respect and learn about the many forms of labor that were conducted formerly within the home and family (see Addams [1902a], 1). This "hands-on" museum became the model for thousands of others, most notably Chicago's Museum of Science and Industry, first sponsored by Julius Rosenwald, owner of Sears Roebuck and a staunch supporter of Hull-House (Werner 1939) and the now popular children's museums that are found throughout the world.

A vital, distinct component of the Labor Museum was Starr's book bindery. Since she began her formal studies in this craft in 1898, two years before the Labor Museum opened, she probably was part of the early planning for the museum. Addams, on the one hand, does not mention her name in this connection. On the other hand, the book bindery was intended to be the most complicated form of labor established and displayed at the Labor Museum and part of its vision of arts and crafts from Europe to America. Unfortunately the display of bookbinding as labor was difficult to arrange because the students and workers were producing their precise, slow, and complicated art ("Miss Starr's Book Bindery" 1900). Thus, the intent of the bookbindery was to present a working model to the masses, but the painstaking work could not be performed if the worker was under observation or rushed. This type of contradiction plagued the work of the artisans and craftsmen who followed Ruskin and Morris.

The Labor Museum, the CACS, and the bookbindery were all popularly promoted through the Chautauqua movement, the national program of adult education that had strong allies at the University of Chicago (Deegan 1988). Their journal, the *Chautauquan*, published ten articles on the arts and crafts movement in Great Britain and the United States in 1903 and 1904 (see tables 3 and 4). These were read nationwide in local Chatauqua classes held in homes, schools and neighborhood centers. Rho Fisk Zueblin even wrote all the "lessons" to be read as a year-long course. Her book length manuscript instructed Americans about Arts and Crafts in their historical, aesthetic, and international dimensions (see list of articles in Tables 3 and 4).

Table 3

**Articles in *The Chautauquan* on the BAAC or the CACS in 1902
and 1903 as part of the *Chautauquan* "Arts and Crafts Movement"
Course, 1902-1903, vols. 36 and 37.**

Zueblin, Rho Fisk. "The Pre-Raphaelites: The Beginnings of the Arts and Crafts Movement." *Chautauquan* 36 (October 1902a): 57-61.

_____. "A Survey of the Arts and Crafts Movement in England." *Chautauquan* 36 (November 1902b): 167-73.

_____. "The Art Teachings of the Arts and Crafts Movement." *Chautauquan* 36 (December 1902c): 284-88.

_____. "Economics of the Arts and Crafts Movement." *Chautauquan* 36 (January 1903a): 409-14.

_____. "Continental Tendencies in the Arts and Crafts." *Chautauquan* 36 (February 1903b): 506-13.

_____. "The Production of Industrial Art in America, I." *Chautauquan* 36 (March 1903c): 622-7.

_____. "The Production of Industrial Art in America, II." *Chautauquan* 37 (April 1903d): 59-66.

_____. "The Education of the Producer and the Consumer." *Chautauquan* 37 (May 1903e): 177-82.

_____. "The Patronage of the Arts and Crafts." *Chautauquan* 37 (June 1903f): 266-72.

Table 4

**Articles in *The Chautauquan* on the BAAC or the CACS in 1903 and 1904 as
part of the *Chautauquan* "Arts and Crafts in American Education" Course,
1903-1904, vols. 38 and 39**

Adams, John Quincy. "The Relation of Art to Work." *Chautauquan* 38 (September 1903): 49-52.

"Hull-House Labor Museum." *Chautauquan* 38 (September 1903): 60-61. Notes on series, p. 77.

Zueblin, Rho Fisk. "Public School Art Societies." *Chautauquan* 38 (October 1903g): 169-72.

Hall, J. Harman, Mrs. "The Beautifying of School Grounds." *Chautauquan* 38 (November 1903): 276-81.

Dopp, Katherine Elizabeth. "The Place of Handicraft in Education." *Chautauquan* 38 (December 1903): 384-86.

Campbell, Matilda G. "Crafts in Elementary Schools." *Chautauquan* 38 (January 1904): 487-91.

Marlatt, Abby. "Crafts in Secondary Schools." *Chautauquan* 38 (February 1904): 584-88.

McBride, Henry. "Crafts in Technical Schools." *Chautauquan* 39 (March 1904): 49-52.

Zueblin, Rho Fisk. "Art Training for Citizenship." *Chautauquan* 39 (April 1904): 49-52.

Addams, Jane. "Humanizing Tendency of Industrial Education." *Chautauquan* 39 (May 1904): 266-72.

The Chautauquan, House Beautiful, The Craftsman, Manual Training Magazine, Industrial Arts Magazine, International Studio, Art and Progress, and related journals often quoted Dewey's ideas as part of their articles and philosophy (Kaplan 1987, 302), as well as the feminist pragmatism of Starr and Addams.

This work was also promoted directly through the *Hull-House Bulletin,* that was widely distributed in Chicago, and through the nationally distributed *The Commons,* edited by Graham Taylor (see references in the bibliography here). Starr also befriended A.L. Simon, trained in sociology and economics at the University of Chicago, and May Wood Simon. The Simons were frequent Hull-House lecturers and visitors. They were also socialists who were active in the Chicago-based *International Socialist Review* (Buhle 1981, 166-69) where they popularized and criticized the CACS. In chapter 7 here, Starr presented in their journal her view of the CACS as an organization for the workers and not for elites like Wright.

The Angel of the Strikers (1910-1916):
Hull-House, the Arts and Crafts Movement, and Labor

By 1910 Starr was a committed Fabian sociologist, influenced by Dewey's pragmatism via the Labor Museum and by Ruskin and Morris via the BAAC. Although she remained an intimate of Addams and shared her intellectual work and feminist pragmatism, Starr's socialism and militancy had grown since the 1890s. By 1910 she was walking the picket line during a long and bloody garment workers' strike. Starr's work here was central in swinging public sympathy toward the strikers (Wolman et al.1922/1915, 30). Mead, the Chicago pragmatist, also had an important role in this strike, as did most of the Hull-House residents and friends (Deegan 1988, 292). Although Starr continued to practice her craft and write about it and remained active in the CACS, she wanted to militantly join workers who were disgusted with capitalism.

Thus, Starr's commitment to socialism increased in fervor between 1910 and 1920 while she became more and more disenchanted with the BAAC and the CACS. Although these latter groups were dedicated abstractly to the laborer, their products were so labor-intensive that they were expensive to make and only the elite could afford to buy them. Starr's shift in priorities first appeared in 1910 with her drive to support the striking garment workers, and this change began to appear in her writings (see chapters 12-19 here). By 1914 her struggle against police violence toward waitresses at Henrici Restaurant became front-page headlines in the newspapers (see chapter 13 here). During this strike, Mary Anderson (1951, 54), the union organizer and later head of the Children's Bureau in Washington, D.C., recalled that "The police were very tough; they yanked the arm of one girl out of its socket and another girl had her arm broken." When Starr was grabbed by a policeman, arrested, and brought to trial, the power of Hull-House became apparent. "The man who was the prosecutor for the city [Harold Ickes] lived at Hull House and Miss Starr was a good friend of his" (Anderson 1951, 55), and Starr was quickly acquitted. Starr was also apparently difficult to live with during these strikes. According to Alice Hamilton, a medical researcher and Hull-House resident who liked Starr but found her intense militancy wearing on her nerves: "Miss Starr is picketing and passionately longing to be arrested. I do hope it will be over when I get there, Miss Starr is so difficult when she is striking" (Alice Hamilton correspondence cited in Sicherman 1984, 174).

In 1915 Starr and several allies associated with the University of Chicago became vocal and visible (See Wolman et al. 1922/1915; see chapters 14-18 here). Her confidant Frances Lillie—wife of a Chicago professor in zoology, daughter of the philanthropist Charles T. Crane, and deeply religious—joined her in many of these newsworthy activities. Mead once again became an important figure (e.g., Ickes, Mead, and Tucker, 1915), this time at least partially moved by his son Henry who was arrested for his participation in the strike (see newspaper clippings in Starr papers, Smith College).

Although Starr (see chapter 17 here) castigated sociologists for their failure to participate in the 1915 strike, on 6 December 1915 a rousing meeting was held at the University of Chicago under the auspices of the Sociology Club. Albion Small, the chair of the Department of Sociology, spoke against police violence and for arbitration ("Stories of Violence of Police are Told," 1915, 1). Hillman also spoke that night (see "Invitations Sent to Mayor and Members of City Council" 1915). Charles Henderson had devised a plan for social justice for garment workers before his death and this also influenced Starr's work ("Garment Strike Has Been Broken Say Employers" 1915).

Starr testified on behalf of workers in 1910 (see chapter 12 here) and in 1915 (see chapters 14 and 15 here). In 1915 she also signed a "Petition to the Mayor on Behalf of the Garment Workers by Mary McDowell, Mrs. Medill McCormick, Ellen Gates Starr, and Sophonisba Breckinridge" (see chapter 14 here). In 1917 Starr's testimonial on "Why I am a Socialist" was published in a socialist newspaper (see chapter 19 here), after she unsuccessfully ran a campaign for alderman in 1916.

Roman Catholicism as the Prism of Starr's Autobiographical and Mystical Writings (1920-1940)

Starr, like Addams, wrote her autobiography but this work and thus much of Starr's writings and life have received far less attention. Addams' first major autobiography, *Twenty Years at Hull-House* (1910) is a lyrical statement of human struggle and Chicago's emerging role as a national model for the new, vital, if problematic, industrial city. It is a classic in American literature. Her second autobiography, *The Second Twenty Years at Hull-House* (1930) is a more critical yet powerful statement of the triumphs and losses of human struggles and the difficult role of creating an international model for the new, smaller world beset by war and hatred. These two autobiographical works are major statements on American life, politics, women, and an era.[19]

Starr's autobiography is far more modest and less charming than Addams' self-reflections, but Starr's work is important, nonetheless. At the very minimum, it provides a dramatic contrast to Addams' work that depicts a bustling and secularized institution in the midst of rapid social change and experimentation. In her autobiography, Starr rejects this active life; not because it is bad, but because it is far less important than her new life of prayer. This is a great turnaround both in her everyday life and as a former Protestant, Anglo-Catholic: she directly challenges the vision and work of Hull-House and its community. Starr critically examines her "first" life of sixty years and finds it wanting in power, meaning, and majesty. While most others who had reached this age were reflecting on what they had accomplished, Starr was starting anew and rejecting one of the most successful American institutions developed by women. Although Starr's writing style is not melodic, her statement is dramatic.

Starr's autobiography is also a significant statement on American Roman Catholicism. Her conversion to Catholicism is the lens for her autobiography and she analyzes her life as a journey toward its sacred vision and rites. Starr discards her former life as a Protestant, an artist, an activist, and a socialist in favor of a convent with its ordered life of prayer and devotion to Christ. Starr reflects on her active life as "A Bypath Into The Great Roadway" (see chapter 22). For Roman Catholics, Starr makes a positive statement about the monumental significance of prayer, ritual, and contemplation, a choice for an "other-worldly" dedication and against the activity and "this-worldly" outlook characterizing her previous, stellar practice of the "Protestant Ethic" (Weber 1976/1920). Because Starr co-founded the most important social settlement in America, became a world-class bookbinder, and a radical supporter of workers' rights, her rejection of these successful activities is a major, religious act.

Starr devoted her intellectual life between 1920 to 1940 to religious writings. Roman Catholic beliefs and practices inform all her writings during this period. Thus she reflects on the meaning of pilgrimages, the practice of the Mass, the Breviary, prayer, and devotions (see chapters 23 to 24 here). Only a small sample of these writings are included here because they amply illustrate the cataclysmic shift that took place in Starr's intellectual approach. Starr became one of the most prolific Roman Catholic, female writers during these two decades, retaining her search for excellence, intellectual labor, and meaning. During this period, she thoroughly rejected the ideas and practices of the arts and crafts movement, with its alliances with the Church of England, as well.

In conclusion, Starr's work at Hull-House, in her numerous art and labor organizations, and her religious search for meaning are documented through her writings included here and these are elucidated more below.

Feminist Pragmatism and Starr's Writings between 1892 and 1920

Hull-House—although modeled after the Oxford-affiliated, male-dominated and defined, Church of England's social settlement Toynbee Hall—quickly emerged as a democratic, co-operative, feminist enterprise. This unique vision underlies "feminist pragmatism." More formally, "feminist pragmatism" is an American theory uniting liberal values and a belief in a rational public with a cooperative, nurturing, and liberating model of the self, the other, and the community. Education and democracy are emphasized as significant mechanisms to organize and improve society.

In this perspective, social inequality for women shares some similar patterns with other forms of inequality: by class, age, race, religion, education, sexual preference, and disability. Each inequality undermines *democracy* which requires equality for all. Democracy emerges from different groups, nonetheless, and represents these distinct perspectives, histories, communities, and characteristic structures of the self. Social change must articulate and respond to these various groups' commonalities and differences (Addams 1902b).

The community, like the self, is based on the ability to learn, educate, and take the role of the other. *Education, art, and play* are social processes that change and structure the mind, self, and society. Feminist pragmatists believe in the essential ability of all people to change, to search for a wider, more inclusive democracy; to develop a world consciousness and community; and to have the capacity to end major social problems such as war, food shortages, and excessive population growth. This is an optimistic theory that empowers people to confront the horrific underlying inequalities and injustices found throughout the world, in each community, and within each self. As Jane Addams expressed it: "The cure for the ills of Democracy is more Democracy" (1902b, 11-12; see also Addams 1930).

Areas of concentration within feminist pragmatism form separate literatures, including: (1) urban sociology, emphasizing the benefits of city life and urban planning, as well as the problems of poor housing and sanitation; (2) criminology, focusing on juvenile delinquency, the court system, and notions of justice; (3) the use of both qualitative and quantitative methodology, especially interviews, bureaucratic records, mapping, and introspection; (4) the study of the life cycle, including youth and old age; (5) the study of social class and labor relations, analyzing the processes of work, unionization, and worker exploitation; (6) the process of making and enjoying art and aesthetics, especially the connections between art and paid labor and between art and the home; (7) the process of play, calling for the need for playgrounds, national and urban parks, the theater, and an examination of the linkages between play, work, and art; (8) the process of education, usually similar to the theories of progressive education developed by John Dewey and George Herbert Mead and applied to kindergartens, elementary schools, and adult education, and the arts; (9) the organization and mobilization of social movements for peace, suffrage, civil rights, consumer rights, and education; (10) the study of ethics and its implementations; (11) the development of an international consciousness and political apparatus; (12) the study of immigration and its impact on the immigrant and native; (13) the study of African American life and culture and the development of practices to eliminate inequality and social injustice especially in the legal system and the marketplace; and (14) the study of feminine values and the natural environment, what Deegan calls ecofeminist pragmatism (Deegan and Podeschi 2001). Each specific area often involved dozens of scholars and activists with Addams as one of the central figures uniting these disparate interests and activities. Starr's role within this vast enterprise is considerably smaller than Addams, and a comparison of their similarities and differences clarifies these relationships.

Starr and Addams as Professional Colleagues and Individuals

Within feminist pragmatism, Addams and Starr have different emphases and interpretations. Human behavior, according to Addams (1905, 1909, 1910, 1930), emerges from a triple, integrated basis in play, work, and art. Human behavior, according to Starr (see all the chapters here), emerges from a triple, integrated basis in religion, work, and art. For both women, these actions are empowered through democracy and education (Addams 1902b), but Starr added prayer and meditation to her model. Democracy for both encompasses a political, social, and economic equality between all members of the community, and this community is global. Education is democratic in structure and includes all stages of life; all occupations, including equality between work of the mind and body, and development of the arts. Addams stressed learning to play, while Starr stressed learning to pray.

Addams embraces all fourteen of the specialty areas noted above while Starr concentrated on six. Thus it is only in comparison to Addams that Starr seems narrow. Starr, therefore, wrote about social class and labor relations; the process of making and enjoying art and its connection to education; ethics and their implementations; international consciousness and politics; immigrants and their relations with the native-born; and feminine values. Starr also analyzed the religious foundations of social settlements, socialism, and female values.

Both women engaged in creating art. Addams particularly loved writing and continually worked and reworked passages until they were a moving articulation of the common good. Dramas, comedies, children's stories, and ethnic visions, furthermore, were welcomed at Hull-House where they were enacted by the major repertory group, the Hull-House Players, and by dozens of community groups that were organized primarily by ethnicity or age. Starr loved to teach and read literary works and, of course, devoted years to the art of bookbinding. She sponsored exhibitions of objects d'art and stressed the need for art in all aspects of life. An interesting juxtaposition of their interests is seen in Starr's teaching of Shakespeare's play *King Lear* (see Appendix B here) and Addams' (1912) controversial and insightful comparison of the paternal capitalist George Pullman to that same doomed and tragic father. Each woman influenced the other, and neither of them footnoted this pattern.

The Mixture of Intellectual and Interpersonal Influences in the Writings of Starr and Addams

In addition to the tradition of Chicago pragmatism, Addams reanalyzed many sociological traditions in Britain, including empiricism, social surveys, Fabian socialism, and the Arts and Crafts movement (especially following the work and practices of Beatrice Webb, Charles Booth, Patrick Geddes, John Ruskin, and Canon Barnett). As noted earlier, many of these ideas were associated with British social settlements, especially at Toynbee Hall. Addams was also influenced by sociologists in Russia, especially by the pacifism and art of Leo Tolstoy and the arguments for human freedom and labor that emerged from the human relation to the land articulated by Petr Kropotkin. Addams (e.g., 1895b) seriously considered the Germanic tradition enacted by Karl Marx and Friedrich Engels, but her dedication to a cooperative and not a conflict model based on the triple foundation for human behavior—including play and art as well as the Marxist emphasis on labor—made this tradition unworkable for her.

Starr was also heavily influenced by the Fabian movement in England and its sociological development. Starr primarily identified, nonetheless, with the Arts and Crafts movement in England prior to 1910. Ruskin, Ashbee, Horsfall, Morris, and Cobdon-Sanderson were major and active predecessors and/or mentors. She probably supported the urban thrust of the policy makers and empirical data collectors, but they were not her major allies. The influence from Chicago pragmatism on Starr can be documented easily through Addams. Although Dewey and Mead shared many of the goals and activities of Starr, their interpersonal relationships are undocumented. Starr and the Zueblins were mutually engaged for many years in the Arts and Crafts and Fabian sociology movements. Vincent, Henderson, and Small may have had various influences on Starr, too.

Starr, like Addams, was also influenced by a Russian, the labor leader Catherine Breshovsky, but her relation to the ideas of Leo Tolstoy and Petr

Kropotkin are unknown. Starr, again like Addams, seriously considered the Germanic tradition articulated by Karl Marx and Friedrich Engels, but Starr was dedicated to Fabian socialism and its counterparts in America.

Starr's religious influences are of great significance beginning with her Aunt E.A. Starr, followed by Father Huntington, then the Toynbee Hall model, and finally Roman Catholic priests (see chapter 22 for a discussion of this process). This latter religious worldview ultimately led her to renounce her former life at Hull-House in 1920. Addams and her friends were, moreover, strikingly less religious in their approach to social settlements and sociology.

Between 1889 and 1920, Addams and Starr surrounded themselves with intense, intellectual, and political friends, but these friends were usually different people. Thus Addams was close to such female giants of American thought as Florence Kelley, Julia Lathrop, Edith Abbott, Grace Abbott, Alice Hamilton, Mary McDowell, Louis deKoven Bowen, and Rachelle Yarros. Many of the men at the University of Chicago were also allies, particularly the pragmatists and sociologists. Mary Rozet Smith, furthermore, was a personal confidant of Addams. Starr, however, befriended such heroic figures in American history as E.A. Starr; Mary Kenney O'Sullivan and Sidney Hillman, two major union organizers; Vida Scudder and Mrs. Frank Crane Lillie, Christian activists and union allies (Anderson 1951, 53). Both Addams and Starr were friends of Mary Wilmarth and perhaps of Julia Lathrop. Alice Hamilton grew to appreciate Starr, but never loved her in the way she did Addams.

Addams' circle of female friends is the subject of considerable scholarship, and these women often found Starr too intense, confrontational, and religious. Understandably, they do not find fault with Addams, but with Starr. In contrast, people who were close to Starr could find Addams tiresome. Thus Mary Collson, a Unitarian minister who lived at Hull-House from 1900 to 1901, identified with Starr who was "always dashing about with a great hustle and bustle from morning until night" (Tucker citing Collson 1984, 45). Addams' calmness, compromises, and moderation, however, irked and angered Collson.

Because Addams is the focus of almost all research on Hull-House, her friendships are idealized and perceived as the only standard. With this bias and the almost separate friendship groups of the two women, this Hull-House scholarship depicts Starr as almost friendless, an outsider, and a rejected, former friend of Addams (see Sklar 1995; Stebner 1997). Katherine Sklar, for example, speculates about a rejected and isolated Starr who turned in 1898 to England and bookbinding to heal her wounds. This nonsensical interpretation ignores Starr's conversion experience to the arts and crafts model in 1889, and her work in 1891 with Horsfall. Her trip to England in 1898 continued this lifework. Starr, moreover, was far from isolated but surrounded by her allies in the labor movement and the Anglican Order of the Holy Cross, especially Vida Scudder and Father Huntington.

Addams and Starr created a remarkable friendship that changed America. While both women were charismatic, Addams was charming, non-confrontational, and diplomatic, and Starr was more introverted, confrontive, and uncompromising. Both women were well loved by their very different friends. After 1920 their ideas and practices diverged, but their passionate friendship never ended. Addams ideas were widely circulated through her powerful writings, while this anthology is the first published collection of Starr's thought.

Conclusion

In 1889 two young friends opened the door to America's most famous and powerful social settlement: Hull-House. One of them, Jane Addams, made friends and enemies in the neighborhood, in Chicago, in America, and around the world. She won international fame and honor symbolized by the Nobel Peace Prize. Many consider her the most important woman in American history. Her forgotten friend, Ellen Gates Starr, also stepped through that door and made outstanding contributions to the social settlement movement, arts and crafts, labor, and public education. She was contentious, exacting, and on a religious quest. Hull-House filled Addams' life, but it left Starr dissatisfied. Only withdrawal from the world, a turning away from that door to Hull-House, could satisfy Starr's mind and spirit. They were two friends on two different paths, and each journey changed America.

Notes

1. There is a vast literature on Addams, but a few recommendations for further reading are noted here. One of the best, easily available bibliographies on Addams and her era can be found in John C. Farrell's (1967, 217-61) *Beloved Lady*. He also provides an excellent overview of Addams' life, public career, and applied ideas. Most of these writings, nonetheless, do not reveal her sociological legacy and its influence that are of primary interest here. Farrell's book, moreover, is well-written and researched but lacks a compelling narrative. These same comments apply to Daniel Levine's (1971) analysis of the liberal influence within Addams' life and ideas.

    Mary Lynn McCree Bryan spent years organizing, traveling, and reading original, archival material to generate a microfilm of the Jane Addams Papers. This meticulous labor provides expanded access to archival documents concerning Addams' ideas and contributions in dozens of areas. The microfilm, however, is often poorly indexed and finding particular items may be difficult.

2. Starr's family background is similar to Charlotte Perkins Gilman's and both developed radical views of society. Gilman later became closely associated with Addams and Hull-House (see Deegan 1997), but her relation to Starr is unknown. They were both involved in the labor movement; briefly had some higher education but were not college graduates; had confrontational personalities and held strong opinions; dressed in ways that were unacceptable for women; were artisans; strongly supported English socialism; and were friends of Addams. Gilman opposed patriarchal religion, however, and this would have been a major difference from Starr.

3. A similar path was followed by another eminent academic at Wellesley College and founder of a social settlement in Boston (Denison House), Vida Scudder. Starr and Scudder also developed an intense friendship (see Scudder 1932, Boonin-Vail 1993).

4. Joel Harris (1999), however, traces a direct connection between Ruskin and the Webbs.

5. As a socialist, Starr was in the contradictory position of profiting from a benevolent friend and capitalist, in a situation analogous to that of Karl Marx's relationship to Friedrich Engels. Engels owned a bourgeois factory that financially supported Marx and his family. Wilmarth, however, was more integrated into the power structure of Chicago and the Hull-House community than Engels was in his hometown or in Marx's "hometown" of London.

6. Christian sociology was popular in the 1890s, but at the University of Chicago the religious influence was Baptist and not Anglo-Catholic. For a discussion of women in sociology and religion during this era see Deegan and Rynbrandt 2000.

7. Deegan was less impressed with Zueblin when she wrote about him in 1988 than she is now. See, for example, Beatrice Webb's condescending remark on Zueblin in Deegan (1988, 265).

8. Some female sociologists were relieved to leave sociology. This is apparently the case for Edith Abbott and Sophonisba Breckinridge (see Deegan 1991).

9. The era was so supportive of women's work and ideas, Deegan (1991) calls it the "golden era of women in sociology." When it ended in 1920, this initiated "the dark era of patriarchal ascendancy" that continued until the mid-1960s.

10. This group had forgotten their early donations of original artwork in the 1890s when they published a brochure at the turn of the century. Here they characterized their early years as supplying primarily inexpensive pieces and copies. They held art exhibits, however, at the AIC in 1905, 1907, and 1908. (See *Chicago Public School Art Society* 1910.)

11. This "craft production" model survived and thrived in other American cities as well, even as small, family-owned shops gave way to large factories see Wahl (1989) and Robinson and Wahl (1990). In most industries, however, craft production was dominated by men.

12. Wright became familiar with Ashbee's work through the CACS and they met on Ashbee's visit in 1900. In 1910 Wright asked Ashbee to write an introduction to a book published in Germany. This and another project made Wright's work available to a wide international audience and greatly influenced the future direction of European modernism" (Wilson 1987, 211). Thanks to Andrea Smiscek for bringing this article to our attention.

13. There is some scholarly confusion about this speech. This lengthy speech, "The Art and Craft of the Machine," was reprinted for the first and only time in 1960. At that time, the editors of the Wright anthology, Edgar Kaufmann and Ben Raeburn (1960, 73), merely noted that this address was delivered at the CACS and again to the Western Society of Engineers in March 1901. Bryan and Davis (1990) inaccurately note that Wright delivered his speech at the founding meeting of the CACS in 1903. This statement has two errors: the founding meeting was in 1897 and Wright addressed the group in 1899. Bryan and Davis then compound their errors by identifying his speech as one published in 1953 in *Modern Architecture*. Although both writings share the same title, the one identified by Kaufmann and Raeburn (1960, 55-73) is considerably longer and more significant than the brief one identified by Bryan and Davis (1969, 85-88). The error in noting the years also makes Wright's work and the CACS part of what they term "the creative years" at Hull-House from 1900-1914 instead of "the beginnings" from 1889-1900.

14. Oscar Lovell Triggs was an important member of the CACS. He founded several Chicago arts and crafts societies. He was a Fabian, a member of the University of Chicago faculty in English, and dismissed from his position there. An adequate biography of Triggs is lacking but Darling (1977, 1984) and Horowitz (1989) mention him.

15. Inexpensive national chains such as Target and K-Mart now reproduce arts and crafts items very inexpensively suggesting that both Starr and Wright were correct in their visions of beauty in everyday life that is available at a low cost.

16. Exhibited articles made by Hull-House friends in 1898 included: thirty-three pieces of Rookwood pottery p. 128-29; 2 brooches and a covered dish, Exhibit by Mrs. Lydia Avery Coonley-Ward; napkin ring, and card designed by Ashbee, p. 133; thirteen Arts and Crafts items exhibited by Lillian Wald, pp. 135-36; immigrants' items, item by Ashbee (bronze cup), p. 136, four issues of *Evergreen* by Patrick Geddes, p. 140—exhibited by Jane Addams; items by Gertrude Howe, p. 136; Tiffany enameled brick co., tiles; three items by William Morris; books with arts and crafts bookbindings exhibited by Mary Wilmarth, pp. 140-41.

17. In an irritating typographical decision, the first article is not numbered, the second uses Roman numerals, the "third" spells out the word, and the fourth uses the numeral "4."

18. There is a complicated history of other museum projects that were related but tangential to this introduction. Thus Zueblin and Vincent (and perhaps Mead through the Chicago City Club) were both involved in the Chicago Municipal Museum that was gradually absorbed by what became the Museum of Science and Industry (see Deegan 1988, 94; Horowitz 1989).

    Hull-House also had a financial enterprise marketing the products of the Labor Museum, the bookbindery, the metal classes, and the pottery work. The Hull-House shops sold these art objects for over fifty years.

19. *The Second Twenty Years at Hull-House* is not appreciated as a classic in American literature because, we believe, it is too far ahead of our national understanding of pacifism and internationalism.

Part 1

Art and Labor

1

Art and Public Schools[1]

"For all modern communities the decision as to whether art shall be used in education is of much importance. It is, in fact, a decision as to whether the people shall be barbarian or civilized."
—T. C. Horsfall

"The only recovery of our art power possible—nay, when we know the full meaning of it, the only one desirable—must result from the purification of the nation's heart and the chastisement of its life; utterly hopeless now, for our adult population, or in our large cities and their neighborhoods. But so far as any of the sacred influences of former design can be brought to bear on the minds of the young . . . . the foundation of a new dynasty of thought may be slowly laid.
—John Ruskin

"I was strangely impressed by the effect produced in a provincial seaport school for children . . . . by the gift of a little colored drawing of a single figure from the Paradise of Angelico. The drawing was wretched enough, seen beside the original, ... but to the children it was like an actual glimpse of heaven; they rejoiced in it with pure joy, and their mistress thanked me for it more than if I had sent her a whole library of good books."
—John Ruskin

With this short gospel of art according to Ruskin,[2] I should be content to leave the subject, could I get it universally understood, believed and acted upon, for, to my mind, it contains, in brief, almost the whole "body of truth" concerning the necessity for good pictures in schools. But in order that it may be understood, believed and practiced by practical people it must needs be not only definitely preached but demonstrated by those already convinced of its truth and importance.

Feeling deeply that children, and especially the children of large towns, who are debarred the enjoyment and developing power of daily association with nature and beautiful buildings, ought not to be deprived of what good pictures can do, not by supplying their places, but by creating an image of them in the mind, I began, last year, to make a collection of such pictures within my reach as seemed to me valuable for schools. The first of these, mostly photographs of buildings of architectural and historic value, I gave to the public school [Jones] nearest Hull-House. After that it seemed better to form sets of pictures to be lent to schools and periodically exchanged, and I began getting together pictures on this plan.

It was my privilege, last May [1892], to be the guest of Mr. T.C. Horsfall, of Swanscoe Park, near Manchester, England, who has been so active in the cause of supplying the schools of Manchester with circulating collections of pictures. He has taken infinite care that these collections shall have their full educational value by means of an admirable and elaborate system of arranging and labeling them, and by constant reference, in these labels, to pictures in the [Manchester] Art Museum and to those natural beauties which still remain within such distance from Manchester as may be reached on a holiday.

From Mr. Horsfall I received many most valuable suggestions, not a few of which might be carried out in our schools.

Great self-control should be exercised in the selection of pictures for schools. The temptation is strong toward deciding unadvisedly that a thing "will do," or is "better than nothing." It was certainly better than nothing for the children in the seaport school, who could not see Angelico's Paradise, to see a colored drawing of it; the more faithful the drawing the better for the children. It was better than nothing because the original of the drawing was entirely good for them, and because the drawing retained some of the qualities which made it so. To decide when the reverse is the case—that is, when the obtainable copy is either a worthless one, or of a worthless original, requires a considerable knowledge of pictures. Pictures for school should certainly not be selected by incompetent judges. It should be remembered that, though a given picture may do something for a child's mind, a better would do more; and that, though the first object is, indeed, to secure the child's attention and interest; the second is to direct them somewhither for profit. It is a legitimate object to entertain and recreate the mind, but care must be taken to recreate it, indeed, into a more faithful image of its Source.

There is great difficulty in getting good color. Colored prints are sometimes "better than nothing." They give some kinds of information about the represented thing but they rarely convey its spirit, and do little or nothing for the art instinct of the child. As soon as a machine intervenes between the mind and its product, a hard, impersonal barrier—a nonconductor of thought and emotion—is raised between the speaking and the listening mind. It is not impossible, however, to get good water color drawings of flowers, and other natural objects. Several have been given me for the school collections, and I have good hope that, when once the attention of artists is called to the necessity for good pictures in the education of children, they will often be willing to contribute them for the purpose.

Necessity may seem too strong a word, unless one reflects how barren would be all literature to one who had no acquaintance with nature. Mr.

Horsfall, in his paper entitled "The Use of Pictures in Schools," read to the Manchester branch of the Teachers' Guild, says:

> The finest literature of all countries is so saturated with the influence of the knowledge of nature that a very large part of its meaning—nearly all that part of its meaning apprehension of which is perception of its beauty—exists only for those who have the knowledge. If literature is to be the means of evoking admiration and love in those who read it, they must know the fields and woods, the flowers and trees of which so many of the words of prose and poetry are but symbols. *Till a considerable degree of education has been reached, words by themselves cannot convey ideas, or touch powers of thought or feeling* [italics in original].

This much to be desired knowledge and love of nature is not to be acquired through pictures alone. The chief motive in supplying schools with pictures of natural objects, is that a sufficient amount of pleasant curiosity about them may be excited in the minds of children to induce them to notice and admire such as do come into their experience; which, again, will give increased pleasure in the pictures.

Following love of nature it is desirable that it be made possible to young people reasonably to admire the work of man. To those who rarely or never see a beautiful building, pictures of noble architecture and lovely streets, such as the streets of Venice or Verona, the cathedrals of Canterbury, Lincoln, Rheims or Amiens [see Ruskin 1895/c. 1858, I and II], may speak a new truth; indeed many new truths. It is my wish to combine as much teaching, and of as many different kinds as possible in these school pictures. For example: I have had framed many photographs and other reproductions of the buildings and streets of Venice. There have also been given and lent me, paintings in oil and water color which add color to the otherwise sadly defective idea which a child could form of Venice. In order that the group may have its full possible value to the children, their teachers should be able to tell them something of the history of the city, and the men who made it great. Something of this may be accomplished by the descriptive labels.

A third most important function of pictures is that of arousing in the mind of the child and youth, love and admiration for truly great men and women, and making them real to him. I wish a really good picture of Abraham Lincoln might be in every schoolroom in the land. I know of no really good portrait of him which is not too expensive. If some photographer would take a large and fine photograph of Mr. [Augustus] St. Gauden's statue,[3] every school might have it.

If the public were aroused to the importance of making the school room a beautiful place instead of the desert spot it now is, I believe that the board of education would co-operate. The first essential for this is the tinting of the walls with some color in itself agreeable to the eye and pleasant as a background for pictures. The second is a somewhat different management of blackboards. All these changes could be brought about if it came to be generally regarded as a matter of consequence whether the rooms in which the children of the land pass their most susceptible days be beautiful and suggestive or ugly and barren.

Notes

1. [Untitled published pamphlet on art in public schools, October 29th, 1892, Reel 52, Hull-House Association Records; UI, Jane Addams Microfilm, hereafter referred to as JAM. There is another published but unsigned circular from 1892 that was distributed about the Public School Art Society that extends the points made here. It also states that the Manchester and Boston models were adopted in Chicago and it was probably written by Starr.]
2. [We did not locate this citation but Ruskin discusses the importance of color, shade, and architecture in *Stones of Venice, II & III* (1895/1851;1853).]
3. [This statue was located in Lincoln Park and was a comfort to Addams (1910, 32) during the Pullman Strike in Chicago.]

2

Outline Sketch Descriptive of Hull-House[1]

Hull-House: A Social Settlement

The two original residents of Hull-House are entering upon their sixth year of settlement in the nineteenth ward. They publish this outline[2] that the questions daily asked by neighbors and visitors may be succinctly answered. It necessarily takes somewhat the character of a report, but is much less formal. It aims not so much to give an account of what has been accomplished, as to suggest what may be done by and through a neighborhood of working-people, when they are touched by a common stimulus, and possess an intellectual and social centre[3] about which they may group their various organizations and enterprises. This centre or "settlement," to be effective, must contain an element of permanency, so that the neighborhood may feel that the interest and fortunes of the residents are identical with their own. The settlement must have an enthusiasm for the possibilities of its locality, and an ability to bring into it and develop from it those lines of thought and action which make for the "higher life."

The original residents came to Hull-House with a conviction that social intercourse could best express the growing sense of the economic unity of society. They wished the social spirit to be the undercurrent of the life of Hull-House, whatever direction the stream might take. All the details were left for the demands of the neighborhood to determine, and each department has grown from a discovery made through natural and reciprocal social relations.

The College Extension Courses

[The College Extension Courses] grew thus from an informal origin. The first class met as guests of the residents. As the classes became larger and more numerous, and the object of the newcomers more definitely that of acquisition of some special knowledge, the informality of the social relation was

43

necessarily less; but the prevailing attitude toward the house of the two hundred and fifty students now enrolled is that of guests as well as students. Many new students, attracted and refreshed by the social atmosphere, come into the classes who would not be likely to undertake any course of study at an evening high school, or any school within their reach. These students, the larger proportion of whom are young women, represent a great variety of occupations. Among them are teachers in the public schools, employees of factories and shops, typewriters and cashiers. The College Extension Course aims not to duplicate, but to supplement, the advantages offered by evening high schools and business colleges. Hence in these classes the emphasis is laid upon the humanities, and no attempt is made to supply means for earning a livelihood. The most popular and continuous courses have been in literature, languages, music, art, history, mathematics, and drawing. The saving grace of all good things, and the developing power of the love of them, have been proved to the satisfaction of the residents of Hull-House. A prospectus of the College Extension classes is published at the beginning of each term for ten weeks.

The College Extension classes are so called because the instructors are mostly college men and women. These classes were established at Hull-House before the University Extension movement began in Chicago, and are not connected with it. The faculty numbers thirty-five, mostly college men and women, some of whom have taught continuously for three years. No charge is made for the teaching, which is gratuitous on the part of the faculty; but the students pay fifty cents a course, which covers the printing of the prospectuses and other incidental expenses. Any surplus is expended upon lectures and reference books. Three University Extension Courses have been given at the centre formed at Hull-House—two in the drawing-room and one in a neighboring church. The lecturers were from the University Extension Department of the University of Chicago.

Summer School

A helpful supplement of the College Extension Courses has been the summer school held for three years in the buildings of Rockford College, at Rockford, Ill. Half the students were able to attend. The sum of three dollars a week paid by each student for board, covered the entire expenses of the school—the use of the buildings, including gymnasium and laboratories, having been given free of rent. Much time was devoted to out-door work in botany and the study of birds, and the month proved a successful combination of a summer vacation and a continuation of the year's study. The *esprit de corps*, fostered by the intimacy of the month's sojourn in college quarters, bore its first fruits in a students' association formed at the close of the summer's term.

The Students' Association

The Students' Association, now including a good proportion of the attendants of the class, is divided into the literary, the dramatic, and the musical sections. The society meets once a month, and each section in turn is responsible for an evening's entertainment. The programme is followed by an informal dance in the gymnasium. Each term's course is opened by a students' reception given by the residents.

Reading-Room

A reading-room in the lower floor of the Hull-House Art Gallery was maintained by the Chicago Public Library Board for three years, with two city librarians in charge. The room was supplied with English and foreign magazines and papers, as well as several hundred books. All the books of the Public Library are accessible to the neighborhood through the excellent system of sub-station delivery. This library has now been moved to a neighboring block.

Exhibitions of Pictures

Owing partly to the limited space available for the purpose, the picture exhibits have been necessarily small. An effort has been made to show only pictures which combine, to a considerable degree, an elevated tone with technical excellence; and at no time can a very large assortment of such pictures be obtained. There is an advantage on the side of a small exhibition carefully selected, especially to an untrained public. The confusion and fatigue of mind which a person of no trained powers of selection suffers in passing his eyes wearily over the assortment of good, bad, and indifferent which the average picture exhibit presents, leave him nothing with which to assimilate the good when he finds it, and his chances of finding it are small. Frequently recurring exhibitions of a few very choice pictures might do more toward educating the public taste of the locality in which they occur than many times the number less severely chosen and less often seen. Hull-House has had two exhibits every year since the gallery was built, which were well attended. They were omitted during the World's Fair, and an effort was made to supply their place by assisting as many people as possible to see the pictures of the fair intelligently. Parties formed for the purpose were conducted regularly by a resident.

The first residents of Hull-House held strongly to the belief that any compromise in the matter of excellence in art was a mistake. They hung their own walls only with such pictures as they felt were helpful to the life of mind and soul. Very much of the influence of the House they believed to be due to the harmony and reasonableness of the message of its walls. One of the residents has been much interested in pictures in the public schools, and has aroused sufficient interest in the subject to result in providing good sets of pictures and casts for several schools in the poorest localities. With the means at her disposal she has been able to put a number of good pictures into each room of the school nearest Hull-House, and one or more into five of the public kindergartens. A society has been organized for carrying on the work.

Working-People's Chorus

[In the working-people's chorus we use] the same principles the House is striving to carry into effect in regard to the music it provides.

The director of the World's Fair choruses has undertaken the training of a chorus of five hundred working-people. He believes that working-people especially need the musical form of expression, their lives being shorn on the art side. He further holds that musical people need for their art's sake the sense of brotherhood; that art is hollow and conventional unless it is the utterance of the common and universal life.

Sunday Concerts

A free concert is given in the gymnasium every Sunday afternoon. The concerts, at first given with the motive of entertaining, are now conducted with the development of musical taste and understanding as the object in view. This may be illustrated by selections from the programme.

SUNDAY CONCERTS, 5 P.M.
BEETHOVEN CONCERT . . . .   MRS. H. L. FRANK.
(Beethoven's Birthday.)

CHRISTMAS MUSIC.—Songs and carols of Eleanor Smith Reineke, Cornelius, and others.

MISS ELEANOR SMITH AND THE SENIOR SINGING-CLASS

MUSIC.—From Wagner's Opera of "Lohengrin," with interpretation. MRS. JAMES HUNT.
(In preparation for the Music MISS STARR will read Tennyson's "Holy Grail," at four o'clock.)

CONCERT. —Choral . . . . . .   Led by MR. W. L. TOMLINS.
(Solos and choruses from "The Messiah" and "Elijah.")

CONCERT. —Organ and String Quartette.
To be given at the house of Mrs. John C. Coonley, 620 Division Street (and Lake Shore Drive), by

MR. W. MIDDELSCHULTE AND THE SPIERING QUARTETT.

The oldest singing-class is now pursuing its third year of study under the instruction of a composer and teacher of vocal music who has never compromised her severe musical standards here or elsewhere. The comparatively small number of students whose intellect and perseverance have survived the test have had the advantage of an unusual training.

The Paderewski Club

A club of twenty children, calling themselves the Paderewski Club, has had a year of instruction on the piano, together with Sunday afternoon talks by their teacher on the lives of the great musicians. Six of the most proficient have obtained scholarships in the Chicago Conservatory.

The Jane Club

The Jane Club, a co-operative boarding-club for young working-women, had the advice and assistance of Hull-House in its establishment. The original members of the club, seven in number, were a group of trades-union girls accustomed to organized and co-operative action. The club has been from the beginning self-governing, without a matron or outside control, the officers being elected by the members from their own number, and serving for six months gratuitously. The two offices of treasurer and steward have required a generous sacrifice of their limited leisure, as well as a good deal of ability from those holding them. This being given, together with a considerable *esprit de corps* in the increasing number of members, the club has thriven both substantially and socially. The weekly dues of three dollars, with an occasional small assessment, have met all current expenses of rent, service, food, heat, and light, after the furnishing and first month's rent was supplied by Hull-House. The club now numbers fifty members, and the one flat is increased to five. The members do such share of the housework as does not interfere with their daily occupations. There are various circles within the club for social and intellectual purposes; and while the members are glad to procure the comforts of life at a rate within their means, the atmosphere of the club is one of comradeship rather than thrift. The club holds a monthly reception in the Hull-House gymnasium.

The Phalanx Club

A similar co-operative club has been started by nine young men at 245 West Polk Street, most of the members of which are members of the Typographical Union. The club has made a most promising beginning.

The Labor Movement

The connection of the House with the labor movement may be said to have begun on the same social basis as its other relations. Of its standing with labor unions, which is now "good and regular," it owes the foundation to personal relations with the organizer of the Bindery Girls' Union, who lived for some months in the House as a guest. It is now generally understood that Hull-House is "on the side of unions." Several of the women's unions have held their regular meetings at the House, two have been organized there, and in four instances men and women on strike against reduction in wages met there while the strike lasted. In one case a strike was successfully arbitrated by the House. It is most interesting to note that a number of small and feeble unions have, from the very fact of their weakness, been compelled to a policy which has been their strength, and has made for the strength of their cause. In this policy it has been the privilege of Hull-House to be of service to them. The stronger unions, such as the carpenters' and bricklayers', trusting in their own strength and the skill of their members, have too often adopted a course of exclusiveness and self-centred effort. The weak ones, as those in the clothing trades, finding it impossible to accomplish much alone, betook themselves to the constant urging of concerted action. The most important illustration of this highly useful policy is in the action of the unions in urging the factory inspection law passed by the Legislature of Illinois during the spring of 1893. The initiative toward the introduction of the measure in the legislature was taken by a resident of Hull-House; and a Committee of Investigation sent from Springfield to inspect sweat-shops, and decide upon the necessity for legislation, was piloted by her upon its tour. The same resident, who was at that time conducting in Chicago a so-called "slum investigation" for the Department of Labor at Washington, was, after the passage of the law, appointed inspector of factories in the State of Illinois. The work of the inspector and her assistants and deputies can be found in the annual report of the Illinois State Factory Inspector, the first of which has already been issued.

Hull-House is situated in the midst of the sweat-shop district of Chicago, and it was natural that the first effort of the House to procure legislation against an industrial evil should have been directed against the sweating-system.

A ward book has been kept by the residents for two years in which have been noted matters of sociological interest found in the ward. Many instances of the sweating-evil and child-labor have been recorded, as well as unsanitary tenements and instances of eviction.

Eight-Hour Club

After the passage of the factory and workshop bill, which includes a clause limiting women's labor to eight hours a day, the young women employees in a large factory in the near neighborhood of Hull-House formed an eight-hour club for the purpose of encouraging women in factories and workshops to obey the eight-hour law. This club has maintained its position, and done good missionary work for the cause. They have developed a strong sense of obligation toward employees in shops where the wages are low, and the employees much less favored than themselves. Their enthusiasm has carried them across a caste line. This club meets at Hull-House, and makes full use of the social factor so essential in fusing heterogeneous elements.

The Working-People's Social Science Club

[The Working-People's Social Science Club] was formed during the first year of residence at Hull-House, and has met weekly ever since, with the exception of the two summer months. In the summer of 1893, however, owing to the number of interesting speakers to be secured from the World's Fair Congresses, the club met without interruption. The purpose of the club is the discussion of social and economic topics. An opening address of forty-five minutes is followed by an hour of discussion. The speakers in the latter represent every possible shade of social and economic view. Working men and women are in the majority, although professional and business men are to be found at every meeting. The attendance averages seventy-five; the discussion is always animated and outspoken. The residents believe that one of the offices of the settlement is to provide that people of various creeds and class traditions should meet under a friendly and non-partisan roof, and discuss differences fairly. Following is a list of ten speakers and their subjects, selected from the programme of 1893:

"THE ENGLISH LABOR MOVEMENT."
    MR. WM. CLARKE. [Fabian]
"WOMAN'S SUFFRAGE."
    Miss SUSAN B. ANTHONY. [Suffragist]
"THE ECONOMIC AND SOCIAL CONDITIONS OF INDIA."
    SWAMI VIVEHANANDE.
"THE UNEMPLOYED."
    DR. CHARLES R. HENDERSON. [Chicago sociologist]
"THE LONDON COUNTY COUNCIL."
    MR. PERCY ALDEN. [Fabian]
"THE NEW TRADES-UNIONISM."
    MRS. ROBT. A. WOOD. [Social Settlement leader]
"CHARITY ORGANIZATION."
    DR. SETH LOW. [President of Columbia University, 1890-1901]
"THE NEIGHBORHOOD GUILD."
    DR. STANTON COIT. [Founder of Neighbrohood Guild]
"THE CONSCIENCE OF THE STATE."
    DR. BAYARD HOLMES. [Surgeon, College of Physicians and Surgeons]
"THE CHICAGO CITY COUNCIL."
    MR. WM. T. STEAD. [Popular minister of social gospel]

The programme for the fall of 1894 is possibly more typical:—
"SOCRATES."
    PROF. CHARLES F. BRADLEY, Northwestern University.
"EPICTETUS."
    DR. JOHN DEWEY, University of Chicago. [Pragmatist]
"MARCUS AURELIUS."
    PROF. J. H. TUFTS, University of Chicago. [Pragmatist]
"ST. FRANCIS."
    MISS ELIZA ALLEN STARR. [see chapter 21 here]
"SAVONAROLA."
    REV. Frank. W. GUNSAULUS, D.D. [Congregationalist minister/President of the Armour Institute]
"SIR THOMAS MORE."
    Mr. CHARLES ZUEBLIN, University of Chicago. [Fabian Pragmatist/Chicago sociologist]

The Arnold Toynbee Club Meets at Hull-House.

The objects of the club are: 1. To offer lectures upon economic subjects. 2. To ascertain and make known facts of interest to working-people in the fields of economics and legislation. 3. To promote legislation for economic and social reform, especially to secure greater public control over natural monopolies. Membership is by invitation. Members of the club offer a list of free lectures on economic and social questions. It is especially desired to aid in the educational work of trades' unions and young people's societies.

The Chicago Question Club

[The Chicago Question Club] meets in the Hull-House Art Gallery at two o'clock every Sunday afternoon. The club was fully formed before it asked for the hospitality of Hull-House. It is well organized and each meeting is opened by presentation of two sides of a question. Occasionally the various economic clubs meet for a common discussion. One of the most successful was led by Father Huntington, on the subject, "Can a Freethinker believe in Christ?" An audience of four hundred people followed closely the two hours discussion, which was closed by Mr. Henry George.

The Nineteenth Ward Inprovement Club

The Nineteenth Ward Improvement Club meets at Hull-House the second Saturday evening of each month. The president is the district representative in the Illinois State Legislature, and one of the ward aldermen is an active member. The club is pledged to the improvement of its ward in all directions. It has standing-committees on street-cleaning, etc., and was much interested in the efforts of the Municipal Order League to secure public baths. Through the solicitation of the league the City Council in 1892 made an appropriation of $12,000 for public baths. Hull-House was able to offer the use of a lot which had been given it by the owner rent free for two years. He transferred the lease to the city, with a satisfactory arrangement for its sale at the expiration of the lease, and a free public bath-house has been erected upon it, which is now in daily use. It contains seventeen shower-baths, a swimming-tank, and a tub. The Nineteenth Ward Improvement Club has formed a co-operative association, the first officers of which are the same as its own. It has opened a co-operative coalyard near Hull-House. The purchaser of a ton of coal becomes a member of the Co-operative Association. At its first meeting the members voted that their dividends be employed in establishing a bushel trade to meet the wants of the poor people of the neighborhood. The purchaser of each bushel receives a ticket, six of which entitle him to a rebate in coal. The association hopes in time to deal in other commodities.

Civic Federation Ward Council

In the fall of 1894 a ward council of the Civic Federation was organized at Hull-House for the nineteenth ward. The active members of the Nineteenth Ward Improvement Club are naturally working together under this new name.

A full set of committees have been organized—Municipal, Philanthropic, Industrial, Educational, Political, and Moral.

The Hull-House Women's Club

[The Hull-House Women's Club,] which now numbers ninety of the most able women in the ward, developed from a social meeting for purposes of tea-drinking and friendly chat. Several members of this club have done good work in street and alley inspecting through the Municipal Order League. The club has also presented to a public school in the neighborhood a fine autotype of Millet's[4] Knitting Shepherdess, and hopes to do more in future for the art-in-schools movement. They have been active in the visiting and relief work which has taken so large a share of the energies of the settlement during the hard times. One winter they purchased a ticket to the lectures given to mothers in the Kindergarten College. One member attended each week, and reported to the club. They are in touch with some of the vigorous movements of the city, and have frequent lectures on philanthropic and reform questions.

A Reception for Germans

[A Reception for Germans] has been held every Friday evening in Hull-House for four years. Two hours are spent in singing, reading, games, etc., and the habituees have all the comradeship of a club. They give an occasional coffee-drinking and entertainment. They are a good illustration of the social feeling too often wasted in a cramped neighborhood for lack of space and encouragement.

During the first two years of Hull-House the residents held receptions for Italians each week, which were largely attended. These were for a time discontinued, as their success depended mainly upon an Italian philanthropist, who has since started an agricultural colony in Alabama. Immigration societies, such as are successfully operated in London, are needed properly to place the Italian immigrants, who might do as much for the development of the Southern States as they have done for South America. Hull-House has not been able to inaugurate such a society, but sincerely hopes that one may be formed, as well as an association for improving tenement houses, those occupied by the Italians being overcrowded and unsanitary.

Children's Clubs

Since its foundation, Hull-House has had numerous classes and clubs for children. The fortunes and value of the clubs have varied, depending very much upon the spirit of the leaders. An effort has always been made to avoid the school atmosphere. The children are received and trusted as guests, and the initiative and control have come from them as far as possible. Their favorite occupation is listening to stories. One club has had a consecutive course of legends and tales of chivalry. There is no doubt that the more imaginative children learn to look upon the house as a gateway into a magic land, and get a genuine taste of the delights of literature. One boy, after a winter of Charlemagne stories, flung himself, half-crying, from the house, and said that "there was no good in coming any more now that Prince Roland was dead." The boys' clubs meet every Tuesday afternoon at four o'clock, and clubs of little girls come on Friday. The latter are the School-girls' Club and the Pansy Club, the Story-Telling Club and the Kindergarten Club. They sew, paint, or make paper chains during the story-telling, and play games in the gymnasium together before they go home at five o'clock. A club of Bohemian girls, called "Libuse," meets every Monday, and studies the heroic women in history. The little children meet one afternoon in the week for advanced kindergarten work. There are various children's classes for gymnastics and dancing; and two children's choruses, of two hundred and fifty each, meet weekly under the direction of Mr. William Tomlins. Dinners are served to schoolchildren upon presentation of tickets which have been sold to their mothers for five cents each. Those children are first selected whose mothers are necessarily at work during the middle of the day; and the dinner started with children formerly in the Hull-House *crèche*. While it is desired to give the children nutritious food, the little diners care much more for the toys and books and the general good time than they do for the dinners. It has been found, too, that the general attractiveness performs the function of the truant-officer in keeping them at school; for no school implies no dinner. The House has had the sympathetic and enthusiastic co-operation of the principal of the Polk Street public school.

Savings-Bank

A branch of the New York Penny Provident Savings-Bank has been sustained for two years. There are six hundred depositors.

Sewing-School

One hundred and twenty Italian girls meet every Monday afternoon in the gymnasium, directed by a superintendent and fifteen teachers. The children make garments, which they may purchase for the price of the material. An effort is made to follow up each new garment with lessons in tidiness. There are smaller classes in darning, knitting, and simple embroidery among the English-speaking little girls.

Cooking-Classes

Three cooking-classes for adults are held each week. The cooking-class for Italian girls has been very gratifying in its results. There is also a cooking-class every week for American children, and a nature class, which meets every Saturday morning. The young members are very happy when the weather permits them to go with their teacher to the park in pursuit of their subject. When it does not, they are most content with the simple microscopes at their disposal.

Summer Excursions

A systematic effort is made during the summer to have each of the four hundred children connected with the clubs spend at least one day in the country or parks. Excursions in small groups are more satisfactory than the time-honored picnic method. Each summer from fifty to a hundred children are sent from Hull-House to the fresh-air homes and country-houses. The residents were able, through the generosity of World's Fair enthusiasts, to assist fifteen hundred children to see the fair.

Playground

During the last year the use of a piece of ground near Hull-House measuring 326 x 119 was given rent free for a year, and in case it should not be sold in the meantime, for a longer period. The owner permitted the houses upon it, which were in bad sanitary condition, to be torn down; the ground was graded, fenced, provided with swings and other enticing apparatus, an officer was supplied from the city force, and a playground was thrown open to the juvenile public. Through the summer evenings many parents came with their children. Several of the residents spent much time there teaching the children games, and regulating the use of the fifty buckets and shovels which were active in the sand-piles. The music furnished by an organ-grinder every afternoon often brought forth an Italian tarantella or an Irish jig with curious spontaneity.

Free Kindergarten and Day Nursery

From the first month of its existence Hull-House has had a free kindergarten, and for three years a day nursery, where mothers who are obliged to work leave their children for the day, paying five cents for each child. The *crèche* averages in summer fifty children, and in winter between thirty and forty. A friend of the House, who makes herself responsible for the financial support of the *crèche*, gives largely of her time in directing and assisting in the work. This nursery is like others in most respects, differing chiefly, perhaps, in the attention paid to the matter of pictures and casts. The Madonnas of Raphael, in the best and largest photographs, are hung low, that the children may see them, as well as casts from Donatello [1386-1466] and Della Robbia. The children talk in a familiar way to the babies on the wall, and sometimes climb upon the chairs to kiss them. Surely much is gained if one can begin in a very little child to make a truly beautiful thing truly beloved. An experienced kindergartner is in charge of the nursery. She has the constant assistance of two women.

Gymnasium

The last building added to the equipment of Hull-House includes a public coffee and lunch room, a New England kitchen, a gymnasium, with shower-baths, and men's club-room, supplied with billiard and card tables. The use of the gymnasium is divided between men and women, girls and boys, at different hours. The evening hours are reserved more especially for men. The gymnasium, being now the largest room in the possession of the settlement, is necessarily used on certain evenings as an audience room, and as a reception and ball room by the various clubs.

The Hull-House Men's Club

[The Hull-House Men's Club] holds a reception there once a month, and an occasional banquet. This club, which rents a room in the front of the building, is composed of one hundred and fifty of the abler citizens and more enterprising young men of the vicinity. Their constitution commits them, among other things, to the "cultivation of sobriety and good-fellowship." They are not without political influence in the ward, and are a distinct factor in its social life, as all of their social undertakings have been remarkably spirited and successful. They are in sympathy with the aims of Hull-House, and are prompt to assist and promote any of its undertakings. Business meetings are held on the first and third Friday evenings of each month, and on alternate evenings the Literary and Debating Sections hold meetings.

Hull-House Mandolin Club

[The Hull-House Mandolin Club] consists of twelve members of the Men's Club, who have successfully sustained an orchestra of mandolin and guitars for a year. They are most generous with their services to the entertainments of the House.

Young People's Clubs

The Lincoln Club is a debating-society of young men, whose occasional public debates are always heard by a large and enthusiastic audience. In their weekly meeting they have a carefully prepared debate, usually upon current political events. They meet once a month with the Hull-House Social Club. This is composed of young women of the neighborhood, many of whom have met every week for four years. Their programmes are literary and social. They give an occasional play. The last one presented was the court scene from the "Merchant of Venice."

Among the other clubs of young people, the Young Citizens boasts the oldest club-life. Their programmes alternate between discussions and readings. An effort is made in both for civic and municipal education.

The Anfreda Club of thirty young girls meets the same evening. After the literary programme is concluded, the two clubs have half an hour of dancing or games together before going home.

Henry Learned Club, Hull-House Glee Club, Jolly Boys' Club, Good-Fellowship Club, Lexington Club, Bohemian Garnet Club, Longfellow Club, Laurel Club, Harrison Club, and others, are composed of young people from fourteen to twenty-five years of age. Alumni associations of the neighboring public schools hold their meetings at the House. An effort is being made toward school extension.

The Hull-House Coffee-House and Kitchen

The Hull-House coffee-house was opened July 1, 1893. The room itself is an attractive copy of an English inn, with low, dark rafters, diamond windows, and large fireplace. It is open every day from six in the morning to ten at night. An effort has been made to combine the convenience of a lunchroom, where well-cooked food can be sold at a reasonable rate, with cosiness and attractiveness. The residents believe that substitution is the only remedy against the evils of the saloon. The large kitchen has been carefully equipped, under the direction of Mrs. Ellen Richards,[5] with a New England kitchen outfit, including a number of Aladdin ovens. The foods are carefully pre-pared, and are sold by the quart or pound to families for home consumption. Coffee, soups, and stews are delivered every day at noon to the neighboring factories. By means of an indurated fibre can, it is possible to transport and serve the food hot. The employees purchase a pint of soup or coffee with two rolls for five cents, and the plan [is extended by service to factory women.]

Noon Factory Delivery

[Noon Factory Delivery] is daily growing in popularity. The kitchen dur-ing the winter of 1893-1894 supplied hot lunches at ten cents each to the two hundred women employed in the sewing-room established by the Emergency Committee of the Chicago Women's Club. This room supplied work to unem-ployed women during the stress of the last winter. Hull-House has also super-intended a temporary lodging-house for the use of unemployed women for some months.

A physician[6] is in residence at Hull-House, and another who lives near is most constant and generous with her professional services. A nurse of the Visiting Nurses' Association has her headquarters, and receives her orders, at the House.

A Public Dispensery

[A Public Dispensary] was undertaken in 1893. It is open every day from three until four, and every evening from seven to eight o'clock. A small charge is made when possible for drugs. In the same house, 247 Polk Street, is the [Labor Bureau.]

Hull-House Labor Bureau

[Hull-House Labor Bureau is] necessarily small at present from the extreme difficulty of finding work for men or women. Hull-House has always under-taken a certain amount of relief work, the records of which are kept with those of the Labor Bureau. One of the residents [Julia Lathrop] served for a winter as a visitor on the Cook County staff, all the cases of destitution within a certain radius of Hull-House being given to her for investigation. She also has estab-lished and maintained with all the charitable institutions of the city a cordial and sympathetic relationship, which has been most valuable to the neighbor-hood. She has more recently been appointed a member of the State Board of Charities. The House has been active in the movement to organize the chari-ties of Chicago, and has recently united its relief office with the ward office established by the new organization.

Residents

No university or college qualification has ever been made for residence, although the majority of residents have been college people. The organiza-tion of the settlement has been extremely informal; but an attempt has been made during the last winter to limit the number of residents to twenty. The household, augmented by visitors, has occasionally exceeded that number. Applicants for residence are received for six weeks, during which time they have all privileges, save a vote, at residents' meeting. At the end of that period, if they have proved valuable to the work of the House, they are invited to remain, if it is probable that they can be in residence for six months. The expenses of the residents are defrayed by themselves on the plan of a co-operative club under the direction of a house committee. A limited number of fellowships has been established, one of them by the Chicago branch of the Inter-Collegiate Alumnae Association [later organized as the American Asso-ciation of University Women].

All the residents of Hull-House for the first three years were women, though much valuable work has always been done by non-resident men. During the last year men have come into residence in a cottage on Polk Street, dining at Hull-House, and giving such part of their time to the work of the settlement as is consistent with their professional or business life.

It is estimated that two thousand people come to Hull-House each week, either as members of clubs or organizations, or as parts of an audience. One hundred of these come as teachers, lecturers, or directors of club. The house has always had much valuable assistance from the citizens of Chicago. This voluntary response to its needs perhaps accounts for the fact that it has never found it necessary to form an association with chapters in colleges, as other settlements have done.

Finances

Hull-House and the adjacent lots are given by the owner rent free until 1920. Two buildings have been built upon these by friends of the House. Three other buildings are to be erected in 1895. One is an addition to the coffeehouse, a second is designed for general class and audience rooms, while the third is to be known as the children's house. The superintendence and teaching of the settlement are volunteered by residents and others, and are unpaid. The running expenses of the settlement proper are therefore reduced to a minimum. Large sums are constantly needed, however, for the initiation of new departments and the expenses of those branches, such as the nursery, which can never be self supporting. These are constantly defrayed by generous friends of the House, many of whom are active in its service.

Notes

1. [This was originally a pamphlet that was reprinted as the "Appendix" to *Hull-House Maps and Papers*, based on a pamphlet co-authored by Starr and Addams. It was headed by a list of residents who had lived six months or more at Hull-House. It included: Jane Addams, Ellen G. Starr, Julia C. Lathrop, Florence Kelley, Mary A. Keyser, Anna M. Farnsworth, Agnes Sinclair Holbrook, Josephine Milligan, M.D., Wilfreda Brockway, Rose M. Gyles, Gertrude Barnum, Ella Raymond Waite, Annie Fryar, Josefa Humpal Zeman, Margaret M. West, Jeannette C. Welch, Enella Benedict, Clifford W. Barnes, Alex A. Bruce, Edward L. Burchard, Henry B. Learned, Chas. C. Arnold, John Addams Linn. Edwin A. Waldo. This was not an exhaustive list, however, and excluded Mary E. McDowell and Charles Zueblin, among others. They added a note that:] The "settlement, Jan. 1, 1895, numbers twenty, including those who are in residence now, but have not yet resided for six months."
2. This outline was originally issued as a pamphlet, Feb. 1, 1893. It is here revised to Jan. 1, 1895.
3. [This British spelling of "center" reflects the early British influence on Hull-House.]
4. [Jean Francois Millet (1814-1875) is most famous for his paintings of peasants. (see "Millet, Jean Francois" 1974, 898).]
5. [Ellen Henrietta Swallow Richards was a major figure in the Home Economics movement. See James (1971).]
6. [Harriett Rice was an African American physician who came to Hull-House in 1894. She did not stay very long and little information on her life is available. See Stebner 1997, ftn. 75, pp. 220-21.]

3

Art and Democracy[1]

What is Art? What is Democracy? Have they ever existed together? Have we reason to assume, by recourse to history—from the facts of past and present—that they will;—that there will ever be a democratic art, the free expression of a free people? Egypt and Assyria are not encouraging, with their august monuments and their slavery. Nor for a modern instance, is Switzerland, the most complete of democracies, producing little art beyond cuckoo clocks and carved toys. Let us try to take a rapid glance at the great epochs of art and the countries which produced it and consider their relative degrees of democratic achievement.

But first, What are we to look for? What is Art? What Democracy? The second question I shall assume the audience I am addressing to have considered with their full powers and shall not go into an analysis of the ideas contained in it and implied by it. But perhaps those before me have not devoted any considerable proportion of their time to the clear formulation of ideas of Art, or its essence, its uses or its limitations. Let us therefore reflect a little together, and examine our concepts of the much abused word.

"Art" has among other debased uses, come to be treated as an adjective, supposedly descriptive of various products for which sale is sought, e.g. "Art Glass" "Art Furniture," "Art Gum" (applied to a kind of soft rubber for erasing) phrases which cause a shudder to a lover of pure English and drive to despair one who hopes for any dawning in his span of life, of popular understanding of and respect for the handmaid of life and of nature, known also, throughout great ages, as the hand maid of religion.

Perhaps a majority of persons who use their minds analytically might say, in effect, that Art is the formal expression of the sense of Beauty. That definition allows a broad interpretation including plastic and linear art, color and musical sound, and thus embracing the arts of painting sculpture, engraving, music and poetry. This definition emphasizes the product, and attempts an analysis and interpretation of it. William Morris was wont to give a definition which focused attention upon the process, or the functioning of the art of faculty, and explained or aimed to explain it. He says that art is the expression of a man's joy in his work. Whenever, so Morris thought, work is done with real pleasure, that pleasure finds expression in some degree of comeliness or beauty: and that beauty or comeliness is, in its degree, artistic: art is produced with and by pleasure in work.

You will readily see that this definition draws no line between major and minor arts. The so-named "fine arts" fall into the same category, under the same classification, with the minor arts and crafts. And, indeed, it is quite true that no definite line can be drawn. The fine arts of Painting and Sculpture were not born full grown and armoured from any deity's head. They had very humble origins, such as the decoration of jugs and all kinds of kitchen utensils, of swords, shields and all manner of weapons. Everything which interested a primitive and developing people, they decorated. Always much interested in their own bodies, they at all times made personal ornaments of one sort and another. And as long as this was done simply and honestly with a single eye to embellishment, they are always in some considerable measure attractive, however crude. Witness the silver and other ornaments of aboriginal Indians, and all savage peoples.[2] It is only when the commercial motive enters (introduced by "Civilization") and the object becomes primarily to sell and only secondarily to please, that degradation and vulgarity set in. (Elaborate and illustrate this.[3])

Morris [1884] protests that commercialism-competitive commerce—created the vulgar; that the peculiar thing we name vulgarity was non-existent before the advent of the commercial ideal. (Read passage on rubbish made by machines—*Art and Socialism* [1884] p. 108).

Turning back, then, to Morris's definition of art (suggested to him by Ruskin whose pupil he was) as the expression of man's pleasure in work, it will readily be seen that, in order to have pleasure in work there must be freedom in it. Slavish work can never be pleasurable and hence never beautiful or artistic in itself, through it may be utilized by a free mind using it as material. Even then the resulting whole will be less beautiful than it might have been if all the material had been, bit by bit, made beautiful and interesting by pleasurable activity. John Ruskin deals very fully and convincingly with this idea in a chapter entitled, "The Nature of Gothic"—in *Stones of Venice* [II. *RW, I* 1895/1858, 152-230]. So important did Morris consider this chapter that he printed it as a separate book on his Kelmscott Press. (Read or quote passages from it and show photos of Greek mouldings, and Gothic ornament from Amiens Cathedral and Ducal palace. Note imperfections accepted in Gothic Art.)[4]

Now if we accept these definitions, statements and inferences, the first question which arises is [:] Why do we trouble at all about trying to produce or encourage the production of art under present adverse circumstances? Why not devote all our energies to making life free, happy and livable, and leave art to take care of itself, as it then will do?

I feel fairly assured that such has been the practical answer to the question given, in conduct, by most of my friends and comrades in this audience. Yet, as a policy to be advocated and urged upon all, it is open to some objections. Morris himself felt the logic of it, and for a time, yielded to it to the extent of giving a very large part of his time to teaching and propaganda lecturing. But when he came to see that freeing the world was a long and laborious process, that meanwhile if art were utterly to languish and die, many souls craving it (he believed that beauty—art—was a necessity for all, not a luxury for the few) would live and die unsolaced without it. When he reflected that, once extinct, many years and much experience must be spent in re-invention and re-discovery of processes and techniques, he was convinced that we must e'en [sic] do our best to keep art alive. But he granted that it was only the specially endowed individual who could produce art under modern conditions, in a world ruled by competitive commerce; that this individual, because he must live a life apart, had, and could have, small influence on the lives of others of his time.

Let us now continue the inquiry as to whether in seeking to actualize our ideal of a democratic art we are looking entirely toward the future or whether such has ever existed, and in what measure. In glancing over the great epochs of art production we find the Assyrian (Ninevite) and Egyptian to fall entirely within Ruskin's grouping of "servile" art; and the Greek as well, i.e. as far as inferior ornament goes [Ruskin, *RW* I, 1895/1858, 382-94; II, 159]. The great sculptors, though also decorators, Phidias of the age of Pericles, and Praxiteles, enjoyed not only freedom but high standing in the state. In the great Gothic periods of the 13th and 14th centuries freedom in work went much farther; for, as I have shown you, even in minor decoration, the workman enjoyed, obviously, entire freedom to deal with his allotted space and materials in his own way. Nobody could claim that in these centuries, the 13th and 14th, democracy in government had been achieved. It was in the 14th Century, 1381, during the reign of Richard the Second, that the famous peasant's uprising took place of which Morris [1913] gives us so wonderful a picture in the most perfect of all his works, *A Dream of John Ball*. So late as 1350 a man who had escaped from his master might be branded in the forehead with a hot-iron, and we have records of the sale of serfs "with their litter" meaning the family of children.

Yet in the vivid and marvelously beautiful picture drawn by Morris in *John Ball* (which Mackail calls at once a romance, a political manifesto, and a study in the philosophy of history,) one meets with men whose spirits are free, whose surroundings are wholesome and beautiful. Morris knew the middle ages, the Gothic ages, with a deeply sympathetic knowledge; and he cared for human freedom with passionate interest. You can hardly suspect that he could be satisfied with or indulgent toward branding of human beings or sales of serfs. Yet we feel sure from what he [and Ruskin] has set forth for us in *John Ball* (with the double charm of the artist and the poet) that he would himself have chosen to live and work under the conditions he pictures there rather than under factory conditions of his day.

And now hear what Ruskin says of the "freedom" of today as compared with that of the Gothic builders, ("Nature of Gothic" pp. 19 & 20. [Ruskin, II, RW 1895/1858, 173-175]). If the testimony of these two students and lovers of beauty and its expression in work is convincing (as the evidence in the monuments was convincing to them) we are thrown back, as they were, upon Gothic architecture as the point at which the path was lost. Morris himself believed that the way must be retraced to the lost trail and that we must take up the road, where we lost it (*Gothic Architecture*, 7)[5]. To many this will seem impossible, to many more, undesirable (undesirable it would surely be if we returned in a spirit of mere imitation of the Gothic form.) Indeed true Gothic could not be produced by imitation, since its first and fundamental characteristics are freedom and naturalness and infinite variation. It is difficult to convince many persons of the freedom of cathedral builders. (Note a conversation about Reims at a Socialist dinner. The problems of superstition, slavery, etc.) Yet, not Ruskin only, but Morris himself, a socialist and a modern—see his estimate of Ruskin's "Nature of Gothic"—in preface—as one of the few necessary and inevitable utterances of the century (see Morris in *Gothic Architecture*, pp. 3 & 4.)

Unfavorable comparisons to the present day—I should think they cannot be quite ignored—given the testimony of two such men, and even by our comrade who scoffs at the Cathedral of Reims and regards its destruction as a matter of no great moment. Assuming for the moment that my audience gives ear to this testimony [of Ruskin and Morris]—assuming, even, that there begins to be a public which tires of ever—increasing miles of drear ugliness, which dimly feels that times were not ever thus, that even cities need not of necessity be wholly hateful to the eye: assuming that an appreciable public has awakened to the wish for something better—what, then, shall we say to them? What advise? Where begin?

First, you must not expect me to say or believe that democracy in government would immediately produce beauty and art. The popular traditions of beauty and art among us are dead. The discernment of beauty has perished in the people. (Examples—Dress, houses of those who begin to be prosperous and of the rich.) We must, then even while we strive for freedom of life for the workers, freedom for conditions of work for them, without which we have seen that there is little or no hope for any national or community development of art, indeed, little or no hope for art at all—we must, at the same time form, as best we may, by the study of the great past and by willingness to understand it, and to believe that we are not ourselves in all respects "the people" with whom "wisdom shall die," some concepts of what a beautiful city has been and might be, and how even "The Brute" (See Wm. Vaughn Moody's poem) may be subdued and made to work for it (Read passages if there is time.) And together with this effort I deem it not futile, at least not objectless, to reflect, occasionally, upon our own worst national defects, as the present day impediments to vision and progress.

We might study them in the young, we elders, if that be more agreeable to our pride! Our "independence," so we think it, and vaunt ourselves upon it, which is, nevertheless, really a copying of others with self-will. Research work in this subject may be carried on most easily in the phenomena of dress and recreation. This vaunting of independence has all the faults of slavish convention and arrogance combined. It has neither the virtues of obedience and humility (which, though highly unpopular in our day are real virtues in their place) nor of courage, originality, inspiration and self-sustainedness. This hybrid "independence" gives to the character, and the corresponding life-products, all of the undesirable traits of slavish copying and of self-will combined. It tends to monotony of the dullest sort together with incessant craving for excitement. (Examples and illustrations)

> Dress—no invention, absolute conformity but constant change of fashion. Amusements—movies, undermining legitimate drama.

> Modern dances—their hideous ugliness—contrast with charming folk dances and stately minutes—no real gayety nor grace—angles and "wiggles."

A society of foxtrots and movies & gum-chewing can produce no art.

When slavish conventions are forced upon people (as they often are) only the strongest characters can resist. The conceit is omitted from the result, but the tasteless slavishness remains. What will free us from all this and replace these odiously vulgar substitutes for the rational play instinct which is art producing?

[Starr struggles for a satisfactory answer to this question and presents a few examples of examples of life around Hull-House.]

> European peasants when they arrive and after. Test to one's democracy to witness what happens. Agonizing period to be gone through.

> Imagine boy born on Halsted Street or Milwaukee Avenue, the effect of always living in that surrounding. How make an artist of him? The dulling effect of 28 years of ugliness even on one who loves beauty and sometimes escapes it.

> Imagine sudden fortune to the youth thus born and reared. His house. furniture, carpets, wallpaper. A nightmare!

> How art developed and grew in all great peoples; first, it is primitive. It began with their infancy and grew with their growth. Literature leading. Shield of Achilles in Homer. (Give a description far beyond playthings.)

Now let us take account of our own position as a nation—the U.S.A. We were never a primitive people. The colonists and George Washington were no more primitive than the English, Dutch and French they left. The same will be the case in all colonies settled from mature civilizations. The art of our colonial forefathers, then, should logically have been a continuation of or a development from the art of their several races and nations. But they could do nothing at all about art. Their energies were entirely demanded by their struggle with the elements and the Indians. Houses, indeed, they must have. And colonial architecture is the only dignified and beautiful architecture we have ever had in this country. Even the village "meeting houses" with their prim fronts and slender "steeples" have a quaint dignity and charm of their own. We are quite rightly returning to colonial after having destroyed many beautiful specimens, and replaced them by Queen Anne, "ginger bread," bedpost porch columns and various architectural enormities. In this retracing of our steps to our own best and only good thing in architecture we can make no mistake. But it does not carry us far, It gives no type or ideal of the structure of a city— the grouping of its buildings of civic importance.

Notes

1. [Typescript. Box 21, folder 273. Ellen Gates Starr Papers, Sophia Smith Collection, Smith College. This was a speech that was not prepared for publication. It has been edited for accuracy and clarity.]
2. ["Savage" was a technical, anthropological term at the time this was written.]
3. [Ruskin's *Stones of Venice, I-III* was the basis of Starr's references throughout this chapter. These volumes contain hundreds of illustrations and pen and ink drawings of architectural features and designs. It is logical to assume that Starr used some of these for her stereoptican examples.]
4. [Ibid.]
5. [Starr used a copy of this book and uses references to it here. We could not locate this book.]

4

Art and Labor[1]

To any one living in a working-class district of a great city to-day, the question must arise whether it be at all worth the cost to try to perpetuate art under conditions so hopeless, or whether it be not the only rational or even possible course to give up the struggle from that point, and devote every energy to "the purification of the nation's heart and the chastisement of its life." Only by re-creation of the source of art can it be restored as a living force. But one must always remember the hungering individual soul which, without it, will have passed unsolaced and unfed, followed by other souls who lack the impulse his should have given. And when one sees how almost miraculously the young mind often responds to what is beautiful in its environment, and rejects what is ugly, it renews courage to set the leaven of the beautiful in the midst of the ugly, instead of waiting for the ugly to be first cleared away.

A child of two drunken parents one day brought to Hull-House kindergarten and presented to her teacher a wretched print, with the explanation, "See the Lady Moon." The Lady Moon, so named in one of the songs the children sing, was dimly visible in an extreme corner of the print otherwise devoted to murder and sudden death; but it was the only thing the child really saw.

The nourishment to life of one good picture to supplant in interest vicious story-papers and posters; of one good song to take the place of vulgar street jingles, cannot, I believe, be estimated or guessed. A good picture for every household seems unattainable until households can produce, or at least select, their own; but certainly a good one in every schoolroom would not be unattainable, if the public should come to regard it as a matter of moment that the rooms in which the children of the land spend their most impressionable days be made beautiful and suggestive, instead of barren and repellant.

Mr. T. C. Horsfall, of Manchester, England, who has developed a system of circulating collections of pictures in the schools[2] of that unhappy city, says that the decision as to whether art shall be used in education is, to modern communities, a decision as to whether the mass of the people shall be barbarian or civilized. Assuredly it has a direct bearing upon the art-producing possibilities of the communities in question.

Let us consider what is the prospect for an "art of the people" in our great cities. And first let us admit that art must be of the people if it is to be at all. We must admit this whether we look into the life of the past or into our own life. If we look to any great national art, that of Athens or of Venice or of Florence, we see that it has not been produced by a few, living apart, fed upon conditions different from the common life; but that it has been, in great part, the expression of that common life. If it has reached higher than the common life, it has done so only by rising through it, never by springing up outside it and apart from it. When Florence decked herself with reliefs of the Madonna and the Infant, the life of Florence was a devotion to these shrines. Giotto and Donatello [1386-1466] only expressed with a power and grace concentred in them what all the people felt; and more than that, had not the people felt thus, there could have been no medium for that grace and power.

If we are to have a national art at all, it must be art of the people; and art can only come to a free people. The great prophet of art in our day, John Ruskin, has said that "all great art is praise" (Ruskin, *Laws of Fesole*, *RW*, 1895/1894, 11-14), showing man's pleasure in God's work; and his disciple, William Morris, expresses another side of the same truth when he says that "to each man is due the solace of art in his labor, and the opportunity of expressing his thoughts to his fellows through that labor." Now, only a free man can express himself in his work. If he is doing slave's work, under slavish conditions, it is doubtful whether he will ultimately have many thoughts worth the name; and if he have, his work can in no wise be their vehicle. It is only when a man is doing work which he wishes done, and delights in doing, and which he is free to do as he likes, that his work becomes a language to him. As soon as it does so become it is artistic. Every man working in the joy of his heart is, in some measure, an artist. Everything wrought with delight in the work itself is, in some measure, lovely. The destructive force of the ugly is its heartlessness. The peasant's cottage in the Tyrol, built with its owner's hands, decorated with his taste, and propounding his morals and religion in inlaid sentences under its broad eaves, blesses the memory with a beauty but half obliterated by daily sight of dreary parallelograms and triangles, joylessly united, which make up the streets of our working-people. The streets of Venice, of Verona, of Rouen, were built by men working in freedom, at liberty to vary a device or to invent one. They were not built by lawlessness or caprice, but under a willing service, which alone is perfect freedom.

The same men who built so nobly the cathedrals and council-halls of Rouen and Venice, built as harmoniously, though more simply and modestly, as was fit, their own dwellings. Had they been capable of making their own houses ugly, they would have been incapable of housing beautifully the rulers of their city or the King of kings.

This is the fatal mistake of our modern civilization, which is causing it to undo itself and become barbarous in its unloveliness and discord. We have believed that we could force men to live without beauty in their own lives, and still compel them to make for us the beautiful things in which we have denied them any part. We have supposed that we could teach men, in schools, to produce a grace and harmony which they never see, and which the life that we force them to live utterly precludes. Or else we have thought—a still more hopeless error—that they, the workers, the makers, need not know what grace and beauty and harmony are; that artists and architects may keep the secrets, and the builders and makers, not knowing them, can slavishly and mechanically execute what the wise in these mysteries plan.

The results should long ago have taught us our mistake. But only now are we learning, partly from dismal experience of life barren of beauty and variety, and partly from severe but timely teaching from such prophets as Ruskin and Morris, that no man can execute artistically what another man plans, unless the workman's freedom has been part of the plan. The product of a machine may be useful, and may serve some purposes of information, but can never be artistic. As soon as a machine intervenes between the mind and its product, a hard, impassable barrier—a non-conductor of thought and emotion—is raised between the speaking and the listening mind. If a man is made a machine, if his part is merely that of reproducing, with mechanical exactness, the design of somebody else, the effect is the same. The more exact the reproduction, the less of the personality of the man who does the work is in the product, the more uninteresting will the product be. A demonstration of how uninteresting this slavish machine-work can become may be found in the carved and upholstered ornamentation of any drawing-room car—one might also say of any drawing-room one enters.

I have never seen in a city anything in the way of decoration upon the house of an American citizen which he had himself designed and wrought for pleasure in it. In the house of an Italian peasant immigrant in our own neighborhood, I have seen wall and ceiling decorations of his own design, and done by his own hand in colors. The designs were very rude, the colors coarse; but there was nothing of the vulgar in it, and there was something of hope. The peasant immigrant's surroundings begin to be vulgar precisely at the point where he begins to buy and adorn his dwelling with the products of American manufacture. What he brings with him in the way of carven bed, wrought kerchief, enamel in-laid picture of saint or angel, has its charm of human touch, and is graceful, however childish.

The peasants themselves secretly prefer their old possessions, but are sustained by a proud and virtuous consciousness of having secured what other people have and what the world approves. A dear old peasant friend of Hull House once conceived the notion that the dignity of his wife—whom he called "my lady"—required that she have a dress in the American mode.

Many were the mediatorial struggles which we enacted before this "American dress" was fitted and done. And then, by the mercy of Heaven, her courage gave out, and she never wore it. She found it too uncomfortable, and I know that in her inmost heart she found it too ugly.

Could men build their own houses, could they carve or fresco upon casing, door, or ceiling any decoration which pleased them, it is inconceivable that, under conditions of freedom and happiness, they should refrain from doing so. It is inconceivable that, adorning their own dwellings in the gladness of their hearts, they should not develop something of grace, of beauty, of meaning, in what their hands wrought; impossible that their hands should work on unprompted by heart or brain; impossible then, as inevitable now, that most men's houses should express nothing of themselves save a dull acceptance of things commercially and industrially thrust upon them.

A workingman must accept his house as he finds it. He not only cannot build it, he cannot buy it; and is usually not at liberty to alter it materially, even had he the motive to do so, being likely to leave it at any time. The frescoed ceiling to which I have referred, as the only example within my experience of any attempt at original decoration, was in a cottage tenement. If the author had any affection for the work of his hands, he could not take it away with him. He would probably not be permitted, were he inclined, to carve the doorposts; and the uncertainty of tenure would deter him from yielding to any artistic prompting to do so. It would be disheartening to find one's belongings set into the street, and be obliged to leave one's brave device half finished.

A man's happiness, as well as his freedom, is a necessary condition of his being artistic. Ruskin lays it down as a law that neither vice nor pain can enter into the entirely highest art. How far art can be at all co-existent with pain, ugliness, gloom, sorrow, and slavery concerns very vitally the question of an art of the people.

No civilized and happy people has ever been able to express itself without art. The prophet expands his "All great art is praise" (Ruskin, *Laws of Fesole*, *RW* 1895/1894, 11-14), into "The art of man is the expression of his rational and disciplined delight in the forms and laws of the creation of which he forms a part" (Ruskin, *Laws of Fesole*, *RW* 1895/1894, 11). A rational and disciplined delight in the forms and laws of the creation of which a denizen of an industrial district in one of our great cities forms a conscious part, is inconceivable. Some of the laws which govern its conscious life may be traced in their resultant forms.

Its most clearly manifested law is "the iron law of wages." Of the workings and products of this law in squalor, deformity, and irrecoverable loss of health, many examples are given in the accompanying article on Child-labor [Kelley 1895].

Of the law of love manifested in the harmonious life of the universe, these little toilers know nothing. Of the laws of healthy growth of mind and body by air, sunlight, and wholesome work, neither they nor their children can know anything. Of the laws of heredity they know bitterly, and of the law of arrested development.

It is needlessly painful to say here in what forms these laws have made themselves known to them, and to all who look upon them. It is equally needless to say that they can have no delight in these forms, no wish to reflect and perpetuate them. Need it be said that they can have no art?

The Greek was compelled by his joy in his own and his brother's beauty and strength to make it abiding, and a joy to all who should look upon it. It was a not unreasonable pride which offered to the gods as a religious act the feats of those strong and perfect bodies; and Greek sculpture smiles forth the gladness of the Greek heart blithely in its graceful runners and wrestlers, solemnly in its august deities, whose laws the people obeyed, and rejoiced in obeying. It may not be quite profitless, though altogether painful, to think sometimes of the weak, small, ugly frames produced by the life we force men and little children to live, and of which we would not dare make an offering to an offended God, whose laws we have neither rejoiced in nor obeyed.

Obedience to physical law results always in forms of physical beauty; love of these forms and happy activity, in artistic expression. From disobedience to law follows physical ugliness, which inspires nothing but apathy or distaste, and results in no artistic utterance. A higher art is born of delight in spiritual beauty, consequent upon obedience to law above the physical. It remains to determine how far the disharmony of disobedience can have expression through art. Discord has place in music only as a negative, to give accent to the positive good. Variety is good, but the eye and ear crave occasional monotony in art-form to make the good of multiform life keenly felt. Beyond that need monotony and discord are both painful. This is the limit of the purely artistic use of these negative values.

The expression of the negative in art-form has, however, within limits, another legitimate use, which bears the same relation to art in its strict sense which pamphleteering bears to literature proper.

Against the infliction or willing permission of pain, there is a gospel to be preached; and for the effectual preaching of this gospel, literature, art, every language in which it can be couched, may be pressed into service.

> "We're made so that we love
> First when we see them painted, things we've passed
> Perhaps a hundred times nor cared to see;
> And so they are better, painted,—better to us,
> Which is the same thing. Art was given for that."

So it was,—to make us love the lovable. But if we are made so, too, that we hate for the first time as it deserves to be hated, and dread as we ought to dread it when we see it painted, the destruction of the lovable and the beautiful by the impious hand of man, then art must descend from her altar service to that hard work of discipline.

As long as we inflict or supinely permit the wilful destruction of life by rapid process or slow, we need to be shocked into the realization of our guilt. But we cannot grow by a series of shocks; and only in so far as we are conceivably responsible for any measure of this woe, and most assuredly only in so far as the sight of it is awful and unbearable to us, can it be anything but harmful to us to see it. So far as it gives any pleasure it blunts or degrades. It is only the faith that God wills that not one of His children should perish, and that with Him all things are possible, in His eternity, which makes it endurable to look for one moment upon the starvation and degradation of mind and soul, the defacement of the image of God by man, in Millet's[3] "Laborer." Strange that we can bear so constantly the sight of the real laborer; that the back bent, never to stand erect in the true figure of a man, the stolid and vacant face, should be looked upon with such equanimity and apathetic acceptance.

The pictures of Jean Francois Millet illustrate well the limit beyond which art cannot go into the realm of gloom and wrong. They are entirely true always. They reflect perfectly the life and work of the people he knew best, and of whose life he was part. They are beautiful and artistic, or painful and inartistic, just in the degree in which naturalness, the joy, the rightness, or the unnaturalness, severity, gloom and slavery of that life predominate. From the child carrying a lamb in her arms, and followed by the loving mother and whole docile flock; the father stretching out his arms to his baby, graceful in his love through the clumsiness of his excessive toil; all the dreary distance to that heartbreaking image of man's desecration he passes, through every step of increasing backache and stolidity, fearless and, indeed, helpless. It is the awful record of a soul seeing things as they are, and recording them as he must in his art language, which ceases to be artistic, and becomes ugly, inartistic, inarticulate, and finally refuses to go farther into the discord of man's desolate, stifled, degraded life. Behind the laborer with the hoe stretch God's earth and sky. "With these open witnesses, you have done that, O man! What you have done in darkness, away from the face of these witnesses, my art cannot say." No true art can. Into the prison-houses of earth, its sweat-shops and underground lodging-houses, art cannot follow.

Whatever the inspiring motive of art, though there be in it pain and struggle, the result must be one of triumph, at least of hope. Art can never present humanity as overborne. It cannot let the hostile principle, pain, sorrow, sin, at the last conquer. Just where it begins to smother and snuff out the flame of life, art turns away.

When life reaches a point at which it can furnish no more material for art, we cannot look to it for an artistic people. If in all the environment of a man's life, there is nothing which can inspire a true work of art, there is nothing to inspire a true love of it, could it be produced. The love of the beautiful grows by what it feeds on; and the food must be the common bread of life. That which makes the art-loving people, makes the artist also. Every nation which has left a great art record has lived an artistic life. The artist is not a product of spontaneous generation. Every Athenian, every Florentine boy, saw daily in the street the expression of the most perfect thought of his people, reflecting their thought of God; and he saw it, side by side with God's own thought, undefeated and undefiled. He saw column and tower and statue standing against a sky, the pure, serene, tender, infinite mirror of the divine intelligence and love; and hills, the unswerving image of divine steadfastness. He saw them unpolluted by the smoke, and undistracted by the din of commercial strife. Poor or rich, the best his nation wrought was his. He must be taught his art as a craft, if he were to follow it; and he did learn it precisely as a craft which must be honestly and industriously practiced. But first and always he lived it, as a life, in common with the life of his nation.

The boy of our great cities, rich or poor (we are so far democratic), has this common inheritance. He sees from his earliest years the mart; not the *mercato vecchio* of Florence, where the angel faces of Della Robbia looked down above the greengrocer's wares in the open booth, from out wreaths of fruit and flowers that vied with those below; but our *mercato nuovo*. He sees there walls high and monotonous; windows all alike (which he who built had no pleasure in); piles of merchandise, not devised with curious interest and pleasant exercise of inventive faculty, but with stolid, mechanical indifference; garish wares, and faces too harassed and hurried to give back greeting. These belong to rich and poor alike. But here the lots diverge. The poor lad goes, not to his sheep, like Giotto, nor to keeping his feet warm, like Luca, in a basket of shavings, while he works cheerily at his art and saves fire; he goes home to the dreary tenement, not fireless, but with closed windows to keep its heat within, dingy plaster, steam of washing and odors of cooking, near discordant voices, loneliness of a crowded life without companionship or high ideals; and for view of hills and sky, the theatre bills on the walls across the street, and factory chimneys.

The son of the rich man goes home to his father's house. Through plate glass and lace curtains he looks across at his neighbor's father's house, with its lace curtains,—perhaps a little less costly, perhaps a little more. Up and down the street he compares the upholstery, the equipages, the number and formality of the servants belonging to the establishments, which represent his social life. He has flowers in a greenhouse; he has fine clothes; he has books; he has pictures. Does he live an artistic life? Can we look to him for the great art of the future? Alas! "The life of the poor is too painful; the life of the rich too vulgar." Rather, is not the life of each both painful and vulgar to a degree which seems almost beyond hope? "The haggard despair of cotton-factory, coal-mine operatives in these days is painful to behold; but not so painful, hideous to the inner sense, as that brutish, God-forgetting, Profit-and-loss Philosophy and Life-Theory which we hear jangled on all hands of us, from the throats and pens and thoughts of all-but all men."[3] Happily, at least for art, there remains that "all-but" modicum,—the tenaciously impractical and unbusiness-like, the incorrigibly unconvinced as to the supreme importance of "selling cotton cheaper." Else "vacuum and the serene blue" would indeed, "be much handsomer" than this our civilization. For the children of the "degraded poor," and the degraded rich as well, in our present mode of life, there is no artistic hope outside of miracle.

There is one hope for us all,—a new life, a freed life. He who hopes to help art survive on earth till the new life dawn, must indeed feed the hungry with good things. This must he do, but not neglect for this the more compassionate and far-reaching aim, the freeing of the art-power of the whole nation and race by enabling them to work in gladness and not in woe. It is a feeble and narrow imagination which holds out to chained hands fair things which they cannot grasp, —things which they could fashion for themselves were they but free.

The soul of man in the commercial and industrial struggle is in a state of siege. He is fighting for his life. It is merciful and necessary to pass in to him the things which sustain his courage and keep him alive, but the effectual thing is to raise the siege.

A settlement, if it is true to its ideal, must stand equally for both aims. It must work with all energy and courage toward the rescue of those bound under the slavery of commerce and the wage-law; with all abstinence it must discountenance wasting human life in the making of valueless things; with all faith it must urge forward the building up of a state in which cruel contrasts of surfeit and want, of idleness and overwork, shall not be found. By holding art and all good fruit of life to be the right of all; by urging all, because of this their common need, to demand time and means, for supplying it; by reasonableness in the doing, with others, of useful, wholesome, beneficent work, and the enjoyment, with others, of rightful and sharable pleasure, a settlement should make toward a social state which shall finally supplant this incredible and impious warfare of the children of God.

Whatever joy is to us ennobling; whatever things seem to us made for blessing, and not for weariness and woe; whatever knowledge lifts us out of things paltry and narrowing, and exalts and expands our life; whatever life itself is real and worthy to endure, as there is measure of faith in us, and hope and love and patience, let us live this life. And let us think on our brothers, that they may live it too; for without them we cannot live it if we would; and when we and they shall have this joy of life, then we shall speak from within it, and our speech shall be sweet, and men will listen and be glad. What we do with our hands will be fair, and men shall have pleasure therein. This will be art. Otherwise we cannot all have it; and until all have it in some measure, none can have it in great measure. And if gladness ceases upon the earth, and we turn the fair earth into a prison-house for men with hard and loveless labor, art will die.

Notes

1.   [Pp. 165-79 in *Hull-House Maps and Papers*. New York: Crowell, 1895. The physical design and execution of the maps is not discussed in the text, but Ruskin discussed this process in detail and may have influenced the cartography (See Ruskin *Laws of Fesole*, "Of Map Drawing" 1895/1877-79, 94-115).]
2.   The principles and plan of Mr. Horsfall's beneficent work may be found in his papers entitled, "The Use of Pictures in Schools," "Art in Large Towns," and "The Work of the Manchester Art Museum." J. E. Cornish, St. Ann's Square, Manchester.
3.   [Thomas] Carlyle, *Past and Present* (1910).

5

Report of the Public School Art Society
March, 1896[1]

The Chicago Public School Art Society is now in the second year of its existence. In answer to many inquiries its officers present this brief account of what the society has accomplished during its first year, and hopes to do in the future.

The published reports of societies for the study of the child's mind make clear that a considerable proportion of the children in our city schools are entirely without knowledge of the commonest facts of nature, and therefore wholly without the capacity to understand either the literature of which it is the theme, or the laws by which it is governed. Investigation revealed that an incredible percentage of the children in the schools of one of our cities had never seen a cow, and did not know what trees were. Children in this condition can be taught nothing which can be said to make them human. Literature, science, art, must alike be out of their ken. The same children have obviously never been where they can see any of man's works which are at all beautiful; and should they, by chance, see a fine building they could not be expected to recognize it, having in their minds no basis for ideas of beauty. Great numbers of children, not in so deep mental darkness as this, are in a state approximating it. If any connection is to be made between them and the real world (not the artificially perverted world in which they live) it must be done largely through the public schools. A heavy duty is thus laid upon teachers in localities where such conditions exist; one which, with the means they have provided them for arousing the child to an interest in the things chiefly interesting to normal human beings, they can hardly be expected to discharge. It is the first aim of the Chicago Public School Art Society to assist teachers in their heavy task, and to add a rightful pleasure to the hours children pass in school.

The active interest expressed in this aim by numbers of the teachers themselves, and their desire to co-operate, is the greatest encouragement the society has had.

Aside from directly familiarizing the children with natural objects by means of pictures of them, whater trains the eyes to discriminate between good and bad in color or form, and cultivates the habit of attention and observation in children is at once training them to make the most of such scant opportunities as they have to enjoy nature, and is making possible to them, also, the enjoyment of literature.

There are two immediate objects in view in the decoration of school rooms—the one directly educational or pedagogic, the other educational through the aesthetic. In the work done by Mr. T. C. Horsfall in Manchester, Eng., where the plan originated, the educational idea has led, and the aesthetic has been quite secondary. The Manchester plan does not, however, omit to call attention to the beautiful as such. A good deal of energy is spent in directing attention through printed labels attached to pictures to places of historic, romantic and picturesque interest which can be reached by short journeys from that city, but no attempt has been made to provide a school room beautiful in color and the aim in the selection of pictures is not so much to make a room attractive to the aesthetic sense as to arouse a mental activity by the subjects before the eye. In order to carry out such a plan as the one adopted in Manchester a great number of duplicates are required and constant passing on of sets of pictures from one school to another. Our society at first aimed to imitate this plan, but so far we have not been able to buy pictures enough even to begin the rotation among our so numerous schools. The size of our school rooms also makes the use of small pictures and printed descriptions impracticable.

Our great need, especially for younger children, is for really beautiful nature pictures of birds, flowers, trees, woods, water and fields. It also seems needful to put before the eyes of school children wholly unacquainted with such things some large and impressive pictures of buildings which are not only of classic beauty but of historic fame.

In our later work, therefore, we have concentrated upon the idea of good color in the walls and for further decoration have found most satisfactory large casts and very large solar prints[2] of such subjects as the Egyptian Pyramids, the Cathedral of Amiens, the equestrian statue by Donatello, [and] the Lion of Lucerne.

The question of color in pictures is the most difficult one to cope with. It is very necessary that the color element be supplied, and at the same time it is almost hopeless to find really good color within a possible cost. For kindergartners, Walter Crane's [1845-1915] "Flora's Feast,"[3] unbound and framed in five groups of eight plates to a frame, has been a source of great delight to both children and teachers. The designs are exquisite both in color and drawing. The price of the book itself is $2.00. Certain of the Fitzroy pictures which can be obtained from the Iron Cross, 45 Joy street, Boston, meet the color need better than anything we have so far found. They are large photo-lithographs (the largest 46 by 31 inches) in bold and flat coloring, distinctly decorative in handling. The best designs, those by Heywood Summer, comprise five subjects from the Old Testament, a St. George and the Dragon, and four beautiful smaller ones of the seasons. The Old Testament subjects cost $2.00 each, the St. George $2.25, and the Seasons $1.25. They are designed for large spaces and long distances.

The visible results accomplished by the society in its first whole year, though encouraging, are perhaps secondary in value to the invisible. For example, a room has been decorated at the Cook County Normal School, the principal, Col. Francis W. Parker,[4] himself furnishing the funds, but allowing the work to be done under the direction of the society. As students from all parts of the country, and from across seas come to the Normal School to study, the effect is far-reaching. Indeed, in a single morning I was visited by a lady from the New York Training College [at Columbia University] and one from the University of Utah, both of whom came to consult me on the subject of school decoration. I constantly receive letters from other cities asking assistance and information about the decoration of schools.

We have been "greatly blessed" in the co-operation of the Board of Education in our last and most ambitious effort, the decoration of the assembly room of the Goodrich School, [on the] corner [of] Taylor and Brown streets. The room was in need of repair, and in consideration of the promised gift by the society of a frieze of the Parthenon casts and two large solar prints, the committee of the Board of Education, which has the direction of this school, consented to paint the walls and ceiling in whatever colors the society should select.[5] "We are indebted to Mr. Lorado Taft,[6] [the] Art Institute [of Chicago], Chicago, for an extraordinary reduction in the price of the casts, ranking it possible for us to buy many more than our treasury would otherwise have afforded. Mr. Taft had the molds of the casts made by his students, and will continue to furnish the casts for the purpose of school decoration at the very low rate of $1 a linear foot.

What has been so satisfactory in this case will doubtless be repeated in many schools. Indeed there seems to be no reason why all schools should not be painted or calcimined in good colors as it becomes necessary to refresh the walls. If the work of coloring the walls were done by the city, the energies and funds of the society could all go to supplying pictures and casts, which should be at once a source of pleasure and unconscious education and an untold assistance to teachers in their work.

It does not seem at all incredible that, so much being achieved, artists should have sufficient amount of public spirit to give some of their work to their city, through its schools. Indeed, I feel convinced that many gifted artists would do this, could they see a good color on the walls for a suitable background for pictures, and perceive in the public and the school authorities a sense of the importance of art in education.

What is common in France—exhibits of collections of good picture, in schools—might also become possible in our cities. Pictures lent by artists for the season might be exhibited for a time in one school and then passed on to another. Real artists are the most generous of people. None are more willing than they to give the world of their best. In order, however, to utilize even valuable gifts and loans, the society must have funds for training and transporting pictures. Its work has proceeded but slowly, for lack of the requisite money. The annual membership fee of the society is $1.00; a life membership, $20.00. Gifts of money or new memberships, it is unnecessary to say, are most welcome. Gifts of pictures are submitted to a committee of censorship, which passes upon their fitness for purposes of school decoration.

While the members of the Chicago Public School Art Society have no hope that, through means so external, art can be developed in lives cut off from nature and the beautiful, some of us do hope that a slender link may thus be formed between these lives and the beautiful, and that it may lead a few, perhaps many, to try themselves to strengthen it.[7]

Notes

1. [This pamphlet is found in the JAM collection reel 52, frames 0515-0520. It begins with a lengthy list of officers including Starr as President and the members.]
2. Address Wm. H. Pierce & CO., 352 Washington Street, Boston. Catalogue.
3. [Walter Crane (1898, 1968) was an artist and designer in the Arts and Crafts Movement in England.]
4. [Parker was a close Hull-House ally and transferred his elementary school to the University of Chicago's Laboratory Schools, directed by John Dewey (see Deegan 1999).]
5. It has since been decided that for purposes of propaganda the resources of the society shall, for a time, be concentrated upon this one school, that it may be an example of what we consider fit decoration for schoolrooms.
6. [Lorado Taft (1860-1936) was a frequent Hull-House visitor and founding member of the Chicago Arts and Crafts Society. His monuments throughout Chicago played a central role in beautifying its public spaces. See Timothy J. Garvey (1988).]
7. [This pamphlet included a "List of Objects Placed by the Society:"Polk Street School, Andrew Jackson School; Andrew Jackson Kindergarten, Goodrich School, and the Jones School.]

6

Hull-House Bookbindery[1]

So many questions are asked about Miss Ellen G. Starr's Bookbindery at Hull-House that she has printed "A Note of Explanation" accompanying the last issue of the Hull-House Bulletin, *which we republish because it bears so vitally upon the educational problem of the settlements to which this issue of* The Commons *is so largely devoted. Miss Starr and her pupils have transferred their shop for the summer to a cottage at Lake Bluff.*[2]

A Note of Explanation

People wonder, I suppose, why a resident of Hull-House chose to bind books and what connection it has with the work or life of the House. I shall try to make this personal explanation as simply as possible.

Before I came to Hull-House to live, and for some time afterward, I used to have classes and give lectures on the history of art. I partly earned my living in this way and partly did it for the pleasure of it. I used to enjoy interpreting to others, as far as I was able, the beautiful things which have been made in the past, and to think it did good. But after a time, living amidst a great deal that is ugly and ill-made in the present, and feeling how many people are forced to do so, even more than I, it began to seem to me not enough to talk about and explain beautiful and well-made things which have been done long ago. I began to feel that instead of talking, it would be a great deal better to make something myself, ever so little, thoroughly well, and beautiful of its kind. The influence of anything I could make would, to be sure, be very small, as I had no special talent for anything. But then, suppose that all the people who had no genius, in the ages when the most beautiful buildings, carving, books, silver and goldsmith's work, etc., was done, had fallen to talking about the work of past ages, and refused to do any work themselves, how much less we should have now to talk about or to enjoy.

Another thing I used to reflect upon was this: All modern life has been tending to separate the work of the mind and the work of the hands. One set of people work with their heads but produce nothing whatever with their hands.

Another vast body work with their hands at very mechanical and uninteresting work, which does not in any way engage or develop the mind in its higher
faculties. Both sets of people are living partial lives, not using all the powers
God gave us, who certainly did not make half humanity with heads alone,
and the other half with only minds. To account for this tendency would
require much space and much cleverness—more than I have. Suffice it to
say that I believe it to be a wrong one, and that I do not think it necessary
to submit to it. So then it became necessary for me, if I were to act as I
believed, to learn to make something worth making, and to do it as thoroughly well as I was able. I thought of various things, and selected books,
being interested in them from several points of view. I went to the man
who, in my judgment, does the most beautiful bookbinding in the world
at this time, was so fortunate as to be received as his pupil, and worked
under him[3] for fifteen months, six hours or more everyday, excepting a half
holiday on Saturday. It is no light matter to learn a craft thoroughly, and if it
is not thoroughly learned it does more harm than good. I promised my master
that I would not teach or sell my work until he thought I might rightly do so.
This was only sensible, since I had undertaken to set an example of good
workmanship, in so far as I was able, and to produce something of a kind
worth making.

I had thought, when I formed the intention of learning a craft, that I should
teach it here at Hull-House on the basis of the extension classes and the
manual training. I have not been able to do this for several reasons: the
implements and material are expensive; the time required to accomplish anything is too long for those who only give an evening or two or three evenings
a week, and the amount of personal attention required by beginners precludes
the possibility of anything but a small class. I still hope to be able to instruct,
thoroughly, a few who care to undertake the work in earnest, if there be any
such, and who can arrange to give the necessary time. Meanwhile I earn my
living, not by talking about other people's work—that I still do for pleasure—but by binding and ornamenting a few books as well as I can do it, and
by teaching three private pupils as well as I can teach them. I cannot take a
pupil for less than a year, nor more than three pupils at a time, tho[sic] more
would like to learn. Indeed, the number of people who ask to be instructed
shows that there is much thought of this question of learning to work with the
hands, and seems to me a very good sign. It takes me a long time, sometimes
two or three weeks, to bind a book as I have been taught to do it. Naturally, I
only bind books which seem to me worthy to last. They are necessarily very
expensive, and the people who most deserve to have choice books, choicely
bound, cannot always, or usually have them. That is to be regretted, but it is
not the main question in doing any piece of work. The chief question is where
the piece of work itself is worth doing. Nobody cares very much for whom a
guildman of the middle ages did a bit of carving or smith's work, or for whom

one of the Venetian binders bound a book. One sees these things in a museum and learns from each its lesson of perfection in its degree and after its kind.

Please do not think that this means that I believe my modest little books will be put into museums for future ages to wonder at. It only means that whatever good any handiwork of today can do must be done by showing forth the same pleasure in the well-doing of it which makes these things give pleasure to us now.

Notes

1. [*The Commons* Whole No. 47 (30 June 1900): 5-6.]
2. [This introductory note was probably written by Graham Taylor, the editor of *The Commons*.]
3. Mr. Cobden-Sanderson, in London.

7

The Renaissance of Handicraft[1]

Within the last decade there have sprung into existence with great rapidity many associations styling themselves Arts and Crafts Societies, or assuming names adapted from that of the London Society of the same name, for the promotion of handicraft. These associations are usually composed of a very small minority of persons who are masters of any craft, and a large majority of those interested in varying degrees and from divers motives. One is forced to suspect in many cases that genuine desire for the exercise of the product of handicraft furnishes but little of the incentive to membership in these societies; that for the greater proportion numerically, this interest has temporarily supplanted, or perhaps only varied, the diversions of Society, the literary club and the charity ball. The rumor that well bred people now-a-days make things and have exhibitions may not infrequently have suggested the relief of ennui.

Another and a pathetic motive toward interest in craftsmanship is that of enquirers the purport of whose plea is this:

> I must work to support myself and help to support others. I cannot earn a living by sewing. I am too ignorant to teach. For the best of reasons I do not wish to be a domestic servant. I cannot dig, to beg I am ashamed. I have heard that there are new industries, agreeable, genteel. Can I learn one by correspondence? In how many months? How profitable will it be when learned?[2]

Of these two classes is the new craft-seeking public partly composed, but not by any means wholly. Even counterfeits and corruptions (and the classes above described are not so) prove the existence of a true thing. Caricatures of the creative craft impulse, successfully advertising themselves and thriving on the desire for real handicraft and its products, prove the existence of a genuine craving for it and impulse toward it. Even for the class which is seeking to kill time, a good craft, thoroughly mastered, would be wholesome and would perhaps clarify the vision and enlarge the horizon.

The causes at the root of the Arts and Crafts "movement" which might be classified as genuine and useful are, I conceive, such as these: the natural impulse to use the hands and to produce something of use and beauty; weariness of useless and frivolous occupations; desire to unite with those who work with their hands and to find a common basis of life and interest with them; reaction against conventions which have assumed manual work to be undignified. The ungenuine and worthless motives are: fashion or "fad;" desire to get money easily and without loss of dignity, and the impression that it can be done in this new way; worst of all, the perception on the part of clever and unscrupulous persons of an opportunity to play upon this new foible of the public for their own advantage. The true motives seem sufficient, despite the false ones, to advance a community somewhat toward a reasonable and comely life. A real and persistent love of doing good and beautiful work must, in itself, tend to bring about the conditions of doing it. Let us consider what these conditions are. First, health—physical and mental buoyancy—and wholesome and comely surroundings. A healthy art cannot thrive on a depressed or morbid condition of mind or body. It cannot thrive on bad air or ugliness and squalor, domestic or civic. In order to produce forms of beauty one must see enough to create and feed a love for beauty. A civic or national art will never be manufactured in evening schools of design and handicraft, frequented by youths who have worked themselves sleepy all the hours of daylight over some dreary business, unlighted by a ray of interest except in the week's pay, and surrounded by squalid monotony of walls and streets.

Then to work joyfully, even to work tranquilly—the artist's first requirement—the must be free from the pressure of immediate need. Though it is well that he should have some wholesome sense of obligation as regards his work to prevent his becoming capricious, it is all but fatal to any lovely development that a bit of work must be done at a given time to meet daily needs. How, then, is the artist's work to go on favorably in this day of luxurious idleness and of overwork. Must it be done as play along with a bread-winning occupation or as play by the rich who need no bread-winning occupation?[3] The difference between professional and dilettante work indicates the answer to the last question. Entirely good and beautiful art or handicraft requires the self-control and continuity of work done under some sense of obligation, together with the play feeling of work done for refreshment. That implies no harassment or pressure of need, no pandering to a false ideal of sumptuousness, set up by the rich to display riches. The very best artist's work, I believe, requires that one is doing or has done some useful work beside, of the elemental sort, ministering to common necessities. There is a feeling of weariness and futility about merely ornamental or decorative work, done in a tooth and nail sort of way, as a means of livelihood. The play spirit is quenched in it. If it is underpaid it becomes labor and sorrow; if overpaid, demoralizing. It is usually either the one or the other, The artist to be an artist, indeed, should come to his work not fatigued, but justified in enjoying himself by having done something serviceable to common needs either that day or at some time not too remote, and by the expectation of again serving others in the natural order of life. It is possible that the fact that the artist's time is devoted wholly to the solace and enjoyment of the community at large might, if the community demanded his entire time as an artist, free him altogether, without loss to himself or the world, from any other work. But the greatest artist would probably still be he who could take his turn at the world's more elemental needs. It is as hard to picture Phidias standing idly by while a block of marble is being lifted into place, as a French miniature painter putting his shoulder to it.

The circumstances, then, which one would conceive as ideally favorable to natural production of good, "artistic" work, are perfect freedom from pressure of personal necessity, combined with a wholesome degree of obligation to the service of others, beautiful surroundings, health and joy. When the conditions have been stated and compared with the actually existing ones the question necessarily arises whether it would not be more economical to devote all energy to making these conditions possible rather than divert any into the channel of an all but hopeless effort to get a fruit artificially grown without its natural soil and elements. Undoubtedly it would be so if we had not to consider at all the individual, who would live and die, as Morris points out, unsolaced by art, while we are preparing for the solace of generations to come; and if we were also to leave out of account the loss to future generations, were Art to die out altogether, and require to be planted anew when new and wholesome conditions of life and work shall have been evolved.

If we grant that it is worth while and effort to keep alive the love of beautiful handiwork, then it is worth while to make certain things as well and beautifully as they can be made.

There is some hope, too, in a nearer view. The indirect value of the really beautiful and well made product of handicraft, through its effect on the ordinary article of commerce, is greater than its direct value to the few who can possess such things or see them. Only the comparatively rich can afford Morris' tapestries, rugs and wall papers. But commercial wall papers, cretonnes and all sorts of fabrics have improved in design to a marvelous degree through the influence of his work, so that he has really done his craft work indirectly for "the masses."

A further and most important consideration in favor of the revival of handicraft is the effect on the life and faculties of the individual who is engaged in making useful and comely articles and his reaction on society. The constant and agreeable use in his daily work of all his faculties, which lie dormant for the most part, during his day of mechanical work in a factory, or are worn dull behind a counter, must make of him a much more effective social factor as well as a happier and more rational human being.

Working men complain of injustice done them in regard to too long working hours, too little pay, insalubrious surroundings, tyranny of one sort and another; but seldom if at all do they cry out against the indignity of the kind of work they are forced to do in the making of so often worthless things or, if not worse than useless, destructive.[4] Nor do they express resentment or indignation at being under compulsion to do bad and unthorough work. This is held to be no part of the workman's concern, nor does he consider it so, so long has he been powerless. How slavish a state of society is this in which the mass of men may not decide whether or not they approve the making of a certain ware, but must perforce go in under a sign of "men wanted" (which should read "puppets wanted") and turn some crank as they are bidden, asking no questions for conscience's or reason's sake. There can be, one would suppose, no hesitation on the part of any one capable of understanding this situation in admitting that it is a degrading one. That the general situation can be at all touched, even at its outer edges by the extension of a demand for good handicraft, will not be so generally conceded. The return to the practice of handicraft will be, not by reason of such conviction but because of love for hand work and reaction against commercial philistinism. The product and the craftsman's life must justify themselves. On one side the argument is gaining support that all work, even the artist's, can be done as well or better by machine. The present writer, though practicing a pure handicraft, has no wish to decry the machine, or even to deny that, judiciously designed, beautiful things as well as useful can be made by it. The judicious designer for the machine would consider its limitations and design only such broad and simple lines as the machine can produce without loss. Designs made for machine work have hitherto resulted in clumsy and vulgar imitations of handiwork. The machine can never take the place of the human hand and its cunning in the field of art, major or minor. Nor can there ever be a return to handicraft which shall abolish the machine. Any expectation of such a doubling back of history upon itself would be childish. The fields are two, but each affects the other. If the "labor saving machine" were carried to its utmost efficiency and the "labor saving" apportioned with justice so that each man might do his share of the community's necessary work and still have time for self-expression, then indeed would the millennium of both Art and Craft be come. The mass of men are now subjected to the machine instead of subjecting it; and the personal problem for those who face the question at all is whether to join themselves to the number of such and try to modify the conditions, or to go out from among them and live a rational life, working "in the spirit of the future"—that future which shall make common the privilege now exclusive of doing the work one likes to do and expressing one's self through it, which, as Morris so often said, is art. The personal problem is solved for each by his individual bent and qualification, and, if honestly decided, doubtless rightly, both as regards himself and his social value.

Notes

1. [*International Socialist Review* 2 (February 1902): 570-74.]
2. Such inquiries concerning book-binding have actually been addressed to me.
3. [Mead, Addams and Dewey all studied the relation between work and play (Deegan 1999).]
4. Never, in the experience of the writer, who has often deplored the fact.

8

The Handicraft of Bookbinding [Article I][1]

When I returned to Chicago in October [1914] from a beautiful country which was sending its young men into the horrors of destruction, it seemed to me that I should be unable to interest myself at all in a nice, constructive process, the result of which is designedly an object of luxury and beauty, fitted to peaceful enjoyment and to a life of harmony and possible contemplation. I practically closed my bindery and did not expect anyone to think either of possessing beautiful books or of learning to make them. But since I find that a few still purpose to continue the tenor of normal life, even including the pursuit of the minor arts, I have readjusted; and I find that there is rest for the racked nerves in a process of construction pursued thoroughly and in quietness. I recall Morris pointing out in one of his lectures that it would be a pity to let art die out altogether, even for the cause of devoting every energy, as one is tempted to do, to bringing about a rational public life, as a fit garden for art.

My dear master, Mr. Cobden-Sanderson, who had betaken himself at about the age of forty from the practice of law and the study of philosophy, to rediscovering the old processes of thorough and beautiful binding, used also to say that he found "making his little patterns" with their balance and symmetry, soothing in the midst of a world of dissolving and vanishing systems of thought.

There is something to be said, too, on the practical side, for the well constructed book as a sort of strongbox for treasure. Many a precious document would never have been preserved for our use had it been entrusted to as frail a protection as a modern commercial binding.

Let us, then, since the mere fact that this series of articles is asked for proves that some believe thorough and comely workmanship worthwhile, proceed to consider the means of attaining it in the binding of books. I will first enumerate in their order the main processes of binding a book by the handicraft method, and then describe and illustrate them as far as will serve an unprofessional knowledge of the subject. Obviously, a few magazine pages are not intended to take the place of a manual or handbook, such a handbook as Mr. Douglas Cockerell's [c. 1901] "Bookbinding;" nor is even a good handbook intended to supplant a course of instruction.

1. Taking the book apart if it has been bound before.
2. "Knocking out" the hinges with a hammer on an iron slab.
3. Mending sheets torn in process of pulling sections apart, and the holes sawed for commercial sewing.
4. Re-folding, if necessary.
5. Cutting tops or "heads" of sections.
6. Cutting or filing edges for gilding a book to be "rough sewn." (See Cockerell, Chapter X for cutting in press, which is too elaborate for this article.)
7. Gilding, which is really a separate craft, usually not done in a bindery.
8. Sewing.
9. Backing.
10. Lining and cutting boards for covers.
11. Lacing in board covers.
12. "Head-banding" and setting head-bands.
13. Paring leather.
14. Covering.
15. Trimming.
16. Decorating.

Perhaps the advantage to the printed book of the careful handicraft process over the cheap and careless commercial one, consists as much in what is not done as in what is done to it. What a book lover most dreads is the sacrifice of margins. This, in almost all commercial binderies is ruthless and wanton. And while, for nearly every other cruel assault upon the book there is some at least partial help, the sacrifice of margins is irremediable. Let us imagine (no imaginary case, but a heart-rendering experience) a beautifully printed breviary, with wide margins. The book was in a temporary paper cover and a well meaning friend offered to have it bound. The confiding owner gave it up and received it back with mutilated margins; [yielding] two thick volumes bound into one, of ungainly bulk and a smaller contour. Tears [are] of no avail; no delectation more, forever, possible to the eye.

Margins are cut by wholesale in commercial binderies with ruthless knives, mechanically worked.

In the handicraft process, they are either not cut at all, except the "heads" (tops), to even the top, if re-folding has been necessary, and to keep out dust; or they are cut by hand, section by section, the least possible and never down to the shortest sheets which are left as "proof" that the book has not been unnecessarily mutilated. Sometimes, instead of cutting at all, we file the edges a little to render them sufficiently smooth to take the gilding. This is done to the "heads," "fore-edges" and "tails" (bottom-margins) "jogged up" one after another before the book is sewn. That is, the heads are evened and filed; then the "tails" are evened and filed, letting the heads go uneven while this is being done; then the fore-edges of the separated sheets are "jogged up" and filed. After the gilding is completed, the heads are again jogged-up, the sheets "collated" (put in order in their sections) and the book sewn thus, leaving the leaves somewhat uneven at the fore-edges and tails, as in a rough-cut book, only less ragged and avoiding the raw look of white edges which, in a sumptuously bound book, would be inharmonious. The perfectly smooth, polished, and, in appearance, solid metal surface, like the inner surface of a gold tube, which is the delight of the commercial binder is, to the taste of some, including my own, most unattractive.

The handicraft binder does occasionally for variety cut a book in the press. Some old binders even tooled patterns upon the smoothly cut edges of books— a process called "gauffing." In our modern vernacular this would be termed a "fad" and as such should only be used to amuse, when the book offers a combination of margins sufficiently wide to have something to spare, sufficient beauty not to render this over-decoration too incongruous, and a value or rarity not too great to make any tampering with its margins unjustifiable. Personally, although I have "gauffed" several books, I shall probably never do so again.

I once bound a book while I was a pupil at the Doves Bindery, with the edges cut in the press. But I never look at it without noticing the lower margins which I cut too much.

Plates in books commercially rebound, are often cut absolutely "to the quick." The word "uncut" in book sellers' catalogs does not stand for a mere collector's fad, but is an assurance that the book has not been vulgarly defaced.

Another method of sparing a book is by "casing" it temporarily, if it is a book worthy of beautiful binding, on the assumption that it may be worthily and permanently bound later on. Instead of maltreating the back by beating the sections into angles which will require them to be straightened again for rebinding and filling them with glue which must needs be removed, perhaps tearing the paper and necessitating mending it, the sections are left straight, and the book, without hinges or cords, is sewn on tapes. All the Kelmscott and Dove Press books[2] are cased in this manner, either in vellum or light boards, covered with paper and with linen backs. The ordinary method of "backing" a book (which should not be done until it takes its final, permanent form), consists of placing the sewn sections, held firmly between two wedge shaped boards, each board as distant from the back edge of the section as the thickness of cover. Thus placed, the back is gently beaten into a curve. The angle formed by the bent outer sections receives and fits the board covers and is called the "hinge." ....

The commercial process of sewing differs from the handicraft method at the expense of the book. Sewing is perhaps the most difficult of all the pro-

cesses to describe without demonstration. Cockerell, in his handbook, de-
votes eleven pages, with illustrations, to the subject of sewing alone. Obviously, this cannot be done in a series of short magazine articles designed, not
to teach the craft of book-binding (the handbook, even, does not aim to take
the place of instruction and practice), but to point out some of the main
differences and the advantages of thorough and permanent workmanship
over the cheap and temporary.

In both commercial and handicraft sewing, the sections which form the
book (i. e. the group of folded leaves inserted within others, sometimes in
twos but more often in threes, fours, and more) are attached together by threads
which run longitudinally through the center of the sections, and to cords
which run transversely across the back of the book. In handicraft sewing,
these cords are on the outside of the book. The sections are one by one
opened at the center; the threaded needle passes into it and out, drawing the
thread (or silk) around the cord. The cords remaining on the outside of the
book, and being ultimately covered with leather, form the bands on the back
of the book which are considered part of the decoration. It will be seen that
the thread being passed *around* the cord brings the strain upon the cord, and
prevents the tearing of the paper when the thread is drawn up.

In commercial sewing a much smaller cord is used and hollows are sawn in
the back of the book to admit it within the book's substance. It will be seen
that, the cord being inside the section, it is not necessary to pass the thread
around it, but it may be drawn straight through the section between the cord
and the paper. Of course, this saves much time, trouble and skill; but it injures
the book very much. If the book should open to the center it would show
these saw marks which are very disfiguring. When a book thus bound is
properly rebound, all these holes must be mended. In commercial books of
the more pretentious sort, the bands are *imitated* by false strips pasted on the
back of the book, and covered by leather. That is, having first damaged the
book by sawing into it and sinking the cords into its substance, which is
justifiable only on the ground of saving time and money, because the product
is not worth the cost and trouble, the effect of cost and trouble is sought by a
deceitful imitation. Leaving the back of the book plain and unmutilated is a
thoroughly respectable way of saving time and money. Hacking it unnecessarily
with a saw, and then pasting wretched little detached pieces of leather upon it in
fraudulent imitation of true, structural cords, which are the book's bones as it
were, is cheap and vulgar. No pains are ordinarily taken to make the false
bands on the surface coincide with the real cord within. And frequently the
marks of the cords are seen through the leather at their points of attachment to
the covers, *at quite different intervals and positions* from the false bands.

One of the beneficial effects of handicraft binding upon commercial binding is the tendency to abandon this sort of cheap and unreasonable imitation,
and to omit processes when dispensable rather than do them badly.

Notes

1. ["The Handicraft of Bookbinding [Article 1]." *Industrial Art Magazine* 3 (March 1915): 102-107. This article and the other three in the series were accompanied by illustrations and photographs, and these were often unclear. One could not follow these depictions and be able to become a bookbinder, as Starr notes. Those interested in more detail, however, could obtain copies of the original articles. References to these images are deleted from the text.]
2. [Morris (1898) founded the Kelmscott Press and Cobdon-Sanderson founded the Doves Press (Nordhoff 1898).]

9

The Handicraft of Bookbinding (Article II)[1]

The task of describing and illustrating any delicate and complicated manual process in popular articles has several distinct difficulties. The audience is necessarily mixed. If anything is assumed as known, those who do not know it are at a disadvantage. If nothing is assumed, the articles expand into a full manual of the process. Also, as in practice, the acquirement of one process overlaps another, so, in treating of processes, it is very difficult to divide them sharply. No subject or process in book-binding is ever really finished in the sense of being put out of the way. Every ill-done process rises up to accuse and harass all through the work.

For this reason I always direct my pupils to go straight through all the necessary processes of "forwarding" (the constructive processes) on at least one book—better two, or even three—in order to enable them to understand the consequences of each ill-done process to all the following ones. After that, it is well to take a group of three or four books and put them all through each consecutive process, with the purpose of fixing the more intricate ones in the memory, and of better acquiring the muscular habits so necessary in learning any craft.

The "moves," so to say, can be learned; i.e., they can be gone through with, in a short time, but each step offers indefinite combinations of possibility of error. I have never had a pupil so unresourceful as not to invent an entirely original mistake! "How interesting! That has never been done before" is a compliment paid to each in turn, and I once wrote in a pupil's early book, "An excellent all-around example of how not to do it."

For acquiring these accurate and dependable muscular habits and experience in dealing with materials necessary for reasonably good work, a full year is the minimum time. I spent fifteen months with Mr. Cobden-Sanderson at the Doves Bindery in London, and found it none too much. My hours were nine to four with an hour at noon, a Saturday half-holiday and only two weeks of holidays in the year. At the end of a year I came home to avoid a second London winter of fog and artificial light, returning to London for three additional months' work in the following spring. During the three months' work at home I discovered a great deal which I did not know.

To resume the description of processes: After the book is sewn and backed, assuming that it is not to be cut in the press, but has been gilded before "rough" sewing—as I prefer and have described in the first article—it is now almost ready to be laced into its board covers. All that remains is to fray out the ends of the cords. The board covers must now be prepared. They are of imported English "millboard." So far as I know, no millboard sufficiently firm and compact for thorough and durable work is made in the United States. The boards are roughly cut to the approximate size. (We do it with a huge pair of shears of which one handle is made fast. I have never seen a pair except my own in this country.) They are then lined with cheap white paper, ordinarily with one sheet on the outside and two on the insides of the boards. The lining, draws the boards slightly; and the object of using two thicknesses on the inner surface next the book and one on the outer, is to counteract any tendency of the cover to be concave, which is very ugly. A slight convexity is much preferable. The leather on the outside draws a little in the opposite direction, but there are still two other counteracting inner layers, the "filling-in" papers and the pasted down end papers to be duly spoken of later.

After the boards are lined, they are cut, together, in the cutting press. It is well to stick the two boards together with a little paste in the center, so that they will not slip at all. The cutting press is the same as the backing press, reversed. An implement called a "plow," which runs horizontally, held in place by a groove, holds the knife, and by means of a screw, presses it further and further into the boards, as it moves, back and forth. After cutting one edgeCthe one which is to fit into the hinge—the top and bottom edges are squared to the back at a length which leaves a projection beyond the edges of the sheath sufficient to protect them. These projections are called the "squares." Their width is a matter of taste, but in a large book they require to be wider than in a small one. The fore-edge squares are then measured by laying the cover down on the book, the back fitting into the hinge and squared by the top.

After the boards are cut, a line is drawn about one-half, or in a large book, three-quarters of an inch from the back of the cover. The board is then laid upon the book and lines drawn at right angles to it, from the cord to this line. A row of holes is then driven through the board from the outside, with a hammer and large punch or bodkin, on a piece of lead. Reversing the board, another row is driven thru, between the first, in the opposite direction. The frayed cords, after removing the glue and filling them with paste, are laced through these holes, the protruding ends cut off, the book laid on a flat piece of iron and hammered down. To flatten them still more a tin plate is put inside and outside of each cover, fitted close to the hinge, and the book is then put into the heavy standing press between boards, and left usually over night. It is always well to have several books on hand in various stages, as at intervals a book must remain for some time in press. The frequent change from one process to another also prevents both muscles and attention from becoming over fatigued.

After the laced in cords are pressed down quite flat so as not to show unpleasantly through the leather, the book is again taken out of press, the back moistened a little with paste and the glue on the outside of the back removed, usually with a bone folder. Only the glue which has sunk in between the sections is of any value in holding them together. At the stage when the back and bands are slightly moist it is a good plan to straighten the bands and, if the arch is not perfect, it can sometimes be made to take a better form at this point by pushing it into shape and leaving it to dry in the backing press. The bands are straightened by band nippers [a kind of small pliers] and they may also have their positions slightly altered if the spaces are uneven, by driving them gently to one side or the other with a hammer and a band stick. The band stick is used later in covering.

The book is now ready to be "head-banded." The head band is intended entirely for ornament. It is of silk wound over a strip of vellum, a bit of sewing cord or a piece of gut. Sometimes the two latter, one larger than the other, make a double head band which is very ornamental. As the making of the head band is a difficult and intricate process to describe, and not a structural one, I shall omit it. In commercial books, head bands are not wrought, but bought by the yard and pasted in—a very "cheap and nasty" expedient and, to a trained eye, not in the least ornamental.

The book is now ready for covering. In the early stages, books are "half-bound" both for economy and because the process is much simpler and easier. A half binding is a book covered with a strip of leather at the back and, if to the taste of the binder, triangular pieces at the corners; the rest of the cover being of paper or cloth. The first thing to be done in preparation is the cutting and paring of the leather. A rectangular strip of leather is cut about an inch and a half longer than the book, allowing three-quarters of an inch to turn in at each end. In the beginning it is well to allow a little more than this, in case of accident to the leather in paring; though the pupil should practice for a time on worthless scraps before beginning on the piece he is really intending to use. The width of the piece varies with the taste of the binder, and the thickness of the book. It may come over on the side of the book one-fourth of the distance more or less. I dislike to see a "half" binding really taking up half the cover space. One feels like asking why, since it came so far toward covering the space, a little more might not have been expended and the whole actually covered. I find more than one-third a very ugly proportion, and corners of leather are not to my taste although they do serve the purpose of protection.

The knife which we of the school of Cobden-Sanderson use in paring leather is of the shape shown in Fig. 12 [like a 1" rectangular putty knife]. The stone should not be so hard as to dull the edge of the knife too fast. A spoiled lithographer's stone is used and should be chosen for the greatest surface and the least weight, relatively, for convenience in lifting it about. The bench should be firm. Men usually stand but it is quite possible to sit on a high stool and pare well. With this cut a long ribbon is pared off the edge of a piece of leather in a bevel. This is the first step in paring a full skin, or a strip for half binding. The knife should be held at such an angle with the stone as to cut the ribbon off as cleanly to the edge as possible. Naturally, the pupil does not succeed in doing this at the first or second effort. In fact, early efforts of paring usually resemble the work of the average rat. So let not the aspiring, unassisted amateur be unduly depressed by such a result. After the first beveled strip is removed, the angle of the knife to the stone may be lessened and a second and wider strip removed. After that the position of the knife being held is very flat. In paring the strip for half binding, the whole piece is thinned evenly; then at the top and bottom where the leather is turned in, for about three-quarters of an inch, it is pared so much more as to make the two folds together not noticeably thicker than the rest of the piece, else there will be unsightly lumps in the top and bottom panels. The very edge of the leather must be "feathered" so that it will leave no edge to be seen or felt.

In cutting a skin for full binding it is well first to cut a pattern of paper from the book in boards, laying the opened boards down on the paper and drawing lines at least three-quarters of an inch from the edge. The skin is then pared around the edge just as in the process described for the top and bottom of the strip for half binding, except that it should be made a little less thin in the rest of the margin than in the part turned in over the back. The slope should be very even and gradual and the rule is, as in most cases, "enough and not too much." If pared too much the skin is not durable; if too little the edges are clumsy. If uneven there are bumps and hollows all along the edge. It is all a matter of practice and experience after good teaching.

In a pared skin, if the dye comes through on the wrong side somewhat unevenly, it does not show the paring as even as it should. A strip is pared first down the back, leaving the central part of each cover surface untouched. This central strip should be done last after the edges are finished, and should be carefully marked off with pencil by laying the open covers on the book.

The book is now ready to be covered. This is the most constructive process of all, which makes the book really a book.

Note

1.   ["The Handicraft of Bookbinding (Article II)." *Industrial Art Magazine* 4 (September 1916): 104-107.]

10

Bookbinding (Article III)[1]

In the last article the book was left ready to be covered; indeed, two books are ready, one for a "half," and the other for a "full" binding.

Half Binding

The "half" binding we shall now proceed with. The pupil, in fact, puts on a considerable number of half bindings before it is sensible to attack a piece of skin of the size for a full bound book. My pupils are furnished with scraps for half binding but they buy their own skins for full bindings, which avoids any self interest on either side in the decision as to when the proper moment has arrived to attack the paring of a piece of skin for a full binding.

Before beginning to cover, the implements and materials are assembled. Good, fresh paste should be ready; paste which has begun to be watery is ineffectual. We make our paste according to this rule: One part flour and four parts water. The flour is first mixed with one part water or a little more, and the lumps are thoroughly crushed out. Then the rest of the water is added, and about a teaspoonful of powdered alum, dissolved in a little hot water, is added to every four cups of flour. The paste is made by cooking it in a double boiler—stirring all the while to avoid lumps—until it has a translucent appearance and loses its raw, floury look.

The book is covered on a paring stone. The other items needed are band nippers [a kind of small piers] and band stick (which is a stick made of polished, very hard wood, perfectly smooth, for rubbing down the bands; the edges should not be too sharp, as they may cut the leather); a dish of clean water, a sponge, scissors and a board made in two levels for holding up the cover when the book is open.

The leather is first moistened with the sponge on the right side, not enough for the water to come through, and paste applied, thoroughly and evenly, on the wrong side with a good brush which does not shed its bristles. The leather is laid, right side down on the stone and the book, after applying paste to its back, not too thickly, is put down evenly upon the rectangular piece of leather, so that the same length will project at both ends, and so that the sides of the strip will come over at even distances upon the sides of the book.

The book is then set upon its fore-edges on the stone, back upwards, the leather pushed downwards with the palms of the hands, and also pushed slightly towards the center of the book from the two ends, to allow a little fullness for going over the bands. Care must be taken at this point not to allow the strip to slip over further on one side than the other. Obviously, there is always a tendency of the leather to wrinkle on the side of the book from the fullness necessary for going over the bands on the back, and this constitutes the chief difficulty in covering. Some leathers are much more obliging than others in accommodating the grain to looseness in the back, and returning to smoothness on the side. Moroccos are infinitely easier to manage in this regard than either pig skin or seal skin because of the artificial grain put into them, which takes up the slackness without showing wrinkles. Morocco can be modelled, as it were, to accommodate the bands, in a way which makes it far easier and more pleasant to manage than any other skin. I should never use anything but morocco, but for the fact that pig and seal come in far more beautiful colors, and the texture of pig skin is very attractive. I always advise pupils to begin with morocco.[2]

Let us return to our strip of leather getting dry on the back of the book, while we are discussing its qualities. From time to time, even if we do not stop to discuss, the wet sponge must be applied to it to keep it moist enough to be flexible and also to keep the paste inside from losing its quality. "Enough and not too much" is again the maxim—to apply it, a matter of experience. If the leather is soaked thru, the paste becomes diluted and does not stick. If allowed to dry before it is closely fitted at all points, it does not stick.

After pushing the leather forward or downward with the palms, and slightly inward toward the middle band, the band nippers are applied to force the leather down about the bands. This is done at first with sufficient precision to determine how much is needed to cover the bands and lie down flat in the panels between. Then, before it is perfectly fitted down, the ends projecting beyond the book must be disposed of. A little paste is applied to just as much of the right side of the leather as is to be turned back in. The strip is then folded back to that point, double over the back of the book, and, at the edges; then the fold is separated, the inner part passing between the board cover and the book itself and lapping down over the inner edge of the board cover. When this has been done the band nippers and band stick are used until the leather lies down smoothly in the panels between the bands, and the bands look straight and sharply defined. No amount of description will properly acquaint the would-be bookbinder with the perfection of this process. It must be learned by seeing it done. After the covering process is finished and the book closed, it should remain over a night before being again opened. The opening should be very carefully done, otherwise the leather sometimes cracks at the "hinges." The leather should be moistened slightly along the whole length of the hinges on the outside of the book, and the turn-in on the inside. When this has been done, the cover is opened and pushed up so that a right angle is formed by the cover and hinge, the level of the book itself being below that of the cover. Sometimes it is necessary to loosen the leather a little at the part of the turn-in next the book, and stretch it, if it has shrunken in drying, as often happens. Next, holding the cover open and pushed up, square, it is gently beaten at the hinge with a hammer to make it lie smooth.

The half binding is now ready for the paper part of the cover to be put on, unless the binder likes leather corners, as I do not. To my eye they give a patchy appearance. The "trimming" and "filling" of the paper are done in one process. [This occurs when] a piece of thickish paper (in a full bound book it should be as thick as the pared edge) a little smaller than the cover, is laid down on it, one edge at the inner edge of the cover. A distance of half an inch, more or less, according to taste and the size of the book, is measured off from the book's edge, and both filling and ragged edge are cut through with a sharp binder's knife, guided by a straight-edge held very firmly. As the filling paper is likely to stretch a little in pasting, it is well to cut off a very narrow strip, afterwards, to allow for this. The half binding is now finished to the point of "pasting down" and lettering, which is the same in all books and will be treated later.

Full Binding

Let us now take, up the full bound book at the point where the process differs from the half binding. The fitting of the moistened and pasty leather over the bands is the same but attended with much greater difficulty, as intimated above, because the slack caused by the necessity of pulling the leather over the bands is much harder to dispose of on the sides. In the half binding, it can be disposed of by allowing the edge to be slighttly out of the straight line, and trimming it after it is dry. Obviously, in the full skin, this resource is cut off and great skill is required, especially in handling pig and seal skin, to prevent an unsightly curtain-like looping of the leather between bands. There is no rule; it is done by doing it, and by him who can. A very clever pupil of mine once said that he should never be able to sell a book; he would be too proud of the good ones and too ashamed of the poor ones to part with any.

The leather is pushed firmly along with the palm of the band, taking care to keep it even so that it does not turn over the edge much farther at one point than at another, and taking great pains also to see that it sticks on the edges. The fitting of the leather over the corners is one of the most difficult and delicate parts of the process. When it is perfectly done the juncture does not show and is tooled over, in the decorated book, like a plain piece of leather.

The process, however, is not completed at one time. At the time of covering the leather is pulled over the corner, and with a bone folder pushed well over and inside the corners, a sixteenth of an inch perhapsCas far as it will go, but well over, so that no opening of the leather will come on the edge. Then, still with the folder, the leather is made to lie flat on the board and the slack gathered into one mass, projected above a straight line, this line terminating at a point well within the corner.

With a pair of scissors this bunch of superfluous leather is now cut off, not so close as to run any risk of its gaping at any point; on the contrary, something to spare is left and the bit to spare is temporarily disposed of by pushing one side neatly under the other and leaving it thus to dry with the rest of the book over night. When dry the book is opened in the manner already described, laid open on the board in two levels and the corners completed by cutting the two overlapped faces of leather through in a bevel, exactly bisecting the right-angle, so that they will fit each other with the slight overlapping of the bevel and still be perfectly smooth. The extra bits are now pulled out and a little fresh paste is inserted. The beveling and fitting of the corners is a very nice process and requires a good deal of deftness and a good deal of practice. A gaping corner is very unworkmanlike. Should it occur, as it sometimes does even to the practiced, the inlay is a last resort. Inlaying (literally on-laying) will be treated of in the fourth and last article on "Finishing."

The last process before "Finishing" or "Tooling" is "crushing." This is done in two ways, either by heat or moisture—never both together! I was taught to crush by slightly moistening the leather of the filled and trimmed book with a sponge, placing the single cover between two japanned or nickeled plates sufficiently thick not to bend, then placing the cover and plates on pile of binders' boards, with the cover centered under the screw of the large standing press, and screwing the press down under hard pressure with a lever. The cover was allowed to remain a few minutes thus, and was then taken out. If the crushing was uneven the process was repeated, sometimes several times, moving the cover so that the central pressure came above the part least crushed, or even putting bits of thickish paper, torn with "feathered" edges, as near as possible to the size and shape of the part to be crushed, between the plate and the board; *never* next the book. The method I now use is that of heating the plates instead of moistening the leather. Otherwise the process is the same. The plates should just have stopped hissing when moistened; if they are too hot the consequences are very dire. Either the leather is burned or sticks badly to the cover and if it sticks too fast, the surface of the leather is disfigured in pulling it off. when both covers are crushed (observe, never at the same time, or the book would be crushed to a ruin between them) the back is polished with a polishing iron (for which purpose it is confined in a hand press between two wedge-shaped leather-lined boards). Our book is now ready to be decorated, and let us hope it deserves to be.

Notes

1. ["Bookbinding (Third Article)." *Industrial Art Magazine* 4 (November 1916): 198-200.]
2. "Levant" which has so fine and luxurious a sound is morocco, i.e. goat skin. When one wishes to sound very impressive and expensive one says "Levant." Common, cheap morocco is not thus glorified. I suppose the best moroccos may have come from the "Levant" originally.

11

Bookbinding (Article IV)[1]

"Tooling" or "Finishing"

After the covers of the full bound book are "crushed" and the back polished, it is ready to be decorated. It is only the well-bound book which has any claim to decoration. Heaping ornamentation upon a cheap and shabbily made book is like covering a coarse and cheap garment with embroidery. One of the services which good handicraft binding has done for commercial binding is to teach this canon of taste. It is now unusual, except in the case of novels, to see decoration on commercially bound books. Dignified commercial books are usually bound in plain cloth, with simple lettering of the title and nothing else. It was quite usual a generation ago to cover books of poems, etc., bound in cloth, with senseless filigree mechanically applied.

The proper decoration for a leather bound book is technically called "tooling" or "finishing" and is of two kinds, "blind" tooling where gold is not used, and gold tooling. The pattern on a commercial book is made by putting it upon a plate and stamping it off upon the cover in one stroke. This is the only way in which thousands of copies can be turned off. The hand bound book is a very different matter; each copy is a special creation and it is presumed that a book is not thus especially bound unless it has some value either in itself or personal to the possessor.

"Tools" technically in bookbinding are the implements for putting decoration upon the book; "tooling" is the process of doing so. The tools are little dies of metal set in wooden handles. They are heated and patterns are stamped with them in the leather by a process to be presently described.

The "tools" and patterns of a handicraft book-binder are personal to him and should no more be appropriated by others than any other sort of design. The tools are made to order from drawings which he furnishes the tool cutter. The most useful tools for designs are simple forms such as a conventionalized leaf, flower, or part of a flower, which can be used in a great number of combinations. The more elaborate and intricate a tool, the less frequently it can be used. An amateur craftsman often makes the mistake, in the beginning, of making his tools too interesting in themselves. A complicated lily, for example, can be used only two or three times, perhaps; a picture of a ship still less often. One cannot cover a great variety of books with a lily or a ship pattern without becoming monotonous, and the more naturalistic the tool design, the less often it can be used. Besides a few simple, fundamental forms, a considerable number of gouges, i.e., of curved lines of various lengths and curves, and of straight lines, are required; also dots and circles. With this equipment, and a pencil, a pattern is made on a handmade paper, which is strong enough not to be broken away by the pressure of the tools, through it upon the leather. The lines are first drawn with a pencil, and then fitted by the gouges of various lengths and curves. The tool forms are roughly drawn in with the pencil; and when placed as desired, the tools are blackened in the smoke of a candle and thus exactly transferred to the paper. As the medium is rigid, freehand drawing or any attempt at naturalism on book covers is in bad taste. The more formal, conventional and balanced the designs are, the better fitted to "tooling." This, of course, does not imply that they need be without grace and charm. The French binders, though the greatest technicians, especially in tooling, often make the great mistake in taste of attempting representations and illustrations on the covers of books, which is bizarre. An inlaid lady with an inlaid parasol, the dress and parasol of different colored leathers, tho perfect in technical accuracy, borders on the outré. Since the pattern should have symmetry, accuracy may be obtained in the following manner. The paper is cut to the exact size of the cover, is folded in half twice, vertically and horizontally. One angle is also bisected by a fold. The pattern is begun in the corner.

Supposing it is to be a border, the design is drawn in from the line folded to bisect the angle, to the line bisecting the paper vertically. The tools and gouges are then blackened by smoking them in a candle, and sharp black outlines of them are stamped upon the paper between these two folds. The paper is then again folded inward at the bisected corner and with a bone folder, rubbed on the back so that the black of the candle smoke is transferred. The corner pattern is now complete, to equal distances from the central line. The rubbing can be reinforced by blackening and applying the tools a second time, taking care to put them down precisely so as not to blur the pattern. The sheet is now folded again, this time in the fold bisecting the sheet horizontally, and the rubbing process repeated. A second time reinforcing it with the blackened tools, it is folded a third time, now in the lateral bisection, and again rubbed off. It will be seen that the border is now complete with the exception of the space at the sides, representing the distance by which the book is longer than its width. This is now composed and filled in on one side and transferred by the same method to the other. Had the pattern consisted of corners only, it would have been complete without the last step. A diaper pattern may be treated similarly as regards transferring one side to the other, but if the unit is not symmetrical both ways it must be managed differently. Each designer has his personal methods for these details. The above sufficiently suggests the general treatment on its mechanical side.

It may be said of designing for books, as for many other, perhaps for all other crafts, that it is impossible to do it well without knowing the medium. General principles of design may be well taught, but quite obviously a design which is suitable for embroidery or wood carving might be wholly untranslatable into gold tooling, and even if it were possible, wholly inappropriate as in the case I have cited above.

The patten duly made, it is now time to execute it. The paper is attached by a little paste to two corners of the book, perhaps three. I always leave at least one comer unattached that I may peep under and make sure whether all the tools have been struck. Care must be taken not to use too much paste, for it sometimes discolors the leather and sometimes the surface comes away with it when the paper is taken off. The tools are heated in the finishing stove. Like the polishing iron and the crushing plates, the tools should ordinarily be used at the point at which they cease to hiss, when moistened. But the degree of heat varies with the quality of leather and also with the moisture of the leather and of the atmosphere. The greater the moisture, the cooler the tool should be. The right relation of these component factors is learned by more or less costly experience. Of course, one does not begin tooling lessons on a book but on a practice board, made by pasting waste scraps of leather on waste scraps of mill board and crushing it slightly. Experiments are first made with separate tools and letters before it is worthwhile even to make a pattern.

The pattern attached and the tools heated, the latter are applied to the intervening paper and pressed through it into the leather. A smooth, thin but tough handmade paper is the best. The position of the hand in grasping and applying the tool is such that the thumb of the right hand is held on the top of the handle, and that of the left is used to steady the tool in putting it down. The tool should be held firm and slightly rocked back and forth once only, to touch each point, i.e., if it has some extent of surface. A dot or circle obviously does not require this movement. And in any case the movement in each direction should not be repeated. If the tool is waggled back and forth, each time incurring the risk of not going back into the same place, the impression is sure to be ruined.

The impression thus produced is called "blind tooling." Usually the first impression is not quite sharp enough and requires going over again with the tools after the paper is removed. This blind tooling is slightly washed over with vinegar, with a very little paste in it. (For white pig skin, which would be stained by the vinegar, paste water is used). It may be applied with the glaire brush. After that has become dry, the glaire is applied. Glaire is made by thoroughly beating the whites of eggs—say three at a time, for two or three persons' use—adding a teaspoonful of vinegar, letting the substance stand for some hours, and then straining it through a bit of cheesecloth. A little more vinegar may be added if it becomes too thick and the glaire again strained. It will last weeks if covered and if the heat is not great.

The glaire is now carefully applied to the tooled surface with a camel's hair brush, taking pains to touch every point of the tooling without slopping it about on the untooled part. It should not be allowed to stand in little pools but be put on as evenly as possible. If one part is much moister than another there is danger of burning it with the tool. After the first application of glaire has dried, the process is repeated. When the glaire has become dry, superficially, for the second time (it ought not to remain dry too long) the gold is applied. Gold leaf is bought in little books at a gold beater's and the necessary appliances for using it are a leather gold cushion, a gold knife, (long, straight and not too sharp) some cotton and an oil. Palm oil is rather the best, but if it is not to be had, cocoanut oil will do. Olive oil dries too fast, and lard, which dries slowly, does not give a bright impression. Perhaps a little lard and a little olive, thoroughly mixed, might answer if the others could not be had. If the atmosphere is very damp and a small surface is done at a time, olive oil alone may answer the purpose.

A single sheet of the gold is now laid flat and smooth upon the cushion. That is to say, the novice *attempts* thus to lay it there. The probabilities are that the first few attempts are crowned with little success and the sheet crumples and blows about and ends on the floor. When picked up it sticks to the unfortunate's finger, becomes worse crumpled and at last disappears in too fine a ball to be seen. Courage! There are different ways of proceeding. Either the knife is held across the middle and the sheet blown across it, very gently, and then blown off again on to the cushion, or the book is opened carefully and laid over upon the cushion, and then lifted off, leaving the sheet there. If it lacks a little, as is usual, of being quite smooth and flat, one blows gently upon it exactly in the center. If the breath is obliquely directed, the last state of the sheet of gold is considerably worse than the first. When it at last lies flat, it is cut with the gold knife into pieces of the size and shape desired. A good sized pad is now made of smooth and good cotton batting and another small one. Some of the oil is rubbed in the palm of the left hand to melt it, if solid, and the small cotton pad absorbs it, and with this piece of oiled cotton, the surface to be tooled is rubbed over to make the gold adhere to it. The second and larger piece of cotton wipes off what oil remains on the palm, as this piece should be only sufficiently oiled to take up the gold. It is carefully, and with even pressure, applied to the piece of gold to be lifted and the gold, which should remain as flat as possible on the cotton pad, is now pressed very gently and without any lateral movement, which would crack it, to the oiled surface of the leather. The gold sinks down into the tooled depressions and they should, if sharply defined, be plainly seen. As it is very rare that no cracks at all are made in the gold, it is necessary to cover each part of the tooled surface twice. Before putting down the second piece, the first must be quite closely adhering. If it is not, one blows upon it a little with a moist breath, close to it, and pats it down with the cotton. Then the second piece of gold must be laid on without disturbing the first.

The heated tools are now applied to this impression one by one. If they do not coincide, accurately, with the first impression, the result is a failure to the extent of the lack of coincidence. If it is considerable and the first impression has been strong it shows to one side and looks, as my master was wont to say, like a galosh, slipped in the mud. Letters are more difficult than any other tools because the slightest inclination in one direction or other is very noticeable; whereas a leaf, turned slightly one way or another, may not strike the eye at all. Long, straight lines are made with a wheel, the line being first made with a bone folder, guided by a ruler. When the surface has all been tooled, it is rubbed over with a piece of flannel (by the present writer) and the superfluous gold removed. Frugal binders use crude rubber, prepared by soaking in petroleum which takes the extra gold up into it. When the piece is quite filled and will hold no more, it is sold to the gold beater who melts the rubber out. If the gold always stuck where it should stick and away where it should not, how merry and diverting a process would gold tooling be! To rub off the surface and see one's lovely pattern smiling before one in all its gay brightness—how complacent a sensation! But, alas! that the next paragraph heading must be the prosaic word Patching.

To patch the parts needing reinforcement, if they need it only moderately, one simply reglaires, once, and lays the gold on again. But if so much is wanting that the portion must be gone all over anew, it is washed over with vinegar and a piece of cotton, removing as much more as comes off thus being weak, and the process is all repeated. Each time of patching there is a little more danger of blurring and a little less probability of ever getting a really clear and handsome impression. If the leather is burned outright, so that there is no surface that can be worked upon, the only recourse is inlaying.

For inlaying, leather must be pared very thin. The leather is first wet—soaked indeed. I was taught to pare for inlays with a rather long, thin and straight knife. The leather was cut into strips, narrow enough to allow the knife (not too thin to be stiff) to take in the width in one sweep. The Scotch finisher who taught me to pare for inlays could pare a strip of considerable length in this way to a marvelous thinness, without going through the leather. But I was never an apt pupil in this process, which requires a strong as well as a firm and skillful hand, and I departed from my instructions in this one particular (as in the process of crushing) and pare for inlays with the regular paring knife. As the pieces required are usually small, it is not fatal if one occasionally does go through the leather. After the strip is pared and perfectly dry the form required is tooled on it with a warm tool (not hot); is then cut out with scissors unless one has a punch. If the colored inlay is small and corresponds with a toolCsuch as a leaf or flower, one should have a punch, but the punch must be made of steel as a brass one is too soft and loses its edge. And I have not been able to find a tool cutter in this country who would make them. I have those I brought from London, circles and various flowers and leaves. And I do not make designs requiring very small inlays in the forms for which I have no punches, as the labor of cutting out tiny pieces with scissors is too monotonous. I cannot advise those who must get their tools here. My mechanical readers may be able to overcome this obstacle. The old bookbinders made their own tools. To use the punch the pared leather is laid on a piece of hard millboard and the punch lightly struck with a hammer. After the pieces are cut out their edges must be "feathered," i.e., beveled to the finest edge, so that there will be no perceptible edge at all after the inlay is tooled over, but the surface will seem to be unbroken. I do this with an oculist's scalpel, my own device. The inlays are pasted over the tooled depression, pressed in thoroughly with the tool, cool; glaire is applied to them as to the rest, the gold is laid on as before, and all tooled as though the inlay were not there. It is obvious that if the inlay is not tooled around with gouges but a tool, the tool must be an "open" one, or the inlay would not show at all, being covered with gold. Sometimes a blind tooled inlay is effective, but even then the inlaid pieces should have most of their surface raised, not depressed. For an inlaid patch, in case of burning, a small bit may be pared dry. It is always a prudent thing to save a bit of the pieces trimmed off in "filling" the book to use if necessary, the edges being already thin.

Lettering

Lettering is perhaps the most difficult thing in tooling. In one sense it should have come first, as half-bound books must be lettered while it is quite out of taste to decorate them. But in learning to tool on a practice board, as I have already pointed out, it is better to take tools first, to get the technique of making the gold stick, and to acquire some accuracy, as lettering requires the highest degree of accuracy. Thence I have passed on to combining tools in patterns and must now turn back to lettering.

Commercial binders set letters in a "palette" and stamp the whole title at once. But handicraft binders use each letter as a separate tool. The pattern of the title must be as carefully made as any part of the pattern. A strip of the tough, handmade paper is cut to the width of the panel, between the bands. The second panel from the top is the right one for the title and the one below it for the name of the author, if that is to be tooled. In some cases the title includes it, e.g. *Sonnets of Shakespeare* instead of *Sonnets*, alone, and William Shakespeare in the panel below which would look rather foolish. The arrangement of titles requires a good deal of planning and some taste and, not infrequently, invention, when the title is very long or very short, or the book's shape and size very unfitted to it. One must often try several arrangements of a pattern and several sizes of letters before finding the right one.

As the lower margin of a printed page, and the lower panel of the book's back should be deeper than the others, the space below the title should be a little wider than that above it; were they precisely equal it would look narrower. (This is easily proven in any of these cases by turning the book upside down.) Hence, a little space is marked off at the bottom with compass or "straightedge," (ruler) to begin with. Then, if the title is to be in three lines, the remaining space is divided in three, leaving a space at the top a little less than at the bottom; if in four lines, in four. The strip should be folded in such a width as to make sure that the lettering does not run over onto the part of the leather which bends in opening the book, else the gold will crack off. The strip should be folded in the center of the panel thus formed, and each line kept centered. A good eye suffices, but may be aided by the compasses. Counting letters is obviously a very inexact method as an "I" and an "M" and "O" do not at all balance. It is not very desirable to divide syllables, but is sometimes necessary and not altogether forbidden. Sometimes the expedient of using a smaller letter inside a larger, or in its lap, as it were, an "i" within an "O" or "L," is not disagreeable. But this should not be done merely for the sake of oddity. It should always be remembered that the object of a title is to inform as to the contents of the book, and the more clearly it does so the better. Playing tricks with lettering for its own sake shows a paucity of inventiveness in other directions.

The date of the edition should be tooled at the bottom of the lower panel in the space by which the lower panel is longer than the others. The pattern in all the decorated panels is the same. The binder's signature and date of binding (if there is no design a signature is unnecessary) should be placed on the inside, lower margin of the back cover. The signature usually consists of initials only.

The proper decoration of a book is now completed unless one wishes to go into the elaboration of the "doublé" or "doublure." The French are very fond of putting watered silks into the insides of their books, a practice which I much dislike. Stuffs of this sort suggest fussy sofa pillows rather than decorous books. Even leather filling the entire inner surface of the cover and tooled over does not seem to me reasonable. The idea of leather is a protection to the book, which may at the same time ornament it. But the protection of leather is not required on the inside. Decorated papers for the "paste down" and first fly leaves or end papers, are pleasant if the paper is really pretty. Pretty Italian and Japanese papers which are strong enough for pasting down, may be had. Marbled papers are usually excessively ugly. The French binders are much addicted to the use of the ugliest of these—those with glazed surfaces. The idea of the glazed surface is to prevent the discoloring of the paper from the oil in the leather. The paper, unless glazed, will eventually turn brown from contact with the opposite leather. But, to my eye, the brown border of the fly leaf or end paper, with the tooled pattern of the leather border stamped off on it, is rather pleasant—far less ugly than the glazed marble paper used to prevent it. The combinations of a usually crude colored watered silk panel and the glazed paper is uglier than one would believe any Frenchman could invent, were it not so common.

The leather hinge, which makes a continuous border around the four sides of the cover, is rather pleasant for a sumptuous book, and, filled with paper like the opposite fly, has not the objectionableness of the stuff fabrics. The leather for the hinge must be pared to the same thinness as the rest of the turn-in, except for the part which covers the hinge itself. That should be somewhat thinner or the book will close badly. The strip should properly be sewn in with the book itself, but that degree of thoroughness which is difficult and intricate, is omitted by some, and the strip simply pasted in after the book is covered. In this case a thinly feathered edge laps down slightly over the end paper, and the decorative end paper if there is to be one, is cut to the exact size of the other end papers, fitted and pasted over it. A leather hinge should indeed not be attempted by an amateur feeling his way. It is far better to do the fundamental processes well. The very last thing to be done is pasting down the end paper which covers the exposed hinge. This is not done until the lettering and all the decorating is finished, for the reason that the ends become soiled in working on the book. The outer end, or fly, which is soiled is torn off unless, as is well, a protective sheet has been slightly attached. That is now removed and the sheet to be pasted down is turned back, folded and creased closely, down over the hinge. Then, with the compasses, a slight dent is made in several places in each side, at equal distances from the edge, just within the width of the turn-in. The sheet is folded back upon the book itself, a sheet of zinc inserted and the "paste-down" leaf trimmed to the points marked with knife and straight edge. Paste is now applied, taking pains that the hinge is thoroughly pasted and the paper rubbed down with hands and folder under a clean piece of waste paper to prevent its becoming grubby. It is quite possible to get the book into a very messy state—almost to spoil the looks of it, even in this last process. If the paper does not stick fast over the hinge when the book is closed (as it must not be until thoroughly dry) it comes loose there and forms what the men at the Doves Bindery used to call a "pencil case." Pencil cases cause almost as great disgust and depression as any mishap that can befall. They are especially wearying because one is anticipating the triumphant close of the whole work. They may usually be averted by applying a not too hot polishing iron over a piece of clean waste paper, ironing gently, after the paper has been well pressed down. If one does develop, it is necessary to wet the paper again with a clean sponge or bit of cotton and perfectly clean water, and then apply the hot polishing iron under a piece of clean waste paper, taking great pains not to slide the piece of waste along for fear of tearing the moist "paste-down," under it. When thoroughly dry the cover is closed and the book is struck rather firmly with a smooth hammer along the hinges. It is then put between plates *under light pressure*, the press being closed down with the hands only. On no account is the lever to be used. If heavy pressure is applied the leather is torn away from the back and longitudinal wrinkles appear. Probably the gold is also cracked off. In fact, if the pressure has been heavy enough the book is a wreck. This final process of pasting down the ends, when neatly and successfully done, though one of the minor processes, makes a very great difference in the appearance of the book, removing the naked appearance of the book's bones, as it were, showing along the hinges, and the soiled and untidy look of the protective sheets. It is like the completion of a toilette and the precious volume which, wrought with affection and interest has come to have a distinct personality to the binder, is now ready to meet the not too discerning public.

Note

1. ["Bookbinding (Article 4): Tooling and Finishing." *Industrial Art Magazine* 5 (March 1916): 97-103.]

Part 2

Labor Intensified: The Angel of the Strikers

12

1910 Testimony by Ellen Gates Starr of the Picket Committee[1]

On November 24th, Miss Starr sent the following telling letter on the "Police protection" for the WTUL Strike Committee to the papers:

"I went first to a dingy hall, ill ventilated and crowded, to meet the pickets and plan our orderly and law-abiding course, and then to the factory of Price at Franklin and Van Buren Streets.

"About the door stood twenty-one or twenty-two men. It must be conceded that they 'obstructed the street' more than a group of three rather small women [Miss Emma Steghagen, Miss S.M. Franklin, and Starr], who are never allowed to stand for an instant, but are ordered, usually roughly, to 'move on' and 'go about their business.' These men, it is true, were about their business of holding the street for Price & Co. I addressed myself civilly to a police officer and asked him why these twenty-two men were allowed to stand on the pavement and I was not. He answered (somewhat shamefacedly; I think that particular officer did not like his job), that they were all sworn officers, and added, "Don't ask me questions, lady." "You have your orders, I suppose?" "Yes, I have." On which I tendered him my sympathy and proceeded to interrogate the so-called 'officers.'

"After a time a superior officer arrived who was insolent and brutal and absolutely outside his rights, as I was entirely within mine. I was then alone, having separated myself from the girls, and was simply walking back and forth in front of the factory. After roughly asking me, 'Who are you?' and 'What are you doing here'" and hearing that I was simply a citizen of the United States and a settlement worker here in the interest of justice and fair play, he informed me that if I passed by once more I would be sent to the station.

"I then withdrew to the opposite side of the street and watched matters from there. Later I recrossed the street and entered an adjacent restaurant which had a large window looking out full upon the street in front of Price's and from there I watched proceedings until the people had all come out.

"The modus operandi was to bundle the strikebreakers out, surrounded by the hired 'detectives,' directly to the cars which halted precisely in front of the door so that no pickets should be allowed to speak to them." The whole thing was, to the descendant of a Revolutionary soldier [Ethan Allen], an American from 1632, a heart sickening sight."

Note

1. [This testimony was published in several places and sent to the newspapers on 24 November 1910. We used the testimony found on pp. 10-11 in *Extension of the Ten Hour Law: Report of the Legislative Committee of the Women's Trade Union Leagues of Illinois*. Chicago: Women's Trade Union Leagues, 1911. Further information on the strike is available in this booklet, too.]

13

Efforts To Standardize Chicago Resturants— The Henrici Strike[1]

A pioneer resident of Hull-House tells in this article something of the diffi- culties encountered by unionists who attempt to keep within the law and yet make a strike effective. In the Henrici strike the police made arrests freely, although the Illinois law permits peaceful picketing. The courts have seemed to lend their aid to this harrassing of the union, for to date not a single striker's case has been tried, although they have sometimes been arrested twice in one day.—Ed.[of the Survey]

At Henrici's restaurant in Randolph St., Chicago—which is not claimed is worse than may others—the bakery is wholly underground. Since February 28, 1910, it has been illegal to build underground bakeries. There is no window whatever in the kitchen and the bread bakery; the only ventilation is by an air shaft; at night there is often no power on for mechanical ventilating purposes though there is a night shift; the sweat of the bakers frequently drops into the bread. These facts given me by cooks and waiters I have veri- fied at the office of the Bureau of Sanitary Inspection.

For six months previous to February 5, the beginning of the Henrici restau- rant strike, unions of waitresses, cooks, bakers, milk-wagon drivers and deliv- ery-wagon drivers had been negotiating with the restaurants in the "loop" district[2] to the end of establishing a scale of hours and wages; in fine, of standardizing their industries in that district.

The waitresses' main demands were for one day's rest in seven, $8 for six days' work (instead of $7 for seven days' work), as a first step toward freeing them from the pernicious tipping system; and, as always, for recognition of the union, without which no contract is of the slightest value.

Why the Strikes was Called at Henrici's

One hundred restaurants had signed the agreement; Henrici's was the first to refuse and was thus naturally, and not arbitrarily as the Henrici manager alleged, the point of attack. The manager not only complained that his restaurant was unfairly singled out, but that it was unfair to proceed against any one restaurant. He maintained that some measure should be adopted applying to all at once.

Obviously, the only kind of measure which could so apply would be a legislative measure, and it must be remembered that, whenever any attempt is made at legislation to improve the conditions of hours, wages, etc., in restaurants, the Restaurant Keepers' Association is promptly on hand to defeat it.

The four union waitresses engaged at Henrici's were dismissed—on pretended charges—after having been followed by detectives to their union meetings. The two union cooks, of a total of four, and six union bakers, of a total of eight were called out on an officially declared strike; also the milk and delivery wagon drivers. No attempt was made, as is usual in strikes, to influence the waitresses remaining at work either to come out or to join the union at that time. This caused misunderstanding which served to allay public sympathy, and was probably a tactical mistake.

The reason for this inaction was that the season had been a severe one by reason of unemployment. Any strike, at any time, implies a tremendous drain upon union funds. The Henrici Company promised to discharge any waitress who joined the union at that time and, in case the union won, to pay the initiation fees of all those who had staid in. It was decided to be the most fair and humane course to fight it out without disturbing those within; but it gave apparent ground to the Henrici adherents, who constantly stated that no waitresses were on strike, and as constantly ignored not only the locked-out union waitresses but the cooks, bakers, and milk and delivery wagon drivers who were on strike.

The public, which had complained in the last garment workers' strike that pickets had attempted to call out all the workers, now objected that they did not. The lockout of union waitresses and strike of union cooks, bakers and milk and delivery wagon drivers, was named solely a "boycott."

Mr. Collins, president of the Henrici Company, by his own statement on the witness stand, paid between $1,300 and $1,400 to the Chicago newspapers for printing his statement of the situation. Only one paper—the *Evening Post*—would print the union statements. There remained to the union the method which is usually left to unionists on strike—to make their statement as well as they could in the open street.

Peaceful picketing has been pronounced legal in Illinois by repeated court decisions. The instructions given to the pickets by their unions were explicit—never to touch anyone, nor to stand still in front of, or near, the Henrici premises obstructing passage. Peaceful picketing, it is maintained, includes the right to give information in a quiet way. It should be remarked that passage was really obstructed by groups of from twelve to twenty nondescript persons wearing no badge of authority—plain clothes men, private detectives and men who stopped to talk with them and who were not ordered to "move on."

"Peaceful Pickets" Arrested

Although the instructions were carried out, arrests were repeatedly made and with increasing frequency, the same persons being twice placed under arrest and released on bonds enduring the interval between 12 and 2 o'clock. More than 125 arrests were made. The charge at first was for conspiracy, a state offense for which the bond required is $1,000. Sometimes both conspiracy and disorderly conduct were charged; in this case the bond was $1,400.

A section of the Municipal Court act provides that judges may enter an order of record authorizing police officers to accept bail. The attorney of the unions, Edgar L. Masters, considering the $400 bond for alleged "disorderly conduct" four times as great as it should have been, sent to find what the order of the court had been, and learned that the court had entered no order, and the police were fixing the bonds at their own pleasure!

The arrested persons were arraigned and assigned to a hearing in the Municipal Court where the cases were perpetually continued on motion of the prosecution. Judge Ryan at last refused to allow any further conspiracy charges until a case should have been tried.

The strike began on February 5 and up to the present time, May 7, no case has been tried either for conspiracy or disorderly conduct, although a committee appointed by the City Council for the investigation of police procedures passed resolutions urging the speedy trial of these cases. Untold time of the defendants has been wasted by the cases being so often called and continued, and more than $130,000 has been furnished in bonds by unions and sympathizers.

Added to this abuse of power, were charges of police brutality, substantiated by the sworn evidence of two injured waitresses and of a physician who attended a waitress whose arm was so badly wrenched that the attending hospital physician (Dr. Hedger) was unable, until she had had an X-ray taken, to tell whether or not it was broken. Also by the careful statement, out of court, of Dr. Bertha Van Hoosen, surgeon at the Mary Thompson Hospital.

On February 22 a meeting was called at Hull-House to suggest measures for investigating the conduct of the police. Jane Addams, head of Hull-House, presided and Mrs. Joseph T. Bowen, president of the Juvenile Protection Association offered resolutions. A committee was appointed by the chair to attend court proceedings. At that meeting was articulated a leaflet, "Facts Concerning Henrici's," issued two days previous to the Women's Trade Union League, stating the grievances and demands of the unions. This leaflet was sent to the daily papers but appeared, so far as I know, in the *Evening Post* alone.

Arrested for Disorderly Conduct

I was present on Randolph Street four days between February 22 and March 2; on the fourth day I was put under arrest. I went there for the purpose of getting first-hand knowledge of the situation, of preventing recurrence of brutality, if I could, by my presence, aid in doing so, and of protesting against illegal and unwarranted arrests.

I composed a fixed formula for use in case of witnessing such arrests which I had occasion to use three times: "As an American citizen I protest against the arrest of these persons who are doing nothing contrary to the law." I was arrested on the third occasion of reciting it in a clear but ordinary tone. No answer was made to my inquiry of the arresting officer as to the charge, but I was booked at the police station on a charge of disorderly conduct, which was sworn to by the officer, and on my declining to send for bail I was placed in a cell but released shortly thereafter on the bond of a friend who appeared and offered bail. (It has not been the policy of trade unionists to decline bail and suffer imprisonment.)

This sworn charge was afterward changed, without any assigned reason, to another charge (sworn by the same policeman) of "interfering with an officer in the discharge of his duty." To my mind it is clear that the charge was made for two reasons: to avoid the incitement to mirth and consequent disadvantage to the prosecution of a middle-aged gentlewoman appearing on a charge of disorderly conduct: and, more important, that my case, pushed on to earlier trial, might not furnish a precedent for the many cases of waitresses arrested on the former charge. It was, of course, precisely to furnish that precedent that I had been anxious for an immediate trial.

The prosecution (the city) adopted the same policy of moving continuances, as in the cases of the arrested waitresses. My attorney, Harold L. Ickes, however, succeeded in urging the trial on after four continuances, against a further motion for continuance on the part of the prosecution. The only witnesses on the side of the prosecution were four police officers who overreached themselves and swore to statements nobody believed, and which made the fabrication of their entire testimony evident. The jury returned a verdict of "not guilty."

This brief outline of my personal experience is interesting only as it gives some very slight idea of the system of harrying to which unionists on strike are subjected, and the illegal excess of power assumed by the police. It would be next to impossible to an outside sympathizer, even if one had the courage to try, to find out by personal experience the extent of what the real combatants suffer, for the reason that methods are immediately and considerably modified by the presence of outside witnesses.

My relation to the Henrici strike was given a significance which it would not otherwise have had by a meeting of downtown business men (some of whom have restaurants in connection with department stores), in which they passed resolutions requesting Miss Adams to "withdraw her representative." Miss Addams' reply was the obvious one—that I was not acting as her representative and that she had no authority to "withdraw" anyone, even if she wished to do so. This action of the business men was telephoned me, the night before its appearance in the daily papers, by a press representative together with the question "Isn't Hull-House supported by contributions?"

A Two-Edged Conspiracy to Injure the Union's Business

A legal procedure of great importance was that in which three judges, McGoorty, Baldwin and Windes, sat together to hear and decide upon an injunction bill filed by the Philip Henrici Company against the waitresses, cooks, and bakers' unions, and a cross bill filed by the defendants in the above, against the Henrici Company and the Restaurant Keepers' Association.

Briefly summarized (from the dictated statement of Edgar L. Masters, attorney for the unions) the bill filed by the Henrici Company charged the above unions with a conspiracy (the stock charge in such cases) to injure the business of the Philip Henrici Company, and prayed that they be enjoined from picketing, distributing literature—particularly the *Bakers' Journal*—and using such phrases as, "We want $8 for six days' work" and "there is a strike on at Henrici's."

The cross bill, filed at the same time, made defendants the Henrici Company, its manager, and an organization known as "the Restaurant Keepers' Association" (being the employers' union) and the members of the latter, charging them with conspiracy to injure the business of the waitresses and of their unions, and to wreck the said unions and to prevent the said unions from increasing their membership and widening their influence in the economic world: and set up that the Restaurant Keepers's Association was "picketing" by means of inserting advertisements in the newspapers, tending to corrupt public opinion and prejudice the public against the unions, and praying that the said Henrici company and its manager, and the Restaurant Keeper's Association, be enjoined from prosecuting said conspiracy. The claim was set aside by the court.

In this hearing, which consumed two weeks, the entire case (and, indeed, much more) was on trial, all the important witnesses and parties concerned having been put upon the stand. Only the merest fraction, editorially sifted, of this most significant testimony ever reached the public.

Undoubtedly, anyone in sympathy with the trade union position would be glad to have the evidence in this case spread out, in its entirety, to public access.

The trial ended on March 19. At the opening of the case the judges directed that there should be no picketing, pending a decision. They also directed that there should be no arrest of pickets. The unions conformed: the Henrici Company resumed its "picketing" advertisements in the daily press.

After two weeks the judges handed in a decision which to the average lay interpreter seems to forbid "peaceable picketing" by the spoken word as "tending to intimidate" those addressed—at least in the vicinity of the Henrici restaurant; but, on the other hand, refused to "enjoin the defendants from printing or publishing printed matter of any kind, calling attention to the fact that the business of said company is not unionized, or that a strike is on at its said place of business, or that it is unfair to labor, etc."

The unions conformed as before and proceeded to get out their printed statements and distribute them at the railway stations. One arrest was made of an official at the Waitresses' Union who submitted peaceably but warned the arresting officer and the booking station that she would prosecute. She was not booked. The waitresses are also employing the method of slides at nickel theaters to make their strike statements.

An interesting sequel is now being enacted in the strike of all the George Knab restaurants in the loop district, nine in number. Knab refused to renew his contract with the unions in order to become a member of the Chicago Restaurant Keepers' Association. Picketing is being silently conducted before these restaurants by means of cards carried in the hands or pinned upon the hats or clothing of the pickets. These cards announce "Strike of cooks, waitresses, bakers and waiters at Knab's. Don't be a strike-breaker." Or sometimes merely "Don't be a scab."

It would seem that the recent conflict for freedom of speech and action had not been in vain, for only two arrests have so far been made in this strike: one of a waitress accused of distributing printed matter and one of a cook who was arraigned before Judge Stewart. This judge discharged the man and instructed the police that he wished no more such arrests made. The strike seems now to have a chance of fair play.

Notes

1.   ["Efforts to Standardize Chicago Restaurants—The Henrici Strike." *Survey* 32 (23 May 1914): 214-15.]
2.   [The downtown area of Chicago has a section circled by the "elevated" train that forms a loop overhead.]

14

Petition To The Mayor On Behalf Of The Garment Workers By Mary Mcdowell, Mrs. Medill Mccormick, Ellen Gates Starr, and Sophonisba Breckenridge[1]

It has been shown that in spite of the fact that Chief Healy's orders to the police were to avoid all unnecessary violence, one girl was beaten so severely that her breast bone was fractured; others have been hit on the head and body so that they carried the marks for days. Still other strikers have been seriously injured by private detectives in the employ of the manufacturers in the presence of the police without interference on the part of the latter. The affidavits as to these instances have been presented to the City Council and are a matter of record. The trials are called for next week.

The strikers repeatedly have stated through their agent, Mr. Hillman, that the they will go back to work and submit their demands to arbitration the moment the manufacturers agree to do so. The manufacturers, on the other hand, have not only refused to make any statement of their position to members of this Committee but have even refused to appear before the Committee of Aldermen appointed by the City Council to investigate the strike, merely sending a representative to say that, as they could not be legally compelled to appear, the decline to do so.

In view of these facts, and in view of the magnificent record made by Chicago through you in the last six months in this matter of a peaceful settlement of industrial disputes, we earnestly urge you to take whatever steps may be possible to settle the present one, and, by signing the Council order to Chief Healy, by offering yourself as an arbitrator, or by any other means that may seem to you advisable, prevent our relapse into the old evil days of labor wars, days which we had hoped after your success in handling the great strikes of the early summer were gone forever.

Note

1.   [P. 101 in Wolmon (1922/1915).]

15

1915 Testimony By Ellen Gates Starr On Her Arrest[1]

"This whole affair is grotesque; the opera bouffe is not to be compared with it," declared Miss Starr. "They arrest us over and over again. Our cases come up and would probably be dismissed, but we insist on a jury trial that our friends may have a chance to find from our evidence what the real state of things is. Our cases have piled up until there are over a thousand of them.

"It is an absurd and laughable circle—arrest, bail out, return to picketing the next morning; arrest, bail out—and so it goes.

"Every time I am arrested, I ask the officer by whose authority he is acting. He usually replies "The boss." I tell him always that his boss in not my boss— that there is no law or ordinance to prevent my walking quietly past a building, that the public highway is mine as well as his."

Miss Starr again asked for a jury trial.

Note

1. ["Mrs. Lillie Defies Police." *Chicago Daily News* (7 November 1915), Box 1, Starr papers, SCA.]

16

The Chicago Clothing Strike[1]

The strike of the Amalgamated Clothing Workers in Chicago, October-December 1915, was a fine piece of human effort. To rate it at its true value it is necessary to turn back to a brief view of the strike of United Garment Workers in 1910-1911.[2] That was more like a peasant's uprising than a modern strike. The workers were practically unorganized until after they came out. Although the movement out of the factories began spontaneously, eight or ten weeks passed before as many workers were out and organized as came out in perfect order and organization in two weeks last October.

The strike of 1910 was lost, though it had the sustained official backing of the Chicago Federation of Labor, and of the affiliated Women's Trade Union League. It would be as fruitless as uncongenial a task to go into the sordid details of the loss of that strike. Suffice it to say that the great majority of the strikers did not trust their leaders; and that less than two years ago (at the Nashville Convention) they seceded in overwhelming majority and reorganized under the name Amalgamated Clothing Workers of America. They elected as their national president a man whom they trusted, Sidney Hillman. Although the new union includes the great majority of the old members, the A. F. of L. charter still remains with the small minority.

There are two clothing manufacturers' associations in Chicago, closely allied, both having offices in the Medinah Building. The Wholesale Clothiers Association (ready made clothing) and the National Wholesale Tailors Association (special order houses). Outside of these two associations are Hart, Schaffner and Marx, far the largest firm in the country, working harmoniously under a trade agreement, and many small independent houses.

In the association houses, although the price of garments rose rather than fell, wages had been constantly falling since 1910, until in the autumn of 1915 they had fallen from 35 to 40 per cent below those of 1910, and conditions were felt to be no longer tolerable. Note that at the houses of Hart, Schaffner and Marx during the same time, wages had risen; the while the firm's profit sheets showed steady and substantial increase.[3]

Aside from wages there were many and grievous complaints arising out of the subjection of women and young girls to brutal and indecent foremen, subforemen and inspectors, in whose power they were. Many such instances were brought before the aldermanic council committee which investigated strike conditions; the proceedings were written up and are accessible at the city hall.

Great numbers of pay envelopes were brought before this committee, showing an average wage of seven to eight cents an hour for girls. The weekly wage in very many cases fell below $3, even below $2 a week. In the only public statement ever vouchsafed by any member of the association (up to almost the end of the strike the manufacturers had refused to appear before the Council or any body of people, or make any statement whatever of their position) Mr. Jacob Abt, president of the Wholesale Clothiers Association, accused Miss [Edith] Abbott (without naming her) of basing a statement of wages upon one pay envelope which she had thrown upon the screen at a citizens' meeting for arbitration. The daily paper which published this statement of Mr. Abt's (following one by Mr. Hillman) refused Miss Abbott the opportunity to deny this charge. Many such envelopes were, in fact, thrown upon the screen, and Miss Abbott distinctly stated to the audience that many others were in her possession.[4] In every case she had given the week's wage, the number of hours and the rate per hour. The excuse was offered by Mr. Abt that the one girl in the one special case which he alleges to have been chosen, had worked very few hours. It will, one hopes, be granted that whatever the number hours, seven or eight cents an hour is not a living wage. Out of this much less than living wage numerous witnesses testified at the council hearing that charges were made for drinking water and towels and soap, only one towel being furnished free for two hundred girls.

The blacklisting system, in all its tyranny, was also brought out before this council committee. The existence of the blacklist has been amply proven.

These being the general causes, the strike was precipitated by the discharge, in large numbers, of union people. Hillman was most anxious to avert it and to that end sent a letter to every association house, proposing co-operation between the union and the employers for the purpose of "establishing and maintaining permanent industrial peace in the clothing trades in Chicago," citing the "protocol" in the cloak industry of New York City as a successful instance; and asking the employers to consider certain demands of the union, and proposing arbitration. *Not one of the firms replied.* Hillman then called out four houses as a warning, and there being still no response from the manufacturers, he called out the entire industry, excepting Hart Schaffner and Marx factories.

It was owing to the extreme orthodox attitude of Mr. [Samuel] Gompers on the charter question that notwithstanding the hearty sympathy of most of the unions and the officers of the Chicago Federation, and the outspoken commendation of the strike by John Walker, President of the Illinois State Federation, the unions were deterred from officially backing the strike; and though a good many contributed unofficially much support was cut off from this cause. Toward the end of the strike Mr. Gompers thought good to "sympathize" publicly. His expressed sympathy at the beginning might have made a very material difference. The manufacturers had, of course, made the utmost use, in their own interests and against the strikers, of what they were very pleased to call a "factional division in the ranks of labor."

The conduct of the police during this strike was reprehensible, even beyond the ordinary.

Some 1,700 arrests were made, of which about 400 have been non-suited. Five test cases were tried of the first 800, in all of which a directed verdict of acquittal was rendered. In no case represented by counsel has any fine or other penalty been imposed. The 1,200 cases (approximately) still undisposed of have been released on their own recognizance. These facts seem to speak for themselves.

On evidence introduced by the clothing manufacturers, through special counsel of their association and by detective agency people, many of whom were "stool pigeons," the Grand Jury returned seven indictments each (four charges of conspiracy and three of malicious mischief) against five strikers, two of whom were union officials.

On the other hand, a fatherly rebuke was read to the police, but no action taken or recommended, notwithstanding the fact that eight affidavits were introduced of private detectives or "guards" hired by the clothing firms and turned state's evidence. These affidavits and several men who testified in person, bore witness to the instructions given them concerning methods of dealing with pickets. One disclosed the fact that an automobile, owned by one of the firms and manned by "private guards," went forth at night loaded with bricks, which were used to break windows of strike breakers. This violence was next day charged to strikers. One "private guard" whose operations were well known to the present writer, testified that his arms and hands were lame from blows administered to pickets. The affidavits were set aside by the grand jury, the foreman of which was Mr. David Forgan, a well-known banker.

Two men were killed during the strike—both strikers. No strikebreaker, policeman or private detective has been killed. The first man sacrificed—a deaf mute—was shot by a strikebreaker. There was no denial of the fact. The argument was "self-defense." The strikebreaker was discharged at a preliminary hearing in the Municipal Court. The death of the second striker was charged to fellow unionists! This case has not yet been tried.

The advertising daily press is an agency naturally much disposed in favor of those who advertise. To guess what each particular new sheet will see its interest in doing next, keeps the guessing faculty flexible. On the whole, this strike began earlier to get itself noticed than strikes usually do, a larger proportion of actual news got printed and, although there were certain adverse conditions not usual in strikes, the awakening of influential public sympathy did force the press to record it, to some considerable extent. One of the principal morning papers began with quite the best reports given of the strike. The reporter who was "handling the story" sympathetically was suddenly "pulled off" and the paper turned abruptly about, thereafter giving no space at all to the strike or treating it inimically. One of the chief evening papers, on the other hand, did little at the outset, but worked up to a very good report. One was sustainedly antagonistic to the strikers and some inexplicably erratic.

An entirely new section of the public came to the front. It was, indeed, an unwonted sight, that of ministers of religion and college professors—even department heads—taking their places, not once but several times weekly upon the picket line. The department of sociology might have been expected to show interest as a species of laboratory practice,[5] but it was the philosophy, biology, Latin and English departments which were distinguished in their representatives. The pastor of one of the university churches was put under arrest for protesting against the brutal violence of a uniformed policeman to a striker; a stately professor of philosophy (who was a clergyman as well) seized by the shoulders, "hustled" and told to go about his business. (He might well have answered "Wist ye not—?")

The Mayor of the city was consistently hostile to the strikers, twice making appointments with a delegation and failing to appear. Shielding himself behind the charge of "violence," the Mayor refused to further, or even confer about furthering, arbitration. Even before the strike was called, the Mayor had conferred with attorney for the manufacturers Martin J. Isaacs, as had the chief of police, and arrangements were made for detailing as many police as they could for the private service of the manufacturers. All efforts failed to induce the Mayor to use his influence for arbitration; the Mayor, who had shown so vivid an interest in the affairs of the streetcar men, mostly voters, was indifference itself when the question was of 20,000 foreigners, mostly unenfranchised, and 60 per cent women.

The City Council, on the contrary, was astonishingly friendly, due largely to the efforts of some five aldermen, two of them Socialists. The intentions of the Council, however, were largely neutralized by the hostility of the Mayor, the chief of police and the corporation counsel. Among the orders passed by the Council were: an order to "investigate the alleged brutal conduct of the police and the unfair attitude they are charged with having assumed in this dispute;" a "police brutality order" asking the Committee on Schools, Fire, Police and Civil Service to "report the result of its investigation regarding the conduct of the police in the clothing strike"; an order "to revoke the commission of special strike patrolmen employed by the garment manufacturers and directing the General Superintendent of Police to present to the Council a list of all these private guards and sluggers in the service of the garment manufacturers with a list of their former occupations and criminal record, if any."

The strike ended, as so many strikes end, with no decisive victory on either side. The manufacturers' associations did not sign agreements or submit the differences to arbitration. Business to the amount of millions was not only lost to them for this year, but was deflected to other firms and cities, so that it will be years before it will return, if it ever returns. Meanwhile, Hart, Schaffner and Marx have enjoyed a season of great prosperity, as well as the smaller independent houses which signed trade agreements early.

The gains on the employers' side—the gain, rather, if it be a gain—is that of having refused to yield to the modern demand of democracy; of having persistently declined, as an organization, to recognize the principle of bargaining collectively with another organization. In effect they have recognized it, by treating collectively, as separate firms, with the people of the various factories in their shop organizations. The people of each shop and factory were allowed by vote of the union to make such arrangements as they could, through their shop officers, with the firm. In most cases the old employees were taken back and the temporary ones—the strikebreakers—sent away. This is to the real advantage of the houses, as the casual employees are, in most cases, incompetent. Most of the shops have reduced the hours from 54 to 48 a week and have raised the wages to make up to piece workers for this reduction in hours. Union headquarters are open, people who have not yet been placed are still being looked after, and benefits paid in small sums.

Notes

1. ["The Chicago Clothing Strike." *The New Review* 4 (March 1916): 62-64.]
2. [Mead had a significant role in this strike. See Deegan 1988, 115-16.]
3. Net profits for 1912
    $524,709.00
    Net profits for 1913
    1,121,689.00
    Net profits for 1914 up to November   (eleven months)
    1,159,766.00
    Capital stock $4,300,000 earning sufficient to pay 7% dividend on all preferred and 6% on the common stock. Evidently the trade agreement has not been disastrous to the financial interests of Hart, Schaffner and Marx.-Figures taken from *Moody's Magazine* for 1915.
4. Miss [Edith] Abbott is so well known as a statistician and authority upon immigration that the state of Massachusetts had thought worth while to invite her to act for six months as a member of a committee to investigate conditions of immigration for the purpose of recommending legislation in that state. It seems unlikely that any informed person could believe that she would base a statistical statement upon a single instance. [See Deegan for a summary of Abbott's career and writings (1991).]
5. [Chicago sociologists were famous for making the city a laboratory of study, but the Hull-House sociologists opposed this view. See Deegan (1988, 34-37).]

17

Cheap Clothes And Nasty[1]

The twelve weeks' strike of the Chicago garment workers which is just breaking up may be looked upon as the most recent chapter in the long struggle of the workers to raise their standard of living in what has been historically the worst paid, or, in the words of the sociologist, the most thoroughly "parasitic" trade that modern industry has developed. What the Christian Socialists of an earlier generation called "the dishonorable trade of the slop-shops" still counts its victims by the thousand score, and the victims still belong chiefly to what is known as the weaker sex. As long ago as the Christmas season of 1843, Thomas Hood immortalized the misery of the sweated needle-trades when he published the " Song of the Shirt" in the holiday number of an English comic weekly. Kingsley was the next prophet in this field who undertook to preach the gospel of the poor, and under the signature of Parson Lot he wrote the famous indictment called "Cheap clothes and Nasty," in which he charged that "slavery, starvation, and waste of life" were the cost of the ready-made garments that men so thoughtlessly put on their backs. "Cheap clothes and nasty " they remain to this day, and anyone who reviews the long history of overwork and underpay in this industry may be tempted to question whether all the ready-made garments in the world are worth the misery that has been sewed into them.

Not only in England but in America the ready-made trade was founded on the misery of the poorest of those who work to live. As early as 1835 Philadelphia's sober economist, Matthew Carey, published a "Plea for the Poor" which was a vehement protest on behalf of the starving tailoresses and other victims of the sewing-machines of that early day— "poor creatures," as he mildly said, who were living "in a situation almost too trying for human nature." But of late years it has not been the philanthropists but the workers themselves who have attempted to raise this submerged trade to the level of a self-respecting industry. As a result of their hard efforts and heavy sacrifices certain unmistakable and permanent gains have been won. We need only recall the Hart, Shaffner and Marx agreement in Chicago, the New York protocol, and the

English Trade Boards act, which was placed on the statute books through the efforts of the Labor party, as evidence that along this line progress lies.

It is scarcely necessary to enumerate the grievances of the striking clothing-workers in Chicago, for these grievances are common to the trade save where they have been remedied in recent years by collective bargaining. Especially interesting, however, was the submission as evidence before the City Council's Investigating Committee of the pay envelopes of the workers in some of the leading strike-bound firms. The incontrovertible testimony of pay envelopes showing, for example, weekly earnings of $2.40 for 32 hours' work, $2.17 for 23 hours' work, $1.24 for 17 hours' work, $1.23 for 13 hours' work, all of which received due newspaper publicity, gave convincing proof of the justice of the workers' demands. The only answer of the employers to this testimony was that the lowest earnings did not represent a full week's work—an answer which overlooks the fact that a full week's work at less than eight cents an hour would hardly set a living wage.

An interesting feature of the recent Chicago struggle was the refusal of Mr. [Samuel] Gompers and the American Federation of Labor to recognize the Amalgamated Clothing Workers because of their secession from the United Garment Workers. This closed the treasury of every Chicago union that might have come to the assistance of the strikers, and the result has been that a union representing the poorest and weakest groups of the community has fought its battle single-handed while the strongest unions, which should be a source of strength at such a time, have been against them. So heavily lies the hand of Gompers upon the trade-union world of Chicago that even the Women's Trade Union League refused to help in this strike in which thousands of women and girls were making their first sacrifices for the principle of collective bargaining. The public mind was obviously confused by this quarrel, and it is a tribute to the honesty and the skill of the strike leaders that public sympathy was not alienated by it. A young Jewish girl, in attempting to explain to a sympathetic club woman the factional differences that had rent the United Garment Workers and produced the new union, finally put the thing with brevity: "I'll tell you what it is, lady, it's like this; they've got the charter and we've got the members, and that's all there is to it."

Practically, however, the failure of support in the trade-union world has been the chief reason for defeat, if the end must be called defeat. The strike has been supported for all these weeks by contribution from the sewing-trades alone. The workers both in New York and Chicago who are fortunate enough to be employed in "fair" shops have been willing to share their earnings with those who are now carrying on the struggle. Nearly $150,000 contributed by clothing workers and other poor Jewish people on the West Side of Chicago represent sacrifices not to be thought of lightly. One recalls the old saying, "Only the poor are good to the poor, and they that have little give to those that have less."

Another significant fact about the present strike has been the opposition of the mayor of Chicago to the clothing workers, and his acquiescence in the unfair treatment of the strikers and strike sympathizers by the police. As is usual in such cases, the strikers have been charged with violence, but real violence may also be charged to the police themselves and the hired "gun-men" employed by the manufacturers. Some of the girl strikers arrested were too young to be "booked" in the police stations and were finally taken as delinquent girls to the Juvenile Detention Home, and yet the police were afraid of the "violence" of these young girls. The scene described in the Chicago newspapers when on a single day more than a thousand strikers who had been arrested on trivial charges overflowed from the municipal courtroom and crowded the corridors of the City Hall made an outsider wonder if the city had lost its humor.

Resentment over the conduct of the police seems to have led the Chicago public to make an extraordinary show of sympathy with the strikers. Broken picket lines were reinforced by social workers, club women, ministers and university students. Representatives of all these classes have been arrested, and it is possible that their experiences in Chicago's notorious police stations may be efficacious in producing some much needed reforms.

Over against the mayor's hostile attitude to the strikers, relatively few of whom, by the way, were voters, may be set the active and sympathetic interest of some of the ablest members of the City Council. An investigating committee sat for several weeks in October and took testimony not only regarding the system of police protection, which had come to mean protection of the employer's interest without regard to the rights of the public or the striking employees, but also regarding the causes of the strike and the refusal of the employers to arbitrate. It is noteworthy, too, that on the basis of a report by this investigating committee the City Council by a vote of 62 to 6 passed an order directing the chief of police to revoke the licenses issued to the special policemen, colloquially called gun-men, who were employed by the clothing manufacturers.

An inconclusive peace seems to have been the outcome of three months of industrial war. Each side claims a victory, but a condition of stalemate seems to have left things much as they were when the struggle began. The strikers were not "beaten to their knees," but they have few gains to show as a result of the strike. Several hundred and possibly a few thousand workers may have temporarily somewhat better conditions of work and wages. But with collective bargaining lost, all is lost, since the sporadic improvements will not be secure. The clothing workers of Chicago go back to their employers in the shadow, as it were, of another strike. It was said publicly in the early days of the strike that plans were already made to renew the struggle within a year if the workers were defeated. The men and women who are going back to work during these holiday weeks, bitter and starved though they may be, are not defeated in spirit. They have known for a few months the joy of battle and the exhilarating hope of victory, and, after all, the misery involved in no wages for a few weeks or months is not so much greater than the misery of trying to live on a miserably inadequate wage year after year. If one must starve, there are compensations in starving in a fight for freedom that are not to be found in starving for an employer's profits.

"Starved out" is the verdict to be passed on the most recent phase of the struggle for collective bargaining and "fair" conditions in the ready-made industry. And it may be well that Chicago should be reminded of the fact that a controversy settled by starvation is still unsettled. A peace that will last has not yet been reached, and preparedness for the next strike is the question of the hour in the Chicago clothing-trades.

Note

1.   ["Cheap Clothes and Nasty." *The New Republic* (1 January 1916): 217-9.This article was published anonymously, but an earlier and politically hotter draft for it was written by Starr and is found here in Chapter 18. Many of Starr's spiritual and radical ideas were deleted in this more sanitized, but significant, version.]

18

Reflections On The Recent Chicago Strike Of Clothing Workers[1]

History, in the making, is of most enthralling interest to the makers but mere onlookers display a disconcerting indifference to the process. No small proportion of those who might, for the looking, see something, appear to those concerned to turn away their eyes deliberately. There are all sorts of reasons for this besides willful closed-mindedness. It is improbable that any single soul ever proclaimed to himself, "I will not try to see things are they are: I prefer to hold a prejudiced, distorted and self-interested view of what is taking place in my own time and surroundings." Few even admit,

> I am too mentally indolent to look, or think, about what I see; above all, too morally indolent to encounter the misinterpretation and criticism of those in my own circles by seeing things as they do not see them, and doing things "not done" by them. For me, the line of least resistance, please. The side in power must be right, especially if it be the side where my belongings, human and material are.

None say so. Is it a cynic's part to presume that most are likely so to react to the test?

The characteristic form of present day injustice is industrial. It is the great field to be crossed before a foot can be set by society at large on any ground named with the varied names of generosity. The eyes of the world must needs be sewn up fast, like those of Dante's [1895] circles of the envious, to keep on forever offering "charity" or "welfare" (poor, dear, long-suffering words!) for justice. "Tag Days", "Bundle Days!" Old clothes, forsooth, in lieu of a human being's right to work and to a living wage! Hospitals for the wreckage after we have made it! How long will this shuffling kind of substitute pass current with people whose minds are vertical and intact?

Many hopeful signs that it is ceasing to pass current, were observed in the clothing workers' strike of 1915 in Chicago. [Starr had crossed out the following sentence—The strike was written of in several magazines and during its progress even the local daily press, naturally disposed in favor of those who advertise, gave it more fair publicity than is usual.]

In many respects this strike was like others. There was the same array of money power, press power, police power, against the relative powerlessness of the dispossessed, and the unenfranchised. Sixty per cent of the strikers were women, and even a larger per cent of the men, were not voters. It is not difficult to see why the mayor, whose interest was vivid in the strike of street car men (mostly voters) in the preceding June, was ossified indifference in this one. He turned a deaf ear to all approaches of well known individuals, representatives of labor, of women's social and political organizations, of settlements, church federations, etc. To their uniform demand, "Arbitration," his uniform response was "Violence."

That violence was charged by both sides; [Starr had crossed out the following phrase—As to the preponderence of violence, this writer is in possession of abundant statistice (were this article of a length to be extendedly statistical):] that arbitration would certainly have ended violence; that arbitration is a modern and acknowledged principle; that the right of collective bargaining for employees and employers alike is no new demand; that trade agreements have worked well for clothing firms both in New York and Chicago.[2] The mayor never touched upon or showed any sign of interest in or knowledge of these palpable points. His one answer, as though to naughty children, was, "Go home and behave yourselves."

The mayor had not said this to the voting street car men. He tells us that no violence occurred in that strike. True: that strike was ended in two days by his energetic intervention, and during those two days the company never tried to run a car.

[Starr had crossed out the following sentence—Notwithstanding the inimical stand of the mayor, the council, in two committees, took up a stronger position on the people's behalf than ever before, not only bringing the facts before such portion of the public as took pains to attend, but even undertaking constructive legislation for the fairer conduct of strikes in the future.] And there were some points in which this struggle stood out characteristically from the average strike. It was exceptionally clean and exceptionally idealistic. Our somewhat jaded American idealism wants reinvigorating. Where is now our colonial zeal for freedom, our jealousy for equal opportunity, our hatred of privilege, our love of liberty even more than of tea—our respect for it even greater than for "property." "I think things are very pleasant just as they are," a rich and self-indulgent young man once said to me—one whom I was vainly trying to stir to a realization of hideous contrasts of wealth and want. There was but one answer and brief, —"Very pleasant, for you." It would seem that it must be re-created, born anew from time to time, that keen sense of justice and freedom, the fervent love of these attributes, the setting them "above rubies" of comfort and personal advantage. This discerning power will deteriorate, else, and cease to flower, like a degenerated plant.

What made the recent clothing workers' strike of 1915 a great experience to one intimately connected with it, an experience which no statistics can set forth or carry over to any other comprehension, was the strength and fullness of that idealistic sense of justice and of liberty, as ends attainable here and now, to be striven for to the limit of sacrifice. These people had sacrificed their orthodox and conventional standing in the Federation of Labor—sacrificed it to honesty and a clean administration.[3] When they seceded, they took their chances of regaining it. "Honesty first," they chose, not "safety;" [Starr had crossed out the following phrases—(they were used to not choosing safety on the Russian border), not necessarily chartered standing or the backing of the strong; that if and when the strong and established chose to grant it.] They fought and financed their own battle for decent conditions and a living wage, and they fought it as revolutionaries fight.

Whenever a brave, clean-cut, self-sacrificing struggle is going forward, some imaginations are seized, and some onlookers cease to be onlookers. La Fayette and Lord Byron so elected. Surely it was "none of their business," judged by the well-known standards ringing familiarly in our ears. And so to this strike of one of the poorest paid industries [4] against one of the richest and strongest employers' associations, there rallied a new group, one which had never before been actively concerned in "labor troubles." It was indeed an unwonted and heartening sight, that of ministers of religion, university professors, even heads of departments, on the picket line with the strikers, not only once or twice, but some two and three times a week. One pastor of a university church was put under arrest for protesting against brutal handling of a picket by a policeman in his presence. And of honorable women not a few, recognizing *noblesse oblige* and *richesse oblige*, put their equipages and their personal presence at the service of the strikers on picket duty. Among those arrested was a woman of wealth and position [Frances Crane Lillie] who took the opportunity to put herself on record unreservedly as against privilege and for democracy, —that democracy of our early tradition, held now with seeming indifference, callousness or even cowardice by the American born, and with the extreme of carefulness by the more seasoned labor leaders.

The "Cry for Justice" always going up in a muffled way, takes on clearness from time to time, and becomes articulate and communicable. This fine struggle was not alone for more comfort for the body, though that so sorely lacked. It was for more freedom of the soul.

Amidst all the squalor and sordidness of surrounding conditions, abundant proof of this spiritual valor was to be found. One reacted each time anew, with admiring surprise to the discovery of poetry, of idealism, of a culture of heart and of mind in the halls and offices where the strikers were crowed together under outward conditions so squalid. "Do not smoke or eat seeds in here," a notice in one of the offices, always moved me to an almost tearful smile. The seed habit, with its consequent litter, for beguiling the empty stomach, was to be reckoned with and legislated for as much as smoking. There was a symbolic pathos about the old man with his huge baskets of seeds—pumpkin and other varieties—always standing in the entry way at headquarters. My mind leapt by association to the desolated plains of Poland and Russia, where the families of so many of these brave workers pursued by hardships are driven to even meaner fare than seeds; and then by contrast to the overloaded tables of their rich employers. And from out of these queer, crowded, dingy little offices, where benefits were given out, complaints were received and all the official routine of the striking army was administered, more than one youth has emerged upon my horizon who cared for poetry, lyric poetry even, the poetry of Shelly, and who spoke of it with an unfashionable enthusiasm. How they read, those Russian Jews? Some arise in the night to read, as they must labor all the day! One told me that he got up between two and three and studied till shop time, half past seven. He ate very casually. He had saved a little money, this one, and took no "strike benefit," but slept on the floor in vicarious self-abnegation, because others were suffering want. It is very difficult for a cool-blooded Anglo-Saxon to understand the boiling point of emotion to which such a psychic thermometer rises. It makes it all the more amazingly praiseworthy that so little violence was done to those who were taking advantage of the sacrifices of their fellows, and were willing to defeat hopes of a better future for all the workers for the sake of their own selfish and temporary gains. There is a wonderful calmness, a depth of quietude which is developed by the trial, as by fire, of their experience. I fell under the spell of it the night of the shooting of a deaf striker by a strikebreakerCthat tragic quietness of the people. It lay on my heart with a strange power of expansion.[5]

I often talked on the picket line with Russians who had been through the too usual imprisonment and exile and who, with exactly the same motive, paced up and down before a factory on picket duty, facing police clubs here as they had faced cossacks and Siberia, all for the hope of liberty, all to set forward a few steps the eternal struggle for human freedom. We cannot stop it and it is worse than idle waste to try. If only that magnificent dynamic could be conserved and turned to its best "efficiency" in our American life.

One morning before breakfast, I was talking "on the line" with a fine faced young fellow and chanced, because he was Russian, to mention Catherine Breshkovsky, that saintly heroine, "Grandmother" of Russian revolutionists. How his face lighted with an unforgettable smile when I told him that I know and loved her. I cannot now recall his features—only his smile. I remember saying, "You Russians circle the world with your fight for freedom; it is all the same to you, the steppes of Siberia or a Chicago factory; nobody has ever yet inspired me as she, your countrywoman, inspired me, except your people, here and now."

God grant us not to trample underfoot and bestrew the waste of a barren and sordid civilization of money-heaping, with the ruins of what might be a precious reinforcement of the early ideals of our democracy.

Notes

1. [Unpublished typescript, Starr Papers, Smith College Archives. This chapter was an earlier draft of the more politically tame, published paper that is Chapter 17 here.
2. Figures for Hart, Shaffner and Marx from *Moody's Manual for 1915.*]
    Net Profits for 1912,
    $524,799.00
    Net Profits for 1913,
    1,121,689
    Net Profits for 1914 up to November, 11 months, 1,159,766
    Capital Stock $4,300,000. Earning sufficient to pay 7% dividend on all preferred and 6% on the common stock. Evidently the trade agreement has not been disastrous to the financial interest of Hart, Schaffner and Marx.
3. At the National Convention at Nashville where the great majority of the old W.G. of A. seceded, reorganized under the name of A.G.W. of A. (Amalgamated Garment Workers of America) and elected Sidney Hillman national president.
4. Statistics on this head were brought out fully in the council committee investigation. Wages of girls averaged seven to eight cents an hour.
5. [A conversation between Starr and Addams about this death was published but it was not stilted and not very believable. See "One Dead, Three Hurt, in Strike Riots 'Angel of Strikers' Bears News of Killing to Hull House." *Chicago Tribune* 27 October 1915, 1, col. 8.]

19

Why I Am A Socialist[1]

The following is a great deal more than one hundred words, it is true, but we have decided to print it anyway. What are rules, except to be borken:
—Newspaper editor

I am asked why I, personally, vote the Socialist ticket, *i.e.*, how I happened to become a Socialist. All Socialists have some reaction in common. But the initial approach is varied. William Morris was a Socialist because he was an artist. He believed that beauty was a necessity for all, not a luxury for the few. And, believing that, he necessarily became a Socialist, since there is no other system by which equality of opportunity for the enjoyment of beauty and other good things of life can be had by all. Morris' approach to Socialism was the artist's approach.

I became a Socialist because I was a Christian. The Christian religion teaches that all men are to be regarded as brothers, that no one should wish to profit by the loss or disadvantage of others; as all winners must do under a competitive system; that none should enjoy "two coats" while others are coatless; that, in effect, "none should have cake till all have bread." "Civilized" life is in grotesque contrast to all this. And the individual, acting individualistically, is helpless to modify it very much. We dispense ourselves from many of the old obligations and responsibilities of individuals toward individuals, because society has become so highly organized and complex, that is impossible now to imitate Abraham, sitting in the door of his tent and entertaining all who come—some of whom were angels. If we were to sit on our doorsteps and pursue this course we might perhaps sometimes entertain angels, but our doorsteps would settle down under a double mortgage. "Society" or "the state" must see to it that strangers are entertained; that the hungry are fed and the destitute provided for. Does it? "Christendom" is a sorry spectacle of "unbrotherliness." Nothing resembling Christianity—nothing resembling the old Hebrew law. If I had space to quote the Prophets I could show you that they had some very good social standards. They were radicals —the prophets. "Very extreme." Isaiah and Jeremiah would not be permitted to talk as they did to or of the maser class in public places nowadays. What to do? One's eye scanned the horizon for any political system which even proposed doing anything to abolish privilege, to stem the tide of concentrating wealth and power, steadily increasing and intensifying in the hands of a smaller and more terribly oppressive minority while the majority increased in ratio and in suffering.

Many Christians who would otherwise be Socialists are frightened because many Socialists are materialists. Socialism does not make a materialist of me; nor does even the capitalistic system; but I can easily understand how the latter drives many to it. I should expect fewer materialists under a Socialist regime.

Socialism only, so far as I could find out, offered any effective method to put down the mighty from their seats and to exalt the humble and meek; to fill the hungry with good things and to send the rich if not quite "empty away", at least relieved of some of their unnecessary and arrogant fullness. Nothing at all in sight to cure it; nothing in the programs of the Republican or Democratic parties hinging at any such procedure. The Socialist Party proposed, without violence, quite lawfully, by the ballot, to tax away the preposterous aggregations of money and power. It proposed that all necessary things should be made for the use of all, not for concentrating power over their fellow men in the hands of those few who control manufacturing and distribution. It proposed to house and feed and clothe and educate everybody decently, it proposed to allow all who were able the opportunity to do these things for themselves. And those who were unable, through youth or age or feebleness, it proposed to care for in comfort and with respect. The methods were modern, practical, scientific, and peaceable. The object was such a society as Christians precept could be practiced in; even Christians admit that it is impossible under present conditions to carry out the teachings of Christ. Well, then, if that be true, what is wrong? The teachings of Christ or present conditions?

Let us face that alternative. I faced it and I became a Socialist. When I cast a vote, I cast it for no "good man" who "has a chance of winning" and might make things a trifle better for his term of office. I cast it, uncompromisingly, for an ideal; for a total and lasting change in our whole unchristian system of life.

Note

1. [Box 2, Starr Papers, "Socialism," Sophia Smith Collection. Identifying information has been cut off the clipping, although the words "Daily Campaign Edition" remain.]

Part 3

Religion

20

Settlements And The Church's Duty[1]

Every genuine impulse which moves people to work out a good for themselves and their kith, freeing them out of bondage into the service which is freedom, risks an evolution itself beset with hazards. First comes the impulse a way for the false and formal toward the real. The ideal of the true must then take shape and be made sufficiently definite to people's minds to be grasped and used. It solidifies, next, with all the imperfections which it needs must have; and then, in process of time, its necessary imperfections become the central point in many minds, and, behold, the time is ripe for another reform.[2]

Some of the first residents in settlements are beginning to feel a great distaste for speaking and writing about them. The increasing demand for descriptions and explanations of "Settlement methods" promotes a fear that they are becoming "popular" as permanent institutions. Nothing, to the mind of some of us, could be more undesirable than that settlements should tend to perpetuate themselves. Their best and only ultimately useful function is to further a state of society which shall have no need of them. Should the tendency increase to regard a "settlement," with what it now implies of chasms to be bridged in our social life, as something in itself ideal and worthy to be perpetuated—another "institution" to be regarded more than the living soul—there will soon need be an organized "Movement" to scourge, chasten and regenerate, if not to exterminate, "Settlements."

What is coming to be known as "the settlement movement" had its origin, in America certainly, in a very real impulse to eliminate, by disregarding them, the unreal and artificial barriers of class and station (differences which exist only because people have chosen separateness instead of union) and to seek to work together for mutual good, as one community, on the basis that the real good for the individual and of society must be at one. The impulse was toward recognizing and acting upon the eternal and fundamental identities and likenesses in men, and toward doing away with separations by minimizing them as far as is possible without affectation. The capacity to do this depends largely on power of vision. What we see determines us. Our Lord saw in several fishermen and a tax-collector His disciples, men to whom He could entrust His truth. [Giovanni] Cimabue [1240-1300; Chiellini 1988] saw in a little lad keeping sheep the artist of Italy, just as Samuel saw in the same sight the true kind of Israel. There were all sorts of other things there to be seen, differences and barriers to minds which could not see the main thing. Some minds cannot see a friend and equal or superior in a man or woman whose speech or manners or apparel differs widely from their own. Samuel and Cimabue could, and Louis IX of France, and Browning's pope, and patrician Dante [e.g., 1895], the life-long friend of the shepherd boy of Vespignano.

One of the beliefs at the root of the impulse which expressed itself in the Settlement movement was the belief that the Holy Ghost is not conditioned by stations in life. We were taught this by the Annunciation and Incarnation, but we have often forgotten it. Indeed, in practice, it is seldom remembered, even in the Christian Church.

It is difficult to proceed upon a simple basis of actuality, so long have artificial distinctions been the foundation of our working hypothesis [Mead 1899.]. People on either side the artificially erected barrier are trammeled by it unless they chance to be of large insight or of a genuineness and directness of character which verities impress rather than semblances, essentials more than accidentals. These can, indeed, establish themselves on an actual basis of relationship without pretense.

But along with good grains tares may grow up. On the one hand sentimentality—the affectation of an equality which does not exists—is in danger of gaining ground in settlements. On the other hand there is the tendency toward a mechanical institutionalism, a danger which increases as settlements grow larger, more numerous, more an accepted fact, and as the "settlement idea" becomes a cult instead of a simple living of life and doing of duty where it is most needed and can be most effectual.

There can be no real friendship where there is any pretense at all. Things which are different must be acknowledged as different with recognition of their due and relative measure of importance, and of their causes and the means of changing them. It is useless to pretend, because we have at length grasped the idea that community of understanding with "working people" is a thing to be desired, that it is in all or most cases wholly possible.[3] It is as useless to affect that education, custom or training make no difference in the possibility of real intercourse and communion as to insist that there is a difference ordained from the foundations of the world which no effort or education can remove. The thing to be determined is what in education is a universal value, and how, with *their* help, to secure that for all who are now deprived of it. For we must work for it together. To work with people and not for them is an essential note of the settlement *motif*.

The second danger, the Charybdis to the Scylla of sentimentality, arises from our business-like way of setting about the making to order of something which has grown. This has largely been the method in this country with regard to the arts and to repositories of scholarship and learning; and it seems about to become a process of reduplicating settlements. We look upon some real and living thing—a growth—and bestow our approval upon it and ex- claim: "Let us have one. How much does it cost? How many people does it reach? What are your methods? What results do you see?" These are the precise questions which are daily asked. One often facies himself approached by an enquiring mind with the demand, " What methods do you apply in the Christian life, and what results do you see in the people you meet?" Alas, it is not wholly a question of methods. The letter killeth. The life-giving spirit reckoneth not results upon requirements.

For generations we have left the "unprivileged classes" to degenerate men- tally and morally as well as physically by giving them too little use of the lungs, their muscles, their minds, too little wholesome and normal exercise for their emotions. Without concern of the fortunate and well-to-do they have breathed bad air, see and heard ugliness wherever they looked, been deprived of all but the meanest reading besides being left no time or light for it. Sud- denly they are offered "model tenements," the privileges of library, concert, [and] picture gallery. And bitter are the complaints if "those people" do not "appreciate" their advantages. It is strange that in an age which prides itself more than all else upon its science, [that] demands so unscientific should be so common. The tendency of every action to repeat itself, the accumulation of inheritance, are set aside; the slavery, cowardice, apathy, dullness, hope- lessness, narrowness of life, [and] fear of starvation which have pursued father and children to the third and fourth generations and far beyond—all are forgotten; and we demand that the last and present generation shall arise at once to full, manly stature, stand upon its feet and open its eyes to the beauty (such as it is) of some one small spot furnished it of our bounty. How unrea- sonable an expectation, how unscientific, is this. Life cannot be thus re- deemed in spots, in any fullness of redemption. We cannot hope, in the midst of ugliness, for any transcendent beauty. Beauty is born of beauty and grows by beauty. We shall have love of beauty and passion for purity among people who open their eyes upon it and are nurtured in its midst. Art is not to be taught to a people whose days are passed in sordidly making, for a livelihood, the ugliest and most useless things, merely by giving them the opportunity of drawing, by gaslight, once or twice a week.[4] We shall have art again when life is artistic. Art must come back to life through the channel of its daily occupa- tions. All life must be redeemed. If society is an organism, no part of it can be thoroughly saved without the whole. Let us not fancy that our little spas- modic efforts at reconstructing life in some particular corner are going to avail much unless they are founded upon principles which, if applied, would reconstruct life for us all. Those principles are indeed included in Christian ethics, but they have not been applied to any extent in the practical teaching of the Church as regards the problems of modern life. For the serious teaching, with religious zeal, of the fundamental Christian doctrine of brotherhood we must look nowadays to the Labor Movement; and if we would make our efforts toward social regeneration most effective we must join them to that movement, imperfect as it is, and beset with dissensions within and without.

In all efforts to help wage-earners it ought to be kept in mind that the sense of justice, not the "philanthropic" temper, is becoming and requisite. What people like to call "charity" is far more popular than the cardinal virtue of justice.[5] The all-including Christian Love, it is to be feared, does not often underlie our "charitable" acts. We ought, however, to understand that one cannot do "a charity" where he is in debt, until he has first canceled the debt; and the debt of society to wage-earners is so large that there is no possibility of charity in any assistance toward life or its ends which society can yet grant to them, as a class. It is painful to observe how few feel the responsibility of this just debt.

Supposing the residents of a settlement to feel the debt and to be animated by the healthy passion for justice instead of the morbid one for "doing good" in its cant and common sense, there are several ways in which they may serve the Labor Movement in its early, trade union stage. Wage earners need to meet together, to associate outside of their workplaces that they may cultivate an *esprit de corps* and overcome, as far as may be, the disintegrating force of difference of language, religion and tradition: that a fraternal spirit, confidence in each other, an understanding of their own needs, may be developed among them, and may overcome, in part, short-sightedness and lack of fortitude, selfish self-interest and fear of want which often drives men to betray their cause. It is a great help simply to offer a place of meeting which will not draw on the slender funds in the treasury of a new and feeble union, even although no sage advice be added, nor anything except kindly human interest. If any of the residents chance to speak several languages they can be sometimes serviceable, supposing them to have the tact and understanding of the situation, as interpreters and in making the social connection between the various groups. They may also be able to help direct the attention of wage-earners to local improvements in their conditions which could be made by persistent and systematic demand; and they may perhaps even help them to see possibilities in legislation for the benefit of their class—the greatest help they could give.

If what has been finely called the "instinct for mutualness" could be extended widely enough it would redeem the world. It is the distinctive note of capacity to be civilized, social, religious. I have nowhere seem more genuine manifestations of it than in trade unions. During the garment-workers' strike of '96 in Chicago, hundreds of Jewish tailors sat huddled together day after day, hungry, uncomfortable, with a dreary prospect of days and weeks of suffering, to win or fail together, no one willing to be saved alone. There was among them an understanding, in many cases intellectual, in others imbibed and instinctive, of their need of each other. They failed. Even the magnificent street-railway strike in Milwaukee which followed soon after, could not wholly win, though the sense of justice and mutual helpfulness impelled citizens to go afoot willingly for weeks, a sight for which we ought to have thanked God.

At its best the trades union is inadequate. It is too narrow of scope. Supposing a perfect trades union (which would be an exercise of the pure imagination) it would not meet even its own necessities in time of great stress. A perfect union would mean one including in its membership all the workers in the trade, one in which there was complete harmony and absolute loyalty to the principle of mutual support and mutual endurance. Such a compact body would have much power in working for the improvement of its conditions of life, but it would be helpless against a more inclusive organization, against all organized labor. So far, wage-earners have little else than their unions to depend upon. Ultimately they must rely on legislation, which they will have chiefly to secure for themselves. In order to secure it there must be a social movement wider than the trades union movement. It is still too much the rule that each union is satisfied of doing well, if it cares for itself. The instinct for mutualness must transcend the line of trade; workers must see that this is their own salvation, as well as feel that there brothers' salvation is their concern.

To some of us in the settlements which are in near relation to trades unions this truth becomes clear, and it therefore becomes part of our duty to proclaim it. But how many of us, wherever we live, feel deeply that there can be no conflict between the real good of society and of the individual? What we have chosen to regard as society's good, the gospel of competition and all its fruits, is, indeed, often in conflict with the individual, mortal to him. If he remains true he is not infrequently sacrificed utterly. Even if he does not stay quite at the level of the hero, the opportunities of the unionist for unpicturesque martyrdom are ample.[6]

If settlements can help people to see a little more clearly and justly the truth about these things, it will avail more than many years of sending little knots of children for country outings, or teaching them to hoard pennies, or mould clay—admirable as these objects are; because, when all workingmen shall be able to feed, clothe and educate their children, and shall not need infant assistance to eke out the family support, all this is of the pennies and the day in the country will not need to trouble us. Wage-earners will be able to look to these matters themselves, and will assuredly much prefer to do so.

The Church's activity in furthering the Labor Movement has been, in this country, very slight. With few exceptions, very slight, also, has been her manifested sympathy with settlements in their broader aims, thought some of them are the homes of loyal children of the Church, whose interests would be unified and whose paths would be made much easier were it possible to attempt, within the boundaries of the Church, all that they feel the obligation to undertake for society. To some of us, I am sure, it has not been an easy question to settle whether our efforts ought not to bear the stamp of the religion which inspires them rather than to be classed with purely secular undertakings. The choice, I fear, is between two sacrifices. In the one case we must give up, together with her help, something of what might accrue to the repute of the Church from any recognized good results of our energies, and her increased power consequent upon that; in the other case, alas, it seems clear that we must sacrifice largely the desired end itself; I mean to say that the social results for which were are working in settlements can not, at this day, be achieved with the Church so well as without.

Now this for one who holds the Faith once delivered to the saints is a sad admission. But it seems to me that nothing is to be gained for the Church by leaving her weakness ignored within and exposed to attack from without.

The cultivation of personal holiness has been the chief aim of the Church, and can never cease to be a great part of her care. It must always be a great part of the aim of each one of us in our function of brother's keeper. But this other great aim, the pursuit of social holiness, it more and more behooves us to keep in view. In time of greater simplicity in the organization of society the former aim was enough. A personal unselfishness towards our brother whom we can see, typified in such stories as that of St. Martin cutting asunder his cloak and sharing it with a beggar, satisfied the moral imagination and fulfilled the moral requirements of a time when the social organism was not sufficiently complex to develop a social conscience. Brotherliness then expressed itself in spontaneous hospitality, untrammeled by considerations of the effect of successful fraud on the pretender. Now a social unselfishness toward our brother whom we do not see is required to satisfy the moral needs of a much more complex social state. It is not enough that we sympathize with and strive to relieve the want and suffering of the beggar in our path, or the poor washerwoman in our alley. We are required by the same faith and self-abnegation which actuated St. Martin and St. Elizabeth of Hungary, developed into broader and more comprehensive methods, to realize, sympathize with, and assist in relieving the wants and woe of thousands of lives crushed and blighted under a selfish and cruel industrial system. Social sainthood is less picturesque than St. Martin's or St. Elizabeth's, but the same truth underlies it. He that would save his life shall lose it; but they that willingly layeth down his life for another or for many shall find it forever. The Church includes in her teachings, as she has always done, this blessed and essential truth of her Lord's proclaiming and embodying. It is for us to translate it into terms of our modern living. If we can do this in a more universal sense outside the visible Church, for a time, it is loyalty to our Lord so to do, never forgetting that it is His truth and His command, nor failing to bear witness to Him.

The cause of the Church's weakness in dealing with social needs seems to be found on the one hand in lack of imagination and on the other in worldliness. Simpleminded, sincere people go placidly on with toilsome effort, sewing garments and distributing food for a mere handful whom undercut wages and other "business methods" have made destitute, thankful for a good, large donation to their charities form some rich parishioner who has practiced the methods successfully and can afford the luxury of benevolence out of his profits. This is blindness on the one part, juggling with Christian charity on the other. If the Church at this time excludes from its functions setting hand to the mending of such a state of things, we, as Christians, must reinforce secular justice, mercy and truth.

The work of clothing the naked and feeding the hungry in body, mind, and soul can not be altogether suspended while the emancipation of labor from bondage goes on. Churches must engage in it to some extent and under some circumstances, and settlements must. The mere bodily ministration, however, should be but a passing expression of sympathy and brotherhood which can never be satisfied except in doing away with the necessity for expression of such kind. While there is need of it, our sympathy might well be doubted were it withheld.

Aside from the function of fusing by the warmth of real social intercourse and friendliness the divergent and estranged parts of a city, which is the chief characteristic settlement function, most of the American settlements, whether wisely or not, have done a good proportion of nursing the sick and relieving the destitute. But it has not been thought wise in most of them to allow personal ministration to the sick and needy, individual care of children, or even practical experiments in education to absorb all our resources of time, energy and space.[7] Whenever a widely effective measure toward industrial reform is in question some residents have held that such measure ought to be of first importance, since all educational and philanthropic ends and, we believe, all moral ends will be subserved by it. For example, much effort and time on the part of several residents of Hull-House was devoted to the passage of a factory law in Illinois.[8] The removal to schools of thousand of children from factories where premature breadwinning under every unwholesome condition is dwarfing them in body and mind, and the replacing their labor by that of men, now idle, with consequent necessary increase of wage, would assuredly be a better and wider service than merely training a few individual children in the hours they can spare from their toil. But it takes a certain mental perspective to include such work in our Lord's command, "Feed My Lambs."

The doing of such work requires, also, especial fitness for it and much knowledge of the conditions; and I would not have it supposed that the settlement has no place in its life for the energies of those whose bent is in other directions. The social side of our life underlies everything we do. Even our connection with the labor movement began and continues largely in social relations, some of which have been very close and dear. Through social relationsChomely human intercourse—all the life of a settlement house is more or less closely united, at least in spirit. As the functions of a settlement become more differentiated it is not always possible for any one resident to follow all the details of another's work, and we may perhaps go our various ways, which may be roughly grouped under the heads of educational, philanthropic, civil and purely social pursuits.[8]

Each of us has his own personal friends, and here, as elsewhere, the best of our life is in our friendships, and of them the least can be said. Here the deepest side of life can be touched, and it is here that the influence of a religious atmosphere would be most felt. The weak side of the settlement is unquestionably in the absence of that religious atmosphere. Were the strong and genuine social life of the settlement wholly pervaded by the spirit of faith, these friendships might bear rich fruit of spiritual life. Because it is not so pervaded shall we, as Christians, leave the field to the apostles of pure ethics?

Such movements as characterize the settlements of wider aim are going forward, if not with the Church's help and blessing, without it, to her and their inevitable loss. Those of us who are jealous of the churches' honor would fain save her from the accusation that she alone of the powers of righteousness holds her hand—that she alone is not represented in this country, in the movement toward a wider social justice. Of the Church of England that cannot be said. There the part of the Church which is alive is in the front line of social reform.

The Christian vocation demands everything that we can possibly be called upon by our personal or social conscience to do. It is the Church's right to claim no less, though she does not do so. Should we not claim it all for our Lord and Master, remembering, as a motive to humility in "the foolishness of preaching" the example of Chaucer's pilgrim parson:

> Christe's lore and His apostle's twelve
> He taught, but first he folwed it himself.

Notes

1. [Publications of the Church Social Union No. 28 (15 August 1896): 3-16.]
2. This is the argument advanced by George H. Mead (1899) on "working hypotheses and social reform."
3. Note-Among a somewhat wide acquaintance with wage earners I have several real friends, but only one with whom my intimacy is free and as unhampered by chances of misapprehension as any relationship I have. There has never been between us any affectation that our standards of English, or our judgment in matters of art and literature were the same. Our relation is much too real to need that.
4. See Chapters on "Workshop Reconstruction" and "Citizenship," by C.R. Ashbee, Cambridge [1894].

5. During the garment-workers' strike in Chicago in the spring of '96, for a living wage and the recognition of their union, this fact was constantly forced upon my attention as receiver of a relief fund. Almost all who were willing to contribute did so not because they felt it to be due to the sufferers, but as alms. The press, during this strike, showed rather more fairness than usual in publishing both sides of the question; and for purposes of public enlightenment, that so much suffering might at least be of some educational value, I attempted a division of the funds I received, on a line of justice and of simple relief, the justice fund to be applied to any need in carrying on the strike. To my surprise and discouragement I found that very few persons thought further than of putting bread into the mouths of the hungry for the time being. Those who reflected at all (with the exception of a few capitalists who could hardly be accused of not understanding the situation) were mostly doubtful and bewildered as to the main issue. The fact that the disruption of the union would mean reducing the garment-workers to a lasting condition of semi-pauperism did not seem to most people a question demanding their thought.

6. A black-listed leader (personally known to me) in one of our great strikes of some time past has not borne his own name since. Unless disguised he is unable to get any work at his trade. Others have spoken to me of an intention to assume a name in order to get work. During a recent strike I knew of a man who was threatened that, unless he went to work on the following day, he would never again be able to work at his trade in any one of five cities named to him.

7. I can speak with assurance on this point of the Settlement in which I live.

8. See Mrs. Florence Kelley's articles in *Hull-House Maps and Papers* [Kelley 1895, 27-45; Kelley and Stevens 1895, 49-76] and reports of Illinois State Factory Inspector for '93, '94, and '95 [See bibliography in Sklar 1995, 410-11].

9. Two of the residents of Hull-House are servants of the state (one is the State Factory Inspector [Kelley], and one a member of the State Board of Charities [Lathrop]) and one holds a city office (Alley Inspector of the Ward [Addams]). One is responsible for the educational side - college extension, concerts, art exhibits, etc.; one for all the children's work - kindergarten, *creche*, clubs, etc.; one for gymnasium work; and the energies of several go to visiting and caring for the poor and sick. A neighborhood party, or a reception of college extension students, brings us all together. Whenever a trade union asks for a room to hold a meeting it is never denied, although several readjustments must be made to grant the request.

21

Eliza Allen Starr[1]

The pioneer pages of this Review[2] belong, of historic right, to the precursor; to that illustrious company of men and women of our State and Church who have in our midst been first, not only in point of residence, but of achievement. Eminently appropriate and gratifying, then, must be the purpose to here memorialize one, whose devotion to revealed Truth, and whose contribution to the sum of Educational service, have been distinguishably marked and felicitous. To Eliza Allen Starr, poet, artist, and educator, recognition to a foremost place in the patronage and interpretation of the Beautiful in Christian Art, must in all justice be accorded. Proof of title to this honored distinction is the evidence of half a century of life work here in Chicago, surpassing in achievement, and eloquent in appeal. If, with [Thomas] Carlyle [e.g., 1910], it may with truth be affirmed, that biography is at once the most interesting and inspiring of all forms of literature, what wealth of instruction and edification is to be found in the life story of this splendid woman! To indicate with any degree of justice her beauty of character, to portray even in miniature, her career so filled with surpassing accomplishment and high endeavor, would necessitate the magic of a pen, discerning as Boswell's, spiritual as Alban Butler's. It is not a finished picture, therefore, that we shall dare here attempt, but rather a simple, free hand sketch; confident in the conviction, that it will be the story itself, and not the teller, that shall inspire it.

Descended from a Puritan New England family which had helped to rock the cradle of Harvard University, Eliza Allen Starr was born at Deerfield, Massachusetts, Aug. 29, 1824. Through her mother, Lovina Allen, daughter of Caleb Allen of the Allens of "The Bars," she inherited in rich lineage, blood that flowed at Monmouth, and Valley Forge, and that thrilled with heroism the heart of Ethan Allen on the ramparts of Ticonderoga.

Her girlhood was cast in the golden age of American letters. [William Cullen] Bryant [1794-1878], [Ralph Waldo] Emerson [1803-1882], [Henry Wadsworth] Longfellow [1807-1882], [John Greenleaf] Whittier [1807-1892], and [James Russell] Lowell [1819-1891], were the philosophers, essayists and poets of her day. Her native New England hills were rich and storied with the best traditions of literature and art; and it was at an early age that her gifted pen and brush found expression in poems and drawings of rare beauty and promise.

Completing her course in the Deerfield Academy she went at once to Boston, where, during two years, 1846-48, she pursued higher studies in Art under such Masters as Mrs. Hildreth, Joseph Ames, and Thomas Ball. In 1849 she opened a studio in Boston; but as the climate proved unfavorable, she accepted the situation of teacher in the family of a wealthy planter at Natchez, Miss., remaining there for two years. During all this period she was a constant contributor, both in prose and verse, to a number of magazines and papers, frequently illustrating her contributions herself.

In 1853 she returned to Brooklyn, New York, as drawing teacher in a large boarding school; later taking up her residence in Philadelphia as a teacher of drawing. Residing in the latter city was her cousin, George Allen, L.L. D., professor of Greek in the University of Pennsylvania. A man of rare intellectual ability and purity of conscience, he had some years before turned aside from the Unitarian faith, that denied the Divinity of Christ, and embraced Catholicity. His conversion made a profound impression on the educational life of Philadelphia; and no one was more deeply effected than the cousin who looked to him with the greatest love and respect. From a fateful hour in 1848, when she heard Theodore Parker, high Apostle of Unitarianism, declare in the tabernacle of Boston, that Christ, the Author of Christian belief, was not divine; that Mary, His Mother, was not a virgin; that the Scriptures rest for their authority on merely human testimony—her faith in the religion she had so reverently received from her parents began to waver. During nine years she prayed and reflected, seeking for some rational foundation on which to build a structure that should be proof against the sharp assault of critical unbelief, and should at the same time satisfy the aspirations and yearnings of her Truth and Beauty loving soul. In the sanctuary of her heart often would she kneel with [Cardinal John Henry] Newman, who had embraced Catholicity in 1845 and say:—

> Lead Kindly Light amid the encircling gloom;
> Lead Thou me on, the night is dark
> And I am far from home;
> Lead Thou me on!

"A contrite and humble heart O Lord Thou will not despise;" and the same Blessed Father, who watches through the centuries over the lives of His children, and leads the clean of heart into pastures green, led her to the one fold, of the One Shepherd. On Christmas Day, 1854, she was baptized and received into the Catholic Church by Bishop Fitzpatrick of Boston. During the nine years preceding her conversion she had formed the acquaintance, through Professor Allen, of the venerable Archbishop [Francis Patrick] Kenrick [Nolan

1967] of Baltimore. There can be no doubt that the meeting with the saintly
and scholarly Archbishop did much to bring about her conversion. In letters
written to her through many years, and that for thought and beauty of expression compare with the writings to Philothea of St. Francis de Sales, he led her
under the Providence of God, out of "the encircling gloom" into the presence
of the Kindly Light! Nor did the solicitude and assistance of the good Archbishop cease with her conversion. Appreciating her rare gifts of pen and brush,
he encouraged her to the profession of Christian Art. This, he indicated, was
evidently the vineyard where she could best serve the Lord.[3] To dedicate her
talents of soul and intellect, inborn and acquired to the interpretation and
expression of that Beauty, found only in the Church which teacheth a Virgin
Mother, and a Suffering God!

The West had always appealed to her; and, cordially encouraged by Bishop
[James] Duggan [Delaney 1984, 158], she opened a studio of Art in Chicago
in 1856. Her advanced methods soon attracted attention, and pupils came to
take lessons from the teacher who insisted upon their drawing directly from
Nature, instead of from copy, as was the prevailing rule in the Art schools of
the city at that time. Taking up the subject of "Art Literature," as she entitled
it, her fame as a teacher and lecturer quickly spread throughout Chicago and
the neighboring cities. Meanwhile coordinating with her expression of the
divinely Beautiful in Art, progressed her work in Literature. In the opening
number of the *Ave Maria* May 1, 1865, we find one of her exquisite poems:

Daybreak

The slow white dawn is coming to my room
To scatter, far and wide the sense of gloom;
How welcome to the weary watch at sea!
How welcome, also, unto one like me!
Pale herald of the glorious August day;
The daily resurrection of this clay!

How well do I recall the pallid dawn
Hastening to dying ones on wings of prayer;
Or looking from low windows on a lawn
Shaded by mighty trees, and knew that there
Death urged its claim, on that same August day,
For grain full ripened from the blades of May!

O pale slow dawn! Come gently to my room,
Dispelling every thought of night or gloom,
On that last day when I am to resign
The place, on this fair earth, so long called mine;
That day of all my days the one supreme,
When earth's best joys are safe with heaven's first gleam.

The Catholic World, The Record, Young Crusader, Freeman's Journal, and *London Monthly*, were her other principal mediums with the public. In 1867 she collected and published the poems written by her in previous years and edited by her cousin Professor George Allen, L.L.D. Early in 1871 she published a volume entitled *Patron Saints*; drawing for it twelve illustrations after celebrated pictures of her favorite masters. During October the great Chicago fire destroyed St. Joseph's Cottage, as her beautiful little home and studio on Huron Street, was called, and where she had lived for eight years. With her art and literary treasures of a life-time destroyed and without a home to shelter her, truly was her plight appalling. St. Joseph, her protector, has a way, however, all his own, of turning to good account the trials of his children. She accepted the invitation of the good Sisters of the Holy Cross at Saint Mary's Academy, Notre Dame, Indiana, to make her home with them while her own was being rebuilt. Here it was her rare good fortune to form an acquaintance and cultivate a friendship that was to be epochal in her life. In all the beautiful and treasured story of sixty-three golden years, from that feast of the Assumption in 1855 when good Father [Edward] Sorin conducted the Sisters from Bertrand to Saint Mary's and installed them in their new home on the banks of the winding river, no name shines with more holy or brilliant luster than that of Mother Angela. Founder of Saint Mary's, and for more than thirty years forming its members and directing its manifold energies, the record of her surpassing achievements shall ever be read on the most inspiring page of our Church's history in the United States. We can easily understand how the souls of these two valiant women were at once drawn together; how kindred sympathies in the domain of the True and Beautiful united them in friendship that must continue even now in heaven! The department of Art in Saint Mary's has ever been far famed in excellence; nor would we have ever deemed otherwise when we recall the talented hands that directed its foundation and development. The lectures upon Art literature really had their origin at Saint Mary's. Beginning in the convent class rooms, the fame of their excellence spread rapidly abroad; and on her return to Chicago in 1873 a universal demand compelled her to repeat and continue them before the most select and brilliant audiences of New York, Boston, St. Louis, St. Paul and Detroit. In the autumn of 1875, through the generosity of friends, Miss Starr visited Europe, spending some months in Rome; afterwards visiting Orvieto , Sienna, Florence, Pisa, Geneva, Paris and London, and studying especially their Christian monuments. Following her return, *Pilgrims and Shrines* was given to the public, a most original and altogether charming contribution to Art Literature, embellished by her own etchings from drawings taken on the most interesting sites visited by her. Closely following came works from her masterly pen which combine with the discerning technique of the artist that sweet underflow of piety, ever characterizing the Child of Mary; *The Three Archangels and the Guardian Angels in Art, Three Keys to the Camera Della Segnatura of the Vatican,* [4] *Isabella of Castile, Songs of a*

Life-Time, Christmas-tide, Christian Art in Our Own Age, What We See, and *The Seven Dolors of the Virgin Mary.* From evidence of such superior talent and service, public recognition could not long be withheld. Church and State turned to her with salutation of deep respect. In 1883 Pope Leo XIII sent her, with his blessing, a Decoration, in the form of an exquisite reproduction in cameo of "Murillo's Immaculate Conception." The University of Notre Dame conferred on her in 1885 the Laetare Medal in recognition of her eminent services to Catholic Art and Literature. On that occasion Maurice P. Egan wrote in her honor the following poem:—

Our Lady's Golden Rose

You, through great love, redeem our English tongue,
>Which most of all, spake harshness of our Rose,
>Our Lily, and Our Lady, from whom flows
Christ's sweetness and Christ's splendor, - blessed among
The women of our race, from whence she sprung;
Your ardent soul, in spite of Northern snows
>And chilly hearts, with love for Mary glows
Redder than scarlet lace or fire wind-flung:
For you Our Lady's golden gift is meet,
>Who on her sacred shrines lay your high gifts, -
>>You, Mary's artist, poet of Our Lord,
Your best lies fragrant, at their royal feet;
>Your love, your work, our half-cold love uplifts:
>We pass beyond the Angel's flaming sword.

The judges of the World Columbian Exposition in 1893 gave her the only gold medal awarded by them to any woman. Before the Catholic Historical Society of New York she read the ode "Christopher Columbus:"

Invocation

O Thou whose way is on the sea,
>Make known to me,
The path thy dread Archangels keep
>Across the awful deep;
Flash o'er the shadowy main,
Light from those stars that wane,
>Beyond your welkin's space;
>That I, a man, may trace,
>Upon adoring knees,
God's highway o'er mysterious seas.

Voyage

Christ, on these shoulders rest,
While I the billows breast;

My only care,
Christ, and His truth, to bear
    To shores unknown;
    Where God is not;
        In His own works forgot!
Queen, on thy starry throne,
Cheer, with thine eyes benign,
This lonely quest of mine!

Landing

Glory to God on high!
    Thine be the praise
    Through length of days!
Fly, royal, Banner, fly!
Christ to His own is nigh,
For on this flowery strand
The cross doth now victorious stand!
Sovereigns of might Spain,
    Joy to your reign!
Castile's most gracious Queen,
    Await, serene,
Thy future's double crown
    Of just renown!

Death

Hush! o'er that bed of death,
Swayed by the failing breath,
    A clank of chains!
"Peace to the noble dead!"
With tears, by men is said;
While Angels sigh: "God reigns."

Fourth Centenary

To-day, what paeans sound
The glad earth round!
    "Colombo!" chime the bells;
Each breeze "Colombo" swells;
"O'er land, o'er sea,
One burst of melody -
"A New World found."

The honors that came to her, while indeed rare, and highly desirable, and officially recognizing that genius and eminence of service her intimates had always known, in no way effected that sweet simplicity and gentle womanliness, that characterized her to the end. Her home life was ever most tranquil, radiating a delightful charm on all her associates. In a letter to her niece, Ellen

Gates Starr, then in London, we are permitted an insight of her beautiful soul and motives of her life:

> Now the birthday letter and being old, you are right. I was seventy-five years old on the 29th of August,— and I will say that the last twenty-five years of my life have been the most fruitful and the happiest years of my life; the most peaceful, interiorly whatever they were exteriorly. It is a different sort of happiness, has a sort of assurance of continued peace whatever may be the exterior circumstances. I am still in my best working condition mentally,— on which I cannot congratulate myself but only thank God that it is so, because I wish to work for His glory and the good of souls, and He graciously allows me to do it. That is all I can say. It is not pleasant, dear Ellen, to feel one's self less capable, even bodily, and my many infirmities are a great trial to me; but they grow less trying even while they increase, because I take them differently; and I find they allow me to *settle* into my real work which God seems to have appointed to me.— As long as God spares my mental activity and allows me to express myself, I cannot feel it anything than a blessing to be allowed to live to be old even with many bodily infirmities. I do not know what old age would be to me without my faith, my devotions. I will not even dare to think what I should have been but for my faith, mentally even. As it is, I see it to have been the ballast of my faculties, their inspiration, their nourishment, as well as the peace of my soul. I would not be one day younger, for each day has brought its graces and on grace we life [sic]—It is our daily bread.

Nor were her many labors at any time a hindrance to her private devotions. On the contrary, so real was her love for God and so devoted her service to His holy church, that of all those hallowed years most truly could it be affirmed of her "Laborare Est Orare" [Work is prayer]. Her greatest comfort and strength she found in frequent Communion and daily Mass; and ever treasured in the sacred memory of the writer shall be the picture of this exemplary woman, in her declining and infirm age, being conducted in a wheelchair by her faithful old servant to the Cathedral of the Holy Name, to assist at daily Mass. On New Year's Day 1901, she caught a severe cold which resulted in pneumonia. Her wonderful vitality for a time sustained her, and she insisted on assisting at daily Mass. "No one knows what, it means to me," she said, "to live a day without Communion or without hearing Mass; it is that which makes me strong."

During the summer of that year she was sufficiently restored to strength to visit at the home of her brother, Caleb Starr, at Durand, Illinois. Her brother, her niece Miss Ellen Gates Star, and her nephew William Starr, loved her most tenderly; and, although not of her faith, provided carefully and devotedly for her every spiritual requirement, deeming it a pleasure to frequently bring the priest out from the neighboring city. But the end was near at hand. On September 7th, surrounded by every care that love could devise, fortified by the last sacraments of Mother Church, she breathed forth her pure soul into the hands of her Maker, and passed to that heavenly beyond which had been the object of her longing. There were no last words; merely the peaceful sweet smile, the quiet going to God a chosen soul. Her remains were brought to

Chicago, and over them on Monday, Sept. 9th, Requiem High Mass was celebrated in the Cathedral. The celebrant was her life-long friend and biographer, the venerable James J. McGovern, D.D. of Lockport. Father Thomas E. Sherman, S.J. delivered the sermon. His tribute was one worthy of the "valiant" woman, whose genius and virtues he extolled most eloquently.

At Calvary Cemetery, last prayers were offered at her grave by Fathers McGovern, McLaughlin, Sherman and the writer. No lofty monument marks her resting place, but more precious than marble or bronze is the memory of her saintly precious life in the affections of a devoted people. May the "Request" she wrote shortly before her death be our concluding word and prayer:-

"A Request"

A strip of earth within a well blessed ground
   Is waiting for me, has waited many a day;
     And yet, whene'er I think of it I say,
Softly unto myself, with sighs profound —
"When I shall lie within this narrow bound,
   This body falling into swift decay,
   Dust unto dust returning as it may;
Not any sense of sight, of touch, of sound;
O ye, my friends, who love and bless me here,
   Let every thought of me become a prayer,
   To win my soul an entrance to the fair,
Sweet paradise of God, where every tear
Shall dry which I, o'er mortal frailties wept,
   In deep contrition, even while I slept.

Notes

1. [Typescript, "Eliza Allen Starr," Ellen Gates Starr Papers, St. Mary's College, St. Mary's, Indiana.]
2. [This article may have been published in some small publication. The typescript was used here and it is found at the Cushwa-Leighton Library, St. Mary's College, St. Mary's, Indiana. Our thanks to Robert Hohl for obtaining a copy for us.]
3. [A large body of correspondence from Bishop Kenrick is found in the Eliza Allen Starr Papers, University of Notre Dame, Archives, Hezburgh Library.]
4. [Starr added a handwritten footnote to the effect that this book] "was universally praised and pronounced a classic both for its rare technical nature and for its surpassing beauty in printing and binding. It was dedicated to Archbishop Feeharo; and its wealth of artistic merit was intended to express the author's high esteem for that worthy pioneer of Christian Education. Some four hundred copies of this magnificent work are in the library of St. Mary's Academy, South Bend."

22

A Bypath into the Great Roadway[1]

Our readers will quickly recognize that this article is an extraordinary account of religious experiences culminating in conversion to the Catholic Faith. Its author bears a name already honored by American Catholics. Her aunt, Eliza Allen Starr [see chapter 21 here], a distinguished convert of the last century, was eminent in Catholic circles as a writer and especially as a lecturer on Christian art. For her work on The Three Archangels and the Guardian Angels in Art *she received a beautiful medallion from Pope Leo XIII. And she was the first woman to receive the Laetar Medal, which was conferred on her in 1885 by the University of Notre Dame, "in recognition of her services to Catholic art and literature."*

A second article by Miss Ellen Gates Starr, containing pertinent extracts from her letters written before and after he conversion, will be published in our next issue. —The Editor

Part 1

New England Unitarianism was my immediate background; behind that the Puritanism of the Pilgrim Fathers. The first of my own Puritan forbears, Dr. Comfort Starr, came in 1634, from Ashford Kent, and settled in Cambridge. His son Comfort was one of the five Fellows named in the charter of Harvard College. Subsequently the family established itself in the Connecticut Valley. The historic town of Deerfield, Massachusetts, was the birthplace of both my parents. My four grandparents were of the first fruits of the Unitarianism of [William Ellery] Channing and [Theodore] Parker,[2] and reared their children in it.

My father, with his family, including his parents, emigrated to the Middle West. My dear and good, unselfish parents gave me no instruction in religion beyond teaching me the Our Father and a few informal, childish petitions. During the life of my father's father, who retained a certain pious Puritan inheritance, it was the family custom, since there was no Unitarian church on the Illinois frontier to which they had emigrated, to read, after breakfast on Sunday, a chapter from the New Testament and a selection from a prayer book in use by Unitarians, *The Altar and the Hearth*, written, while still a Unitarian, by Frederic Dan Huntington, afterwards Episcopal Bishop of Central New York.

I was never urged to read the Bible, and when I began to do so of my own motion, my father seemed a good deal amused by my comments. I recall his saying that he had always felt a curiosity as to how the Scriptures would impress a quite unbiased mind; and he seemed to feel that the opportunity for gratification was at hand. I remember, also, to have felt some self-congratulation at what I deemed freedom, and to have compared myself, to the advantage of my own situation, with young people whom I met, later on, at a boarding school or [Rockford] seminary to which I was sent for a time. But religion occupied my thoughts very little as a young girl. And the very Protestant and evangelical form of religion which was first urged upon me at school, never really engaged my interest or attention. It was quite alien ground, regarded not wholly without condescension, and remained indifferent to me, except for a temporary interest aroused by the personality of a Protestant minister under whose influence and instruction in literature I came for a time at the age of eighteen or nineteen. But after that episode, as before it, evangelical religion made no appeal to my interest.

On taking up my residence in Chicago, at the age of twenty, I began attendance at the Church of the Unity, of which the pastor at that time was Mr. (Dr.) Robert Collier,[3] a benign old gentleman, of an engaging personality. Going to church on Sunday appealed to my New England sense of decorum, and no further demand was made upon me by it than an ethical one, always quite taken for granted in my upbringing, and a certain vague religious sentiment or sentimentality, not at all a strain upon the average young girl's capacity. After Mr. Collier's departure no memorable successor remains in my recollection. One withdrew for the stage. Whether I sat out more than one I am not sure.

But my next pasturage was supplied by Prof. David Swing,[4] an ex-Presbyterian, of intellect and cultivation and unique, though ungraceful address, of much local popularity in the eighties. I do not remember how long I frequented his preaching services in Central Music Hall. But, though they furnished me a good deal of mental enjoyment, I felt, even at that time, the lack or rarity of any devotional atmosphere. Prof. Swing, whom I still like very much, as I remember him, held me partly by his general culture, partly by his kindliness, and not a little by a whimsical humor and quaintness,—personal traits. There was no difference in spiritual attitude or apprehension, that I can discern in looking back, between this epoch and that of Unity Church. Both experiences consisted in a mild intellectual enjoyment—spiritual only in a very vague and somewhat sentimental way—of discourses by two elderly gentlemen, both of agreeable personality, neither of whom, so far as I remember, ever remotely referred to dogma, except in negation of it.

During the latter epoch I must have begun to discover in myself some rudiments of spiritual craving, for I began to browse in different pastures, seeking; and soon thereafter my associations led me to a trial of the Episcopal Church. At the age of twenty-five [in 1883] I was baptized and confirmed therein. I came in at the "low" end, entirely "Protestant-Episcopal;" indeed, protesting actively, receiving the minimum of dogma, and putting the freest and vaguest interpretation on that. (In after years I heard Father [James Otis] Huntington, the founder of the Anglican Order of the Holy Cross, speak of a lady who said of herself in a self approbatory way, "I am not a creedist." "That is," said Father Huntington, "she congratulated herself that her thoughts about God were utterly vague.")

After five or six years of "Low Church" Episcopalianism I saw for the first time Father Huntington, my impression of him on that occasion is perfectly clear and distinct. It was at the time of the great dock strike in London, in 1889,[5] and Father Huntington spoke of the extraordinary self-restraint of the men, assembling day after day in such vast numbers without committing any act of violence. "And I hope," he said, "that you thank God for that magnificent spectacle." It was his deep concern for justice to the workers which first drew me to Father Huntington. Later he aroused my interest in the welfare of my own soul. Henri Bremond, in *The Mystery of Newman* [1907], continually refers to "his first conversion." My "first conversion" did not occur at the time of my baptism and confirmation in the Episcopal Church, but after I came under the influence of Father Huntington. It was the beginning of my interest in Catholic truth; and as my spiritual director, so far as he could direct me with only occasional meetings, for long years he led me steadily toward the Catholic Faith. My gratitude to him and his Order is increased, rather than diminished, by the joyful termination of my spiritual journeyings, which, thank God, have been always true to his original impulse.

Notwithstanding my Unitarian upbringing, I had been accustomed from earliest childhood to observe Catholic devotion, from association with my aunt, Eliza Allen Starr, a very devout convert, who had been received into the Catholic Church in 1854, at the age of thirty. She was the only Catholic in the immediate family, and notwithstanding their admiration for her gifts, her religion was regarded by her affectionate New England kinsfolk as an idiosyncrasy. A an example of freedom from bigotry, it gratifies me to relate that my father, though not in the least interested in the Catholic Faith, during the summer months which my aunt passed with him on his Illinois farm, was accustomed to drive his sister a long distance over country roads to Mass on Sunday mornings whenever there was a Mass within reach, waiting for her outside the church.

A cousin of my aunt and father, Prof. George Allen, of the University of Pennsylvania, was the only other educated Catholic in my family's circle of acquaintance. He had been an Episcopal clergyman. After his conversion and during the remainder of his life, as a marriage made him ineligible to the priesthood, he occupied the chair of Greek at the University of Pennsylvania. My childish recollection of "Cousin George" is one of a grave, to me almost august, personality, deferred to by my aunt and regarded with awe by us and with great respect by our parents on account of his learning and character. That he should also have been a Catholic must have been accounted for on the ground of some inexplicable mental twist in an otherwise sane and intelligent person. It seems to have had no effect of turning the attention of my family to any examination of the faith he had embraced. But among the many greater and lesser impressions and influences, most of them unconscious ones at the time, cumulative through the years, drawing one's faculties, oh! so slowly, almost imperceptibly, toward the beauty and perfection of the Catholic faith, is a poem written by my aunt, entitled "A Family Motto,"[6] and "inscribed to Professor George Allen, LL.D."

To my aunt's poems and other writings, and of course chiefly to her prayers, throughout her loving life on earth, and, I am sure, in paradise, I owe, more than to any other one source, except God's grace, my ultimate, long-delayed conversion.

It was considerably later than the time of my baptism and confirmation in the Episcopal Church that I began to be attracted to the beauty of certain offices of the Catholic liturgy, especially those of Holy Week. My aunt, in consequence of this predilection gave me a book of all the offices of Holy Week. From that time on I have always been present at the offices of Tenebrae[7] and for some twenty-five years or more have scarcely ever missed the Mass of Palm Sunday [see Starr 1937]. I became very familiar with these offices and always followed them carefully and conscientiously. To lose my place in the long Gospel of the Passion was a calamity, as it was difficult to find it again and I never got help from my neighbors. It has always been hard for me (and it still more difficult now, as a Catholic) to account for the indifference of average Catholics to the extreme beauty of the words of the Mass and all the liturgical offices. I recall my surprise many years since, on looking over at a neighbor, hoping to get some help toward finding my lost place in the Tenebrae office, to see the page heading of the book in her hand, "Meditations for the Month of June." The recitation aloud (or singing) of other devotions, during the Mass, with however devout an intention, is a great distraction and trial to me.

After my dear aunt's death (an inestimable loss to me, yet in some sense a gain), her Breviaries, Latin and English, her rosary, a large bronze crucifix which hung over her prayer desk, with many other devotional objects, pictures, and books, including Dom Guéranger's [1868-1883] *Liturgical Year*, came into my possession by her bequest. While I was assisting in nursing her during her last illness, she had referred to *The Liturgical Year* in a way which arrested by attention, and I fell to reading it, and for several years went through the seasons with it, laying thus a fairly solid liturgical foundation, from which I passed on to the habitual use of the Breviary and Missal, constantly adding to the days, both festivals and fasts, on which it became necessary for me to assist at the offices of the Roman Catholic Church because I could not find them at all in my own "branch of the Catholic Church," or found them so impoverished and incomplete as to give me no delectation.

How well I remember my discovery of that thrilling office of Holy Saturday morning, the lighting of the new fire! My aunt, in the old days of my enthusiasm for Tenebrae, had more than once said to me, "Tenebrae are very beautiful, certainly, but why do you stop with Tenebrae? Holy Week is filled with beautiful and impressive offices." And she then described to me that Holy Saturday office. And I remember the light in her eyes as she told me of the "Lumen Christi!" [Light of Christ] thrice sung by the subdeacon, each time on a higher note, while the procession, bearing the tripartite taper lighted from "the new fire," from which the paschal candle should in turn be lighted, passed up to the steps of the altar.

Since I began, long ago, to attend upon that office, which in some churches takes place very early (I have "assisted" at it as early as five o'clock), it has astonished me to find how few Catholics seem to care for it. The functions are, of course, very long, and the congregation continues to assemble for the Mass which ends them. But it has been usually my experience—as a Protestant—to arrive first; and during those first few ecstatic moments of the "Lumen Christi!" to constitute a half or a third of the congregation, one old man or one old woman or both, the remainder.

Why did I not follow my aunt's advice? Why, indeed! Why must we discover everything for ourselves? I kept on going to Tenebrae as obstinately as though I had invented Tenebrae; sang its praises to others as though it were a private affair of my own. Every Wednesday and Thursday of Holy Week I assembled as many persons as I could provide with books, instruct in the office, and induce to go with me. And there I stopped, for years. A Holy Week—a Holy Saturday—I once passed in London many years ago, where I might have gone to the Oratory for that office as I did go for Tenebrae and for the Palm Sunday Mass.

"Death is often a great grace in families." That sentence I found in a letter from a friend—a priest[8]—to my aunt, after her own death. "I will not forget your intention." Well did I know the intention she had asked him to remember: that what she had not been able by her devoted life to do for those dear to her might be accomplished by her death. And yet so many years were to pass before that intention was realized in the unworthy one for whose sake so many holy prayers were said. "Oh, slow of heart to believe!"

As the richness and fullness of the Catholic liturgy impressed itself more and more upon my heart and mind, the curtailed and impoverished ritual of my own Church's *Book of Common Prayer* [The Episcopal Church 1845] grew correspondingly less satisfactory. I seldom looked into it except at church, and more infrequently there. The *Roman Breviary* became my book of private devotion, and long years before I began to think definitely of the possibility of being received into the Catholic Church, I carried the Missal [for daily prayers at Mass] to early "celebrations" and used it as a book of private prayer, replacing form it those beautiful and solemn portions of the Mass omitted from the Communion Service of the Anglican prayer book.

Thus I went on for perhaps nine or ten years more,—I cannot with definiteness say,—not often or much disturbed by the inconsistencies and lapses of logic which finally became insuperable to me in the Anglican position, nor assailed more frequently by doubts than fancied Christians ordinarily were in this age not characterized by faith. I more or less firmly believed myself to be a Catholic of the "Anglican branch" of the Church. And I felt it quite natural and fit that I should cull what I could not find in one branch from another,— "help myself from both Churches," to borrow a phrase used of me by a member of my family.

My affiliations had been, after the first five or six years of Protestant Episcopal transition, out of my original Unitarian background, more and more with groups of devout men and women, of the Order of the Holy Cross and the Community of St. Mary and, less closely, of St. John the Evangelist, the Holy Nativity, and the Sisters of St. Anne. Of the first two of these religious Orders I was an associate. The members of these communities take the three monastic vows [poverty, chastity, and obedience], recite the monastic office, and live the religious life. I often attended retreats given by the Order of the Holy Cross, the Society of St. John the Evangelist, and others, in the houses of the Community of St. Mary and elsewhere. My debt of gratitude to these Anglican communities is profound and sincere for the teaching of so much of Catholic truth as undoubtedly led me toward embracing it in the end, and for an atmosphere of devotion in which I have passed many serene hours.

It is quite clear to me that, humanly speaking, I should not have passed, as did my aunt, directly from Unitarianism into the Catholic Church. Some, perhaps, are deterred from the goal by finding so much of Catholic faith and devotion on the way and resting satisfied with it. I can but give my own experience. Faith is a gift and, to those not born into it, must always, I think, seem a miraculous gift, whether it comes suddenly or by long and slow development. Even so, the final steps must seem sudden, however long delayed. Yesterday on one side of that dividing line, to-day on the other side; the partition worn thin and at last breaking down; one cannot say how or by what precise means one has been able to pass through it finally, into the life of the one great Mother.

And those last steps are strenuous and sometimes agonizing. All converts tell much the same story—especially all Anglican converts. Allowing for differences in age, and in states and vocations from a bishop to a laywoman, one reads the life histories of Father Hugh Benson [1913], Father Maturin [1912], R.A. Knox [1918], and Dr. Kinsman with the response of an intimate knowledge; e.g. Knox's figure (in *A Spiritual Aeneid*, [1918]) of an elaborate and round-about approach, by a back door, and attempts at locked and winding passages, to find at length, that the front door had stood open all the while!

But how does the discovery of that great fact ultimately come to pass; the final re-focusing of one's spiritual vision, so that what one could never before see, now lies clear before one; and the hitherto impossible shall become the only possible and inevitable; the once foreign land, now the only home of the soul? One retraces the logical steps in one's story and recounts to one's self the falling of one barrier after another, the removal of one misconception after another. But all that, though necessary to the inner action of the spiritual drama, is not it. The ultimate miracle can only be written by the mystic and the poet. A miracle it remains.

An infirmity befell me in the summer of 1918 which made it seem probable that a good deal of time must be passed in physical inaction and seclusion; and in order to encourage myself to more devotion, I proposed trying the rule of the Confraternity of the Love of God, associated with the Order of the Holy Cross. One of the articles of this rule calls for "visits to the Blessed Sacrament" as often as may be. And I began going as often as I was able into Catholic Churches. That was "fatal." When one begins to pass much time alone in the Sacramental Presence, one's undoing (as an eclectic) is at hand. The frequent visits went on for a year, with the result of even greater inclination to go into Catholic churches, and disinclination for those of my own communion, until at length I never went into an Anglican church except for an early "celebration," always to High Mass and Benediction in some Catholic church.

During this year the thought often came to me that it was a situation which could hardly continue indefinitely, and a distinct wish that the Church which was coming to seem more and more my natural home were home, indeed, to me. But obstacles[9] remained, and I assumed that they would always remain and that I must make the best of it. Everything but the sacraments I would enjoy in the Roman Catholic Church. That was clear.

In the summer of 1919 more trouble dawned. Although my difficulties as to the Roman Catholic Church were not all cleared away, difficulties as to the Anglican began to loom larger, so that I glimpsed an awkward possibility of being left stranded, high and dry, between two impossibilities. I decided on what I conceived might be, for me, a kill-or-cure remedy; and it really proved so. I attended the General Convention of the Protestant Episcopal Church, at Detroit, in October, 1919.

At this point begins my real embarrassment as a narrator of my own story. I have always felt indignation against people who speak with disrespect or lack of consideration of those from who association they have withdrawn. And from what I have written above, of those smaller groups[10] in the Protestant Episcopal Church who prefer to call themselves Anglican Catholics, it will, I think, be evident that I am fully conscious of my debt of gratitude to them. And yet it was precisely their position which had now become, to me, the least logically tenable. "It is a solemn thing," says Newman [1890] (p. 94) in *[An Essay on] The Development of Christian Doctrine*, "to accept any part of Catholic truth; for before you know where you are, you may be carried by a stream of logical necessity to accept the whole."

Between twenty and thirty years had passed by, since I had called myself or thought of myself as "Protestant." But now I discovered that I could no longer hold the position of "Anglican Catholic." It appeared to me that logic and candor and events, as well as overwhelming numbers, were on the side of the avowed Protestants in the Protestant Episcopal Church. Every question, practically, which came up on the floor in the joint meetings of the Upper and Lower Houses, at the Detroit Convention, divided the members into "Catholic" and "Protestant;" and the Catholics were a mere handful. I began to see myself as an ostrich, hiding its head in the sand. I had surrounded myself with these small groups of Sacramentarians—had insisted that they were the "Anglican Branch of the Church" and that they would ultimately absorb the Protestants; and, lo! the numbers were on the other side.

In answer to Bishop Kinsman's statement of his position on leaving the Anglican Church, Dr. R. H. McKim, an exponent of the extreme Protestant position, came forward with a letter in *The Living Church* (Sept. 17, 1919), in which he proceeds with his proofs that the Protestant Episcopal Church has always been and always professed to be Protestant. The following is an extract from Dr. McKim's letter:

> But why should the Bishop have just now found out that the Protestant Episcopal Church is Protestant? As a student of Anglican history, shuld [sic] he not have known that the Protestantism of the Church of England has been repeatedly affirmed, not only by judicial opinion, but by a long line of her most illustrious divines from Elizabeth's time down to the middle of the nineteenth century?" [Many names cited.] One would think also that Bishop Kinsman was too intelligent a man to fail to perceive that the doctrines embodied in the *Prayer Book* and the *Articles of Religion* are distinctly Protestant.... He complains that the Episcopal Church does not "definitely teach the sacramental character of Confirmation and Penance.' But didn't Bishop Kinsman know when he was ordained that this Church, following the Church of England, teachers both in her Catechism and in the *Articles of Religion*, that there are only two sacraments, Baptism and the Supper of the Lord? [Quoting Bishop John H. Hopkins, of Vermont:] "This doctrine (that the body and Blood, Soul and Divinity of the Lord are united to the bread and wine in the hands of the priest on the altar by virtue of prayer and consecration) is thoroughly inconsistent with Scripture, with the Reformers, with the Fathers, and with the standards of our Church.'
>
> When Bishop Kinsman declares that the Real Presence and the Eucharistic Sacrifice cannot claim the authoritative backing of the Episcopal Church, he is absolutely

right. But why should he have expected it, since these doctrines were never taught by the reformed Anglican Church?... 'He [Bishop Andrews] utterly repudiates the doctrine that Christ is present in, with, and under the forms of bread and wine. The same is true of the Anglo-Catholic divines in general.'..Again the Bishop has reached a sound conclusion. The Episcopal Church does not teach that 'Orders is a sacrament necessary for valid ministrations.' But why did he not know this when he was ordained? In her twenty-fifth Article she declares that there are only two sacraments, and Orders is not one of them. In her twentieth Article she defines her doctrine concerning 'the Church,' and there is not one word there about apostolic succession being necessary for valid ministration of the Gospel....Why should he have been entangled in this network of misunderstanding? Is it not because, instead of taking the standards of the Church, and its doctrinal definitions at their face value...he has been beguiled by the strained and non-natural interpretation put upon the *Prayer Book* and the *Articles* and the *Ordinal*; by the school of which Newman and Pusey were the founders? These men deluded themselves by a vague appeal to "Catholic custom" and transferred their loyalty from their own national Church to an indefinite entity which they call the Catholic Church, and of whose doctrines and customs they are themselves the judges.

They are loyal to a Church of England (wrote Dr. W. C. Magee, Archbishop of York), but it is a Church of their own imagining,—a Church which is not Roman, for it rejects the Roman obedience; not Anglican, for it accepts nearly all Roman doctrine; nor yet Catholic and primitive, for its worship and teaching are mainly medieval; a Church which dislikes its own history, despises its own ritual, and doubts its own orders.

This letter seemed to me straight-forward and convincing; and Dr. McKim's intimation that the Catholic Church was the proper place for Catholics struck me as unanswerable.

To an Anglican friend who wrote me after my reception into the Catholic Church, "Of course I do not know how you have gone," I replied, "Via Detroit, and at the earnest invitation of Dr. McKim, who seemed in a sufficient majority to have the right to invite us." Of course, as R.A. Knox [1918] (*A Spiritual Aeneid*) discovered in his own case, "a decent doubt of Anglicanism" is not sufficient to secure one's entrance into the Church Catholic, Roman, and Apostolic. Knox records that he had always, through his years of mental conflict as to the authority of his "branch" and the validity of its orders, thought of the Church of Rome as a comfortable blanket stretched beneath, into which he could drop, if and when he loosened his hold on the "branch." And great was his surprise, he relates, when Father Martindale (Monsignor Benson's biographer), to whom he first spoke on the subject, said to him, "Of course you couldn't be received like that."

My own experience equips me to undeceive any who still hold the Protestant superstition that Catholic priests are out with a dragnet to catch and draw in all whom they succeed in entangling. I paid my first visit to a Catholic priest for the purpose of a preliminary test of possibilities for myself just before going to Detroit in October, 1919. That good Father distinctly put me off. It was impossible, in the short time at our disposal, to tell him how far back and down the roots of my attraction extended; how gradual the drawing process had been; and he naturally feared that it was late (at the age of nearly sixty) to pull up successfully roots so deep and to transplant so old a tree. "A vast deal of lopping off of branches," I was reminded by one of my family, is entailed in such a process. Then, too, being a man of a good deal of knowledge of the world, he postulated superficial attraction on the one hand and superficial discontent on the other.[11]

"Why, at your time of life," I seemed to read between his courteously non-aggressive words, "have you only just thought of this?"

The answer was that I was far from having just thought of it; and I was to think of little else for months, until I had found my way out of buffetings of contrary waves into harbor.

My first Catholic consultant, then, wisely attempted little—controversially nothing; but advised me, in case I continued to be interested, on my return to Chicago to call on one of the Paulist Fathers, who was himself a convert and knew the convert's difficulties. Accordingly, after the Detroit Convention, which showed me plainly enough that it was only a matter of a little time when I should be unable to remain where I was, I took Father Gallen's advice and betook myself to the Paulists to consult with this convert as to my predicament. My gratitude to him, who is now my director, is almost too intimate to say much about,—like praise of one's own family. What one may say is that he is a lineal spiritual descendant of Father Hecker. One of his favorite phrases—"You have the perfect liberty of a child of God in that matter"—has lifted me over many an imaginary obstacle; and his deep mystical devotion, fervent love of God and of souls, together with a sense of proportion and a lively humour, opened up to me the beauty of the Catholic life and threw impediments into their perspective.

They were not so much removed at that stage, as made relatively unimportant by comparison. By the same method were overcome many of the common Protestant misconceptions about what the Catholic Church really does hold and teach on such subjects as, for example, that perennial Protestant bugbear of indulgences. The old misconception on this particular point was so deeply embedded as to required the efforts of two theologians to dislodge it. My Paulist consultant went over the ground once, with some preliminary effect. The final elimination was effected later in the story by the Abbot of the Benedictine monastery, where I was received, the Right Rev. Abbot Paul, O.S.B., of St. Joseph's Abbey, St. Benedict, Louisiana.

By this time it was apparent to me that if I was ever to be a Catholic, the thing must and would be accomplished by the positive method: by growth in experience of actual faith, and tasting its fruits, rather than by attacking one "objection," "obstacle," and "difficulty" after another and getting it felled or done away with. I likewise discovered that such difficulties as remained were not for the most part, dogmatic or theological, and that such as came under that head were not distinctively Roman.

The word which I truly found hardest to utter in its context, in making my "submission" and profession of faith, was the good old Calvinistic word "hell." And the real difficulty lay in Our Lord's words, in the Gospel. The new thing in the situation, for me, consisted in the fact that I was for the first time obliged to accept the Church's dogmatic teaching. In the Protestant Episcopal Church one was never faced with an inescapable dogmatic difficulty, since every grade and variety of belief can be found among its teachers, and there was, accordingly, always a way of escape from anything one found unpalatable. So far as distinctive "Roman" doctrine was concerned, the ordinary Protestant difficulties—infallibility of the Pope, the Immaculate Conception of Our Lady—had ceased to trouble me, if indeed they ever had caused me any trouble. I was fleeing from the confusion of a Church where there was no unity because no discipline and no authority.

One of the last and most disconcerting episodes of the "varieties of religious experience" [James 1902] which the Episcopal Church held for me was this: A bishop, a former member of a certain religious Order in the Anglican communion,—one of those mentioned above which take the three religious vows,—gave a retreat at which I was present. In one of his addresses he spoke distinctly and strongly against "reservation." I had recently assisted at "Benediction" in one of the chapels of his former Order; and I knew that "reservation" was commonly practiced in the Order. So, apparently, being a bishop had Protestantized this good man; and the same thing I knew of another. Evidently, then, even within the intimate boundaries of a small religious community, one could not look for uniformity of doctrine, which would stand the test.

And equally evident was it to me, from this and many other episodes, that, if Catholic practice was to be brought back to the "Anglican branch," it must be done either more or less furtively, or in open opposition to the shepherds and governors of the flock. There was nothing new in this experience. Many have had it. (R.H. Benson wrote after his conversion, "It is such a relief to find my Bishop as High Church as I am.") But nothing one hears or reads saves one wholly from the shock of one's own personal discovery. How baffling must be the experience of those boys and girls who are taught in schools under the management of Anglican religious Orders that confession is a sacrament of vital importance to their souls, and who, perhaps, never again live in any parish of the Episcopal Church where confessions are heard.

I clearly saw that authority was necessary to unity, and that it was unreasonable to object to the one and still insist on the other. Also I perceived that it was no more difficult to accept an infallible Head of the Church than an infallible Church; and that an infallible Church we must have to escape all that Protestantism, with its innumerable sectarian divisions, implies and involves. The dogma of the Immaculate Conception of Our Lady had really never troubled me, after I understood it and believed fully in the Incarnation.

I cannot remember to have confused this dogma, as I find many Protestants do, with the Virgin Birth of Our Lord.

At the last, as one sees it in looking back, conversion must always seem a miracle. It is "a leap in the dark." It comes out of many moods of swinging back and forth between necessity and impossibility. "What if I do make this venture of faith, take this leap, cut myself off from all my old moorings,—and then am disappointed, find my old difficulties, or a set of new ones, worse, perhaps? Instead of the warmth and brightness and security one has imagined and longed for,—the sharing of the "communion of saints,"—suppose one should awake to realize that one had staked all on the venture and was again a stranger, a wanderer, with no abiding-place, and even the hope of one now gone forever. I suppose all converts from other faiths must know something of those moments and hours of the "dark night" and the desert.

Of the end of the pilgramage, in its outer circumstances, I want to give a slight outline, chiefly in gratitude for the wholly unforseen, unimagined, and unmerited sympathy, comfort, companionship, and sweetness in which it was my heavenly fortune to be received into the Church Catholic, in a Benedictine abbey.

I might say here that the Benedictine tradition has always had a strong attraction for me. The *orare et laborare*,—counting work as prayer,—the scholarship and elegance so often combined with the life of renunciation and hardness, the desert blossoming in some measure wherever the Benedictines strike root, are elements of the appeal. At Monte Cassino in 1888, I had fallen under the spell of St. Benedict and all the generations of his spiritual sons, down to that holy and humble man of heart, then Prior, afterwards Archabbot, Dom Bonifazio Krug,—a true descendant and exponent of Benedictine meekness, virtue, love of consecrated art, letters and music. To his love and patience the Beuron (Benedictine) school of art owed its maturest and most developed work, the decoration of the tower crypt at Monte Cassino. I had met "Father Boniface," as I never ceased to call him, years before at my aunt's house, where he promised that he would remember me whenever I should come to Monte Cassino. "I shall never forget you, my dear child. I have prayed for you a great deal already." What may I not owe to the prayers of that saintly soul?

Once again, in 1910 (after Abbot Boniface's death, alas!), I visited the sacred spot, and also the Sacro Speco, at Subiaco, built over St. Benedict's cell in the wilderness—pilgrimages which could hardly be without fruit except to a barren soul. The fruit was long in maturing. But St. Benedict's resources are not confined to Italy. The are found in unexpected places.

In a remote and inaccessible spot in Louisiana, reached by traversing for three hours (if one is fortunate) an unsightly desert,[12] there came into existence in 1903, St. Joseph's Benedictine Abbey, of which the post office address is St. Benedict, Louisiana. One supposes that the abbey is at or in "St.

Benedict." One errs. St. Benedict, the post office, is in the abbey, and the postmaster is one of the Fathers.

To the Abbot of St. Joseph's I carried a letter from my Paulist friend in Chicago, when I went to pass a few weeks near New Orleans during the winter following the, to me, momentous General Convention of the Protestant Episcopal Church at Detroit in 1919. So out-of-the-world and inaccessible did St. Benedict, Louisiana, seem on recourse to time-tables and information bureaus, that I gave over the first attempt. Of no use. It would take all day to go and return, and what assurance that anything would be achieved? Perhaps the Abbot wouldn't be there. Perhaps if he were there, he would feel no particular interest in my problems. Why should he? What a strange idea that a woman who has had access to the privileges of the Church Catholic in various lands for thirty years is any more likely to embrace them by taking a train at an unearthly hour and journeying to an unheard-of spot. But how persistent he was! St. Benedict? "Father Boniface?" Which of the saints, dead or living, or what combination or company of them?

I wrote then, to the Right Rev. Abbot Paul, O.S.B., as to the possibility of passing a night at St. Benedict's. Was there a guest house where women could be received? (At Monte Cassino I had stayed for two nights, each time, at a little guest house for the mothers of the boys of the school.)

No guest house as yet, the Abbot regretted; but there was a convent of Benedictine nuns hard by the abbey, and if I did not mind inconvenience and a little discomfort, they could take me for a short time. They would welcome me with cordiality, whether a Catholic or not, "and if by the grace of God, you should be ready to be received at that time, our joy would be the greater." PAX, as always, stood at the head of the letter, and its atmosphere breathed through it. I determined to make this one more Benedictine pilgrimage.

The strangeness of those hours of the journey! I shall never forget them. Setting forth before any breakfast was to be had at hotel or station, traversing a species of "blasted heath" covered with unsightly stumps, a monologue running in my mind of this nature:

"Why am I doing it? What do I expect? I have talked with various authorities, heard and read innumerable statements and arguments. I have never seen these people; perhaps I shall find them unsympathetic and alien. And this hideous barren country! Ominous! Portentous! But, on the other side, did you ever see a Benedictine place where things were not made to grow? Don't they always attack the wilderness to good purpose? Perhaps it will be better when you arrive. Perhaps these Benedictines will be like what you have found them in the Old World. Perhaps—perhaps—perhaps."

Arrived at the station,—no better. I alight and catch sight of a Benedictine habit, but without the cowl. A student in the seminary. "Father Abbot has sent me to fetch you." We drive toward a strip of forest!—left undevastated, by the mercy of heaven, with a creek or little river running through it. Wild flowers beginning to spring up! The omens changing.

The Abbot comes out to greet me as we drive up to the abbey portal. No ceremony—no aloofness—the simplicity, the cordiality, the true hospitality of the Benedictine tradition. I begin to understand why I came on this pilgrimage.

I am to go at once to the convent for my luncheon and a little rest, and the Abbot is to come to me there, for our first talk. How vivid that conversation is to my memory and how impossible to reproduce! It was not that, with perhaps one exception, anything essentially new to me, theologically, was presented; but all fell into relation, to be taken as a whole—a related and reasonable whole. Just what "happened" and how it happened I cannot recount. At the end of it the portals of Mother Church seemed swinging open to me at last.

But I had certainly not been precipitate hitherto and would not be so now. I would go over to the abbey in the morning and give my decision. In the meantime there was the peace in poverty of the convent, the humble little chapel, with the Holy Presence in it, and the same lovely, simple cordiality and hospitality.

"What has happened since yesterday?" the good Abbot asked with his smile, when I at once said that I was now ready to be received. What, indeed, but the completion of the miracle?

"When do you wish to be received?"

"To-day."

In a little book of devotions which the Abbot gave me as a memento of the day of my reception, he wrote this beautiful and fitting passage from the *Canticle of Canticles* (occurring in Matins in the office of the Feast of the Visitation):

"Jam enim hiems transiit, imber abiit et recessit, flores apparuerunt in terra nostra." *

---

* The winter is past, the rain is over and gone; The flowers appear on the earth."

My thanks to Robert Gorman, Classics and Religious Studies, the University of Nebraska-Lincoln, for his help in this translation.

Part II[13]

This is the second and concluding part of "A Bypath into the Great Road-way," the first installment of which was published in the May number. It contains excerpts from letters written by Miss Starr on the subject of her conversion. Unfortunately we are prevented by lack of space from printing the letters in full. But even these extracts will enable the reader to follow intimately the progress of a questioning soul to its journey's end, and to note the helps and hindrances met with along the way. One may well say of this article, as Miss Starr herself has said of Ronald Knox's Spiritual Aeneid: "One can read it through like a romance. What more romantic quest than that of a soul in search of religious truth?" Miss Starr's article is not only a fascinating personal record, but also a very noteworthy contribution to the psychology of conversion.—The Editor

I.

Extracts from letters written to Prof. C. H. A. Wager, Oberlin College, during the winter of 1919 and 1920.

November 10, 1919.

Now to the momentous subject of my spiritual status. It is astonishing—isn't it?—that after all these years, when I supposed I had threshed that matter out and settled peacefully down to browsing here and there, where I best liked the pasturage, for the rest of my days, I should find myself being drawn into the current with a pull that is quite different from anything I have ever experienced before. At first I said to myself, "Oh, it's the same old thing; it's due to present itself every now and again—the Roman "crave." One weathers it and goes on as before—as one always has." "We can't do it," as you said to me the last time we talked about it. But the other side of it is that maybe we—or I—cannot *not* do it. I grow colder and colder to the Protestant Episcopal Church and warmer and warmer to my devotions at Mass and Benediction in the Church Catholic, Holy, Roman, and Apostolic. Once this summer, in Chicopee, I was kneeling quite alone, on a week day, near the altar, in the Polish church, a large, more or less European-looking structure. That strange feeling came over me of the past and future being confused,—do you know it?—as though at some time before I had knelt there,—or was it something that was to be? The Church, which I had recently discovered, was not at all like Chicopee. It might have been European. So that I lost the sense of place as well as of time. Of course, one could maunder along for pages; but "I spare you that."

Then one comes up against "the form of reconciling a convert" in some Catholic manual, and cannot away with it, nor with St. Athanasius,[14] and his "Unless a man receive, without doubt he shall perish everlastingly." But perhaps one isn't asked to, any more than one is asked to sign the articles of the Protestant Episcopal Church. I'm planning to take measures—Paulist measures—to find out.

November 17, 1919.

I told you I intended to take measures to find out, definitely, how much and how little of intellectual submission is requisite. I've been to see the Paulist Father and liked him a good deal; but some weird little books were conferred upon me,[15] one advising the contemplating convert to learn the *Our Father* and *Credo* by heart, so as to be able to say them at his conditional baptism. Really, wouldn't you suppose "they" would have *some* discrimination, and not assume that everybody outside the Holy Roman Church is necessarily wholly heathen and illiterate, to be assigned, without modification or grading, to Borrioboola-gha? That do irritate.

I've been reading over the Franciscan MS.[16] Of the Visitation of the Sick: "And shall communicate the sick man, saying nothing." Think of the impertinence of a Protestant minister, coming and intruding himself with mere talk about your soul and your feelings. Impossible! Protestants have so much to say about a man's "coming between the soul and God," when he is the merest instrument, his personality submerged as much as possible, so that your forget him; and then excellent Mr. So-and-So, in his coat and trousers, with all his personal twists of language and mannerism, comes and harangues! *That* would come between me and heaven.

December 6, 1919.

Do you remember my sending you an article some years since from the *Holy Cross Magazine* on "Validity of Orders?" There were some interesting statements in it, but you raised the question, then of the probability of Anglican orders being invalidated by schism! You, Sir, *advocatus diaboli*, did so. And permit me to quite a paragraph from a letter of yours dated May 28, 1917. It is a letter mostly about the Visitation MS.[17] And Mrs. [Wilifred] Ward's *Out of Due Time* [1906]. "And how can one answer it? —George's argument and the confession of the old priest. Isn't it unanswerable? Is there any other earthly name given among men, whereby we must be saved? Is there any other voice, at once human and divine, that speaks with such authority?" Your words, Sir. But you and Mrs. Lillie are exactly alike in this. You say these things yourself, but when I say them and seem to be facing toward acting upon them, you either fall into "panic" or adopt the rôle of Devil's Advocate. Which is right. I'm glad you do. If I manage to take action in spite of your able obstructive policy, I shall at least feel that I haven't been precipitate or hysterical. Considering the last twenty years, I'm not perfectly sure that I should charge myself with the former. But do go on. I want you to. If I can be stopped,

I ought to be. There's no doubt of that in my mind. And up to now it would
have been a great relief to be stopped.

Chicago,
January 2, 1920.

It grows harder to write. I'm becoming worn with the duration of this
attack. I wrote J. quite flippantly to-day: "'Roman fever' is an awful thing to
have month after month. Your run a high fever spiritually and can't digest
your food."

Chapter IV. Of the *Life* ([Wilifred] Ward's *Life of Cardinal Wiseman* [1894])
made me feel so much at home. [Richard] Hurrell Froude [1838-1839] and
Newman seeking "whether they would take us in on any terms to which we
could twist our consciences" and finding that they couldn't get forward a step
without swallowing the whole Council of Trent. Worse. You're actually made
to say that you accept it "especially;" and then you are perhaps told that you
needn't read it; that the priest who is at the time instructing you hasn't himself read it. That isn't the way we proceed in putting our signatures to mere
worldly documents; is it?

How thrilling Chapter VI. is! (Ward's *[The Life and Times of Cardinal]*
Wiseman [1894.]) Those poor, hounded English Catholics weeping aloud at
the Elevation. So much more convincing—what they were willing to endure
for their religion—than any council's formulae could be. It really comes all
down to that; whether or not you come to feel the Sacramental Presence so
that nothing else counts. If you do, you're a Catholic. If you don't, you're not!
i.e., you don't become one—"migrate."

Yesterday at Mass and Benediction I thought it was quite over. I almost
washed the congregation out of their seats. If Father H. had been there, and
had said, "Come right along, *now*, and be conditionally baptized and read the
form of reconciliation," I would have done it. BUT—IF—There you are again.

Father H. came over on New Year's Eve and staid [sic] two hours,—God
bless him,—coping with what he calls my little quibbles. (He doesn't think
writing them out of much importance.) I became quite rude several times;
telling him that I wished that I might never again hear of the liquefaction of
the blood of St. Januarius,[18] and other like tawdry miracles; that it was a
matter of complete indifference to me whether St. Januarius's blood was liq-
uid or solid; as edifying, and no more so, in one state as the other. "Yes," he
made haste to say, "you have the perfect liberty of a child of God in that
matter." (One of his favorite phrases.) He made me feel superlatively unworthy about shrinking from coarse types I might have to encounter; saying that
"the love of Jesus makes one willing to rub shoulders with all sorts of people."

January 4, 1920.

I have really done my best to get these reasons pro and con set down, as you advised, for the sake of clarifying them. And it does help a little; in this way, that you see how trivial some of you *contra* "reasons" are as soon as you have written them. I've set down the unworthy as well as those which seem to me good and valid ones. Some practically disappear in the stating. The other suggestion, of its being "of interest afterwards," doesn't appeal to me. It is almost impossible to do, except around the fringes. When it comes to the important consideration, it seems almost indecent to go about it in that cold-blooded way. I staved off, as long as I could, formulating my real grievance even to myself, because of the fear of deepening it by recognition and expression, as long as there seemed to be any chance of returning. And of course I have done so. It would be some kind of miracle,[19] now, that would reopen the door behind. But apparently a miracle is also required for opening the door in front. God knows which one He is going to perform.

Reasons Pro and Con

Contra.

I. Inertia. Tendency to remain if possible, where one is, without disturbing the sense of stability. (Note on rereading January, 1920: The sense of stability already profoundly disturbed.)

II. Difficulties remaining in the profession of faith. "Everything defined by the sacred canons and *particularly by the Council of Trent* and delivered, defined, etc., by the General Council of the Vatican, *especially concerning the primacy of the Roman pontiff and his infallible teaching authority*." I have not read the decisions of the Council of Trent, nor, I understand, do many priests read them through. And a very substantial difficulty exists, for me, in subscribing to a statement of the contents of which I know nothing.

"I detest and abjure every error, heresy, and sect opposed to the Holy Catholic Roman Apostolic Church." I do not detest the sects. (My consultant's suggestion is that one detests whatever is un-Catholic and erroneous in each sect, not what is true and Catholic, of which there is something in each sect. That helps.)

III. A full, unwavering, and whole-hearted conviction as to the authority of the Church on all points of faith would alone cover these and all other difficulties; and this has not yet been given me. I am praying for it. It is obvious to me that I shall never become a Catholic by trying to thresh out the faith point by point. Even if one could be received with mental reservations, there would seem to be no use in moving unless one could move into a complete and assured state of assent. The Sacraments might given one that. But—in order to receive the Sacraments one must profess it!

IV. (An unworthy deterrent.) The vulgarity and apparent unspirituality of many Roman Catholic priests one meets, and the extreme businesslike type. (To this oppose the stodgy, self-satisfied, un-Catholic Episcopal clergyman, and contrast again with that type the many exquisite examples of sanctity and humility in the Catholic Church.)

V. A good deal of education, both in Catholicity and in social justice and democracy, is going on in the Anglican communion, and one may hope for a little share of usefulness in it. In the vast Roman body, even if one's activities in behalf of these latter were not "silenced" (as I am encouraged by all my Protestant friends to believe they would be), one would expect to have no influence. (Note, three weeks later: I am already beginning to cease to feel this. Of course, it has nothing whatever to do with the truth.) (Another note, still later, June 13, 1921, some months after I had been received: Nobody above me has shown the slightest disposition to "silence" me or to interfere with my secular activities.)

VI. The greatest obstacle of all (and this one I do not find recorded in the experience of any convert) has been my observation of the reactionary attitude of the Roman Catholic Church in matters of social and political progress; its organized and authoritative opposition to socialism, and its obstructive policy toward social reform and educational movements. One understands that a Catholic body must move slowly, cautiously, and cannot stand back of every promising theory which presents itself, and which may be supplanted by other promising theories. But, until recently, there has been in our day, little indication of much interest on the part of the Church in social and industrial welfare of the people, and none at all, to my knowledge, of any impulse to lead them. Now, however, the Church is putting forth,—if not officially, at least with its implicit sanction,—through the National Catholic War Council (continued as the National Catholic Welfare Council), a strong reconstruction program, which, if followed up, will remove this obstacle for me and for others who meet with this difficulty. One should add in regard to this "difficulty" that the majority of the Anglican communion held the same reactionary opinions. But one is not in danger there of one's own opinions and utterances being restricted, as authority does not exist there.

Pro.

I. A perception and recognition, beginning almost or quite unnoticed and many years ago, and developing slowly throughout a long period, of the note of Catholicity in the Roman Church; a sense of its oneness and universality; of historical connection almost always and almost wholly lacking in the Anglican communion.

II. A sense of impermanence and lack of uniformity and coherence in the Protestant Episcopal Church. One is never sure of what one will find; a relatively high degree of Catholic atmosphere and practice in one church, none at all in the next. In the great majority of Episcopal churches one could probably not get one's confession heard.

III. A longing for peace for the last of one's life (possibly slothful and unworthy; I have been told so)—to cease pulling against the stream and to go with one's impulse and inclination.

IV. An ever-increasing love for the full and glorious liturgy of the Church.

V. An increasing sense of and belief in the communion of saints, and their interest in us. One sometimes finds this highly developed in Anglicans, but not often. I experience a sense of friendliness and warmth and homeliness among the altars, the statues, and the emblems in Catholic churches, even when they are crude and inartistic, as they usually are in this country, as one might feel among family scenes and mementos. A minor, but somewhat potent motive.

VI. The strongest and most important motive. An increasing devotion to Our Lord in the Blessed Sacrament. A sadly diminishing sense and conviction of the actuality of the Sacramental Presence in Anglican churches, even where "reservation" is practices. The Sacramental consciousness, always so strong in Catholic churches, usually not present at all. One cannot absolutely draw a negative conclusion, as "that good and sweet affection" "cometh and goeth;" and "on that thou must not too much rely." If one came to be sure that the Sacramental Presence was to be found always in the one Church, and not (or not always) in the other, no other consideration would have any weight. (Note, July 13, 1921: I did not come to be sure, and that was decisive.)

A Note Written a Little Later At

Pass Christian, Mississippi,
February, 1920:

The separate points that principally constitute obstacles to me, now, are not at all what one used to expect would be the last difficulties—indulgences and papal infallibility (as such); still less the great essential of the sacraments; but really special points not characteristic of the Roman Church at all, like the eternity of the punishment of the wicked, the impossibility of their repentance and forgiveness after death. That is going to be the hardest thing for my lips to utter as an article of professed belief. And that, of course, is professed in Calvinism and in the creeds of the Church I am leaving. But the difference is that I have never, there, been required to subscribe personally to my belief in it, nor to state, explicitly, that I hold on faith all that the Church teaches. I am trying to pass form the confusion of a Church where the principle of private judgment has caused disintegration into innumerable sects of the separated bodies, to the original Mother Church, where all are held to unity of one faith by the principle of authority. I want the unity and see that it is secured by the authority—can only be so secured. But I find the obstacles occasioned by the authority—not the principle itself, theoretically—almost insuperable. I could forget this point—not think about it at all; it isn't essential to my peace to settle it. But I am not allowed to forget it or to merge it. I am called upon to state it as a belief, personally and separately. Then there are points in the Church's legislation about marriage with do not personally concern me at all, but which seem sometimes to conflict with what would be a rational and just disposal of many individual cases. It seems like something that the experiences and wisdom of the race would have to work out, changing, perhaps, with changing conditions; but it is legislated for absolutely and by those who have no personal experience to guide them. (I think I know the answer which will be given to this.)

Then the great and final obstacle is the long established Protestant habit of mind of consulting, finally, my own judgement. I may more and more "agree with" the Church in its judgements and pronouncements; more and more see their wisdom as looked at from the long perspective of all the ages, past and to come, and inclusive of all grades and types of people; but that is a very different thing from the acceptance of the principle of authority, which cuts me off from exercising that judgement at all in matters of faith on which the Church has decided.[20]

Pass Christian, Miss.,
January 15, 1920.

I dropped in to see the Bishop[21] on Monday, and confronted him with the Council of Trent. He gave me a thickish book of it to read, though he intimated that he expected it to do me about as much good as reading a medical book about one's disease. He said I was the first person who had ever asked him for it. (And he smilingly suggested my not attempting to reform the Catholic Church.)

Pass Christian,
February, 1920.

I am sending you Father [Basil William] Maturin's *Price of Unity* [1912]. Of course, it is addressed to people in precisely my position; a very small group in the most illogical and untenable position that any group ever bravely attempted to hold. We surround ourselves with each other and protest that we are Catholics of the Anglican branch of the Church; all the rest, the great majority of that "branch" meanwhile *protesting* as stoutly, that it is *Protestant*, as it quite obviously is; they—the others—are consistent. Let any Protestant who simply prefers the ritual of the *Book of Common Prayer* and the decency and order of the Protestant Episcopal Church and its abundant elbowroom, physical and spiritual, remain and enjoy them: the Catholic-minded, too, if they can keep up the illusion. But I no longer can. And, of course, like all converts from this exclusive little group, I marvel that I have so long been able to do so. But it is finished now. I can never go back. And so, of course, it is only a matter of time when I shall go forward. I am, I hope and perceive, going forward daily. The Archbishop of New Orleans, to whom Father H. gave me a letter, wouldn't let me be received until I had more formal instruction; and sent me back to the Bishop of Natchez who lives here. The good Bishop, I fear, finds me a trying "proposition"...He is no convert,—knows nothing at all of our type and its particular mental quirks.

Father H. has given me a letter to the abbot of a Benedictine monastery near New Orleans. I have been something of a Benedictine pilgrim in my day, as well as Franciscan, and I would like the sentimental association of being received there.

February 9, 1920.

I did have an uncommon good time with Knox. At first I was a bit tried with him by reason of his pert attitude—it seemed to me so—toward, *e.g.*, the Cowley Fathers, who had been so good to him. It was very unlike the respectful manners of Father Benson to the Mirfield Community and of dear Father Maturin to everybody whom he left behind him. Father Maturin's book I find very lovable, though doubtless it is, as Mrs. *[Frances Crane]* Lillie says, a tired book. It is a tiring process when put off so long. I become reconciled to "Ronnie" after he begins to suffer! The young are—the young. The contrast between the brilliant Ronald—on the run to begin setting down his exciting spiritual experiences before they get cool—and poor, dear, precious, old Father Maturin, beaten and bruised and humble, feeling that he has nothing to give anybody for ever so long, and waiting fifteen years before he begins to tell the world what happened to him, is interesting. Few people, I imagine, will care to hear it, compared with the number who will enjoy Knox's brilliant voyage of discovery. I certainly enjoyed it myself; and found it companionable on my young side. One can read it through like a romance. What more romantic quest? And it was a good antidote for that terrible self-distaste and distaste for the whole subject—almost for religion itself—that comes over you when you have worked over it too long and too hard.

February 26, 1920.

I am going in to New Orleans on the 28th and out to St. Joseph's Abbey on Monday. Perhpas I shall write you from there. God knows. Night alternates with glimpses of day.

St. Benedict, La.,
March 3, 1920.

PAX.

This is the first time I have put pen to paper—the first written word—since being received into the Catholic Church. My profession, conditional baptism, and general confession took place yesterday at the abbey and my First Communion this morning at the convent chapel.

It is a comfort that I do not have to explain things to you. The letters I must write seem mountainous. I am not nearly so tired as I expected, not consciously tired at all, though I've not been having full night's sleep; but I dare say I may be later. The strain got worse and worse until all at once it stopped. I kept on fearing that it was only a temporary respite, but I have felt quite quiet ever since I came here; and Father Abbot, though he didn't push me at all, thought there was no reason why I shouldn't go on. There is a great deal I want to tell you sometime, but not now. The Abbot is, indeed, "a mercy." I could easily have been thrown back. Well, thank God, I wasn't. I don't think it is going to seem very strange being a Catholic. I have been one at heart for a good while.

Chicago,
March 11, 1920.

I can't tell you the consolation your letter gave me. It was the only one of its kind—expressing joy for yourself in what I have done. I mean, of course, among my old friends—among non-Catholics. And the other letters—all quite Christian and mostly affectionate; but you know what else they are.

Every mail brings me a wail or so, but except for the dears themselves, for whom I say a great many prayers, I don't mind them any more. I gave up three or four days of my Catholic life to being downright unhappy about it, and that is all I can afford, especially as it does them no sort of good.

II.

Extracts from letters written to the Rev. John Handly, C.S.P.

Dear Father Handly:

Your *White Harvest*[22] has impressed me very much. It is very Christian and very Catholic. That is the way to do it. I'm sure that if all Catholics were like that, most difficulties of my sort would disappear.[23]

That second column of page 14 is very moving,—very familiar. "Suppose" it were true—the priest's claims. ("Think, Abib, dost thou think?") But there is one thing that I have never expressed to you and perhaps cannot altogether. In proportion as the claim is vast and all-inclusive, and the "drawing" intense, the "suppose" on the other side becomes alarming. "Suppose" one threw one's self out; made this terrible hubbub in one's little world; renounced one's old religious haunts,—some very lovely and touching associations,— incurred the suspicion, distrust, perhaps even dislike, of some of one's old friends (all of which might indeed be counted well lost for the Pearl of great price); and then "suppose" one were disappointed; didn't find the Pearl so very different after all, and encountered some terrible "politics" in ones new position, to entangle and disconcert. The step can always be taken if its ahead of one; never undone, with self-respect. One becomes like the man in *The Statue and the Bust* [Browning 1900]. *De te fabula* [God is wonderful to you.]. The answer, of course, is the saints who have found the Pearl all. Some are outside, like Father Huntington. But the great army!

Well, "if I do come to be certain—"[24] There it hangs. I'm working at it.

The alleged "politics" of the Church trouble me greatly. I've been told that "the Roman Catholic Church broke the steel strike."[25] That, if it were true, would set me back permanently. It would reduce the assumption of the "Reconstruction Series" of the National Catholic Welfare Council, which was such a help to me, to nothing. I am not saying that I believe it, but I do wish that the Church would hasten to act in such a way, and publicly, that that kind of thing could no longer be said.

It is you that are earning a crown for patience.

Pass Christian, Miss.,
January 19, 1920.

Bishop Gunn gave me the *Question Box*.[26] I admire the fair and patient way in which even unfair and culpably ignorant questions are answered. Some of them were so obviously meant to be nasty, yet are respectfully considered and straightforwardly and painstakingly answered. That is the way to do it; the "patience of Christ." I'm becoming very much of a Paulist. St. Paul I always call the Apostle to the grown-up; and I love him, though he did sometimes "speak as a fool" about women. In my "beautiful Christian humility," to use C.W.'s phrase, I should like to take the greatest of Apostles for a patron! St. Joseph, who is my patron by birth, furnishes the humility, and St. Paul the example of a great pride an self-will laid at the feet of Our Lord.

New Orleans,
January 22, 1920.

Well, I went to see the Archbishop, and my fervor got quite a dampening. No mad hast to get us in on the part of his Grace, though he was very kind and pleasant. He had evidently not gathered from your note that I was not a Catholic. He gave me a children's catechism! And recommends my going back, on my return, to Bishop Gunn; no time in those two or three days to instruct me, and my general reading he evidently deemed quite insufficient for the purpose. But I'm not sure I shall act on his suggestion. I was at the point where, if he had said, "Come and make your profession of faith and general confession *now*, and be conditionally baptized and received into the Holy Catholic Church without any more hesitation or delay," I would meekly have said, "Yes, my Father" (or "your Grace," I suppose), and obeyed....

The catechism doesn't refresh me very much. I went to a 6:30 Mass in the Cathedral this morning. That refreshed me.

Pass Christian, Miss.,
January 27, 1920.

The Archbishop was quite right, as I find on going through with the catechism. There are numerous things in it which would have disconcerted me a good deal had I been received first and read them afterwards. I am becoming impatient now, to get on. It is very trying and painful to be hung up in this way, between heaven and earth as it were, with no abiding place and with the consolations of "the household of Faith" out of reach.

Pass Christian,
January 30, 1920.

I went meekly back to Bishop Gunn form the good Archbishop (of New Orleans). I wasn't especially eager to go over the catechism, but they both said it was the way to do it, and the Bishop seemed decidedly pleased when I appeared with the penny version in place of the Council of Trent,—as though now we were were on the road at last. The first day it went well enough. But today he was vastly annoyed.... "What prayers do you say, child?" "The prayers of the missal and the breviary, the Catholic litanies, and sometimes the rosary." He couldn't find any fault with that. So at last he sent me away, quite kindly. But he said we had been through the catechism sufficiently; and, curiously enough, after telling me not to do any more of that kind of reading, he gave me a Jesuit book more or less interesting and informing, with a name I don't care for. It sounds like some sort of patent prescription, *The Catholic's Ready Answer*. I have read a chapter on evolution and several others, showing that some Catholic authorities think it worth while to take notice of things which might constitute substantial difficulties to people brought up in or on the outskirts of the modern scientific world,[27] and to rephrase, if not actually reinterpret them. The "six days of creation" having been expanded into a choice of interpretations, scientific or poetic, at which nobody need boggle, perhaps the good and able Jesuits will some day take a hand at Adam. In the meantime, I am going to accept the word of my instructors that all a catechumen is required to embrace is embodied in the catechisms. And if I am to be allowed to "submit" to the Catholic Church with as much faith in her future interpretations as in her past and present, I can proceed.

Pass Christian,
February 10, 1920.

The Bishop seems to have been perfectly right in saying that I would never be a Catholic if I insisted upon threshing out, item by item, everything that presented itself as an intellectual difficulty. He intimated clearly that he had done as much as he thought useful, and that I would now have to do the rest myself, by prayer, until I could make a genuine act of faith. I accepted the verdict of both, and in both cases obeyed. I suppose (if my conversion is in the purpose of God) that, as Father Martindale said to Knox, when he was in the midst of what seemed an endless struggle, there must be a point somewhere between waking and getting up, where it becomes possible to rise. There is a great deal in that book ([Knox] *A Spiritual Aeneid* [1918]) which has been most companionable to me....

I certainly haven't been "hustled." If anyone ever again begins to talk to me about "proselyting priests," I shall say, "O be quiet!! They push you off."

Pass Christian,
February 20, 1920.

It takes a brisk, gay young soul like Ronald Knox to begin to lay about him straightaway, in his newly achieved position. *A Spiritual Aeneid* [1918] relieved the strain for me delightfully. He is full of amusing phrases like "invincible indecision," on the plea of which he used to hope he might perhaps get to heaven. And, referring to the higher criticism, he says, "I could not accept the doubts they proposed for my acceptance. If I am to go to heaven with the Higher Critics, it must be because invincible ignorance has blinded me to the light of doubt." It would be a good book for you to read while you are resting. Longmans.

Pass Christian,
February 24, 1920.

It is best to tell you, I think, that I am suffering a terrible—what shall I name it?—submergence in gloom, whether of Protestant reaction, or a final contest with the "terror, I can't say. But here I am, in the "dark night." Oh, very dark night. I don't know what I should do without the breviary and missal. How wonderful they are! The psalms and canticles of Lauds, with "Dr. Newman's" exquisite translations of the hymns. (The Marquess of Bute's translation of the breviary is the one I have used for years—my aunt's copy.) This is Friday, at Lauds." I stretch forth my hands unto thee; my soul thirsteth after thee as a thirsty land. Hear me speedily, O Lord; my spirit faileth....Cause me to know the way wherein I should walk; for I lift up my soul unto thee." And Tuesday Lauds. "O Lord I am seized; undertake for me. What shall I say or what will he answer me, seeing Himself hath done it? I will call to remembrance before Thee all my years in the bitterness of my soul. O Lord, if by these things men live and in such things is the light of my spirit, so wilt thou chasten me and make me to live. Behold mine anguish is turned into peace." (If it might be!) And for Wednesday, this! "Let your old arrogancy depart out of your mouth; for the Lord is a God of Knowledge and by Him thoughts are judged." (That might seem to be applicable, mightn't it?) Don't you love the hymns of Lauds? Of course, you read them in Latin. I prefer Newman's translations. Lauds, Friday:

> Rise within us, Light Divine!
> Rise and risen, go not hence,
> Stay and make us bright,
> Streaming through each cleansed sense,
> On the outward night.
> Then the root of faith shall spread
> In the heart new fashioned.

Then I must get back to some work. One of the inky clouds that break over me early in the morning is the thought of all the unfortunate people who are being harried and persecuted for their political opinions in this land of the (so-called) free; and I doing nothing about it. They are martyrs for the truth as they see it.

I have been defending the Faith. I defended it valiantly; and I feel better. You will be amused to know the special point of attack. It was the attitude of the Catholic Church on Socialism! And I read for the assailant some quotations from [Karl] Marx, [August] Bebel, [Frederick] Engels, and [Wilhelm] Liebknecht, that I had copied down from the article on "Socialism" in Father Hill's book—an article which irritated me somewhat, from its general attitude; still, I couldn't help acknowledging that the Catholic Church, as such couldn't very well countenance a system represented by people who (even as individuals) talk about religion as those four acknowledged exponents of Socialism talked. I wrote their remarks down (from the article) to have them ready to hand when needed.

New Orleans,
February 28, 1920.

I'm going to tell you this serial story just as it occurs.

Your letter came yesterday, just in time, as I was leaving Pass Christian this morning. I meditated long on its suggestion and this afternoon betook myself to the old Jesuit church. I love the church. It was wonderful there to-day; people passing in and out all the time by dozens to the confessionals, and making stations and devotions of one sort and another; all "at home in Zion;" so warm and glowing in atmosphere. I began to feel at home, too; but it was a long time before I could go into a confessional. You cant think how strange it seemed,—like crossing an irretraceable path; that strange feeling of a chasm and a leap. The priests were in plain view,—no screen before them,—and I looked at several, and selected one whose face I liked, and went and kneeled near that confessional, and watched people going in and out; and then suddenly, without any apparent volition of my own, I darted into it. And then,—did I do what you suggested? Not at all!! I told him at once exactly how it was; that I was a convert (I am, it seems, I said to myself); that I had not yet made my profession of faith, that the Paulist Father who had mostly had me in hand advised my going to a Jesuit, if possible, for my general confession; that I was pretty sure I had been validly baptized, but supposed I would be given conditional baptism. When I had said to the Father at the very first, "Perhaps you will not hear me," he asked, with the kindest, pleasantest inflection, "Why not?" But he wouldn't. He said no, the profession of faith must come first. If I were staying a week he would "take me under instruction," and give me conditional baptism and absolution; but as I was going to the Benedictines I would best do it all there. And then he said, "God bless you, my child," and I withdrew. But do you know, it made a great difference. It isn't going to be nearly so difficult anywhere. The strangeness is taken off it. I have looked at confessionals hundreds of times, and wondered if I should ever be able to go into one, though I have gone to confession, as an Anglican, for years.

New York,
June 6, 1920.

I don't mean to reduce you to being private chaplain to my especial prospectives. And do pray that I may be quiet and restrained and not headlong about pushing my religion into the foreground. I mustn't get to thinking that I am important to the conversion of all and sundry, you know. The Church has worried along a good many years without me, hasn't it? And doubtless God will find means to take care of souls without my intervention. That I try to remember.

The music I heard to-day seemed pretty bad and of a variegated badness after those three glorious Gregorian Masses (the Gregorian festival in New York). "How our Holy Father the Pope would dislike this," I murmured to my companion.

Deerfield, Mass.,
July 8, 1920.

As I was walking the Deerfield[28] meadows at 6:30 this morning, reading Lauds and Prime, the ghosts of my Puritan forbears hovering over, I thought that I had indeed boxed the compass, spiritually.

August 17, 1920.

The more I stay about with people who haven't the faintest conception of the faith, the more important it seems to me that they should be enlightened, when possible. But the Protestant mind is opened to information only just so much at a time, and sometimes you can see it snapped suddenly together again, as though to say, "Oh, I'm not going to let you *in*. You can stay where you are, and I'll take a good look at you." But that may be a beginning. Years after something may happen. Look at me, and at the sixty-three who wrote *Roads to Rome* [Raupert 1908].

Chicago,
September 5, 1920.

I *cannot* go to Communion on Sundays, except when it is of obligation (external and internal). I did my best this morning to be recollected, but that money-collecting I cannot rise above. *How* can one keep one's thoughts on one's devotions with a coin clutched in one's hand and a box or a man's hand advancing steadily, but either faster or more slowly than one computes? Will he arrive before or after the Elevation? Pray heaven, before and get it over. It *is* too much. Devotion oughtn't to be put to such a strain. I protest; and some day, if I'm not put under obedience, I shall cry out publicly against that undevout practice. I feel it coming. It is a scandal, especially to Protestants. Mrs. L. says that at the Madeleine it goes on all through the Mass. Societies are allowed to collect for all sorts of purposes. Something is constantly shoved before you face, with *Pour les pauvres* [for the poor] or the something else. I think it is a Cause with a big C and merits a champion. Somebody must begin preaching on the episode of Our Lord and the money-changers in the Temple. Let the collectors stand at the door, or let there be a committee to beset people anywhere or at any time, except when they are preparing to meet the King of kings and Lord of lords. Surely one wouldn't rush in with money baskets when people were being presented at court, or going out backwards before a royal presence. And The Royal PRESENCE must suffer this constant indignity.

November 3.

When I sent you that letter of the Rev.—I had forgotten that it contained the passage about "my opportunity" of "focusing a movement" in the Catholic Church. *My* opportunity!! Imagine the humble and obscure Benedicta, lost, joyfully, amidst the great congregation of the saints, Jerusalem, the Mother of us all; treading her streets, each day more happily at home in them, and gazing upon all her towers and battlements with so much delectation as almost to forget to go about her daily business in the sordid and corrupted and defaced earthly cities that we have made of what ought to be her counterpart on earth.

Woods Hole, Mass.,
July 1922.

I had a lovely time on Sunday at Our Lady of Good Voyage in Gloucester, a Portuguese fishermen's church. I am always particularly grateful and happy for being a Catholic when I am brought in contact with people from whom I would otherwise be quite separate and foreign. Mass is just the same; though, quite at home, one notices and enjoys all the foreign aspects and touches of our Mother's other children. The church itself was fascinating; rather nice architecture, not unlike the old missions in the West. And between the two towers, lifted high against the sky, Our Lady stands with a ship in her arms,— in one arm, rather, the other raised, blessing her fishermen children, bluey green waves dashing up around her. Inside is a perfect riot of saints—missionary saints, with cross in hand, armored saints, and saints of every variety. Like C. W., "I liked a lot," especially if they are naive, and don't savor too much of manufacture by the gross. In one sense, if images are not really art, "the worse they are the better they are," as a friend of mine says. The truly awful thing occurs when a church begins to have money enough to do something creditable to the complacency of the congregation.

There was a precious old woman just opposite me; one of those whom you can look at all you like, because she would never dream that anybody could be looking at *her*. She wore a kerchief and her mouth was somewhat one-sided from loss of teeth, but of a heavenly sweetness, and her whole dear old face a solemn peace. All her sons were fishermen, I'm sure; and perhaps all dead, so that she could sleep now, o' nights, in storms. Do you remember that piercingly touching passage in *Riders to the Sea* [Synge 1903], in which a mother of fishermen says something like that when her last son is brought in drowned? Can you fancy any church but the Catholic Church as a setting for a face like that?

I went to Mass and to Benediction, which was preceded by the dedication of a chime of bells—the square outside filled with all sorts and conditions and with flags. Very foreign and gay. "Light the candle, ring the bell, sing *Laus Deo* [praise the Lord]."

Final Note, May 25, 1924.

Thus far I wrote as I felt and thought in my progress toward full acceptance of the Catholic Faith. I said things that a Catholic would not say, but I was not a Catholic. The writing was informal, some of it intimate correspondence; and I cannot avoid feeling that there are many more reasons against than for its publication. Those reasons are plain. There is only one in favor of giving publicity to matter so personal, covering the life of a private individual. That is the possibility that the experience of one obscure pilgrim may afford any light, or, better, any sense of companionship in isolation, to some of the many who are treading similar paths, leading, through the varied providences of God's mercy, into the same great Way.

Great intellects, like Newman; vivid and winning personalities, like Robert Hugh Benson; exaltedly sincere and unworldly souls, like Frederick Joseph Kinsman; to whom truth is all and worldly place nought, set in the light by circumstance and endowment,—these from time to time illuminate the broad roadways. But there remain always the little paths, some winding and difficult, and the many who tread them, faltering and unsure, often alone and bewildered. So much needed help was sent to me on my journey that I can scarce refuse the chance of leaving in some bypath, for a possible fellow pilgrim, a hint of the next turning, and of obstacles as I found them. No soul is unique. And the less unusual, the more fellow travelers one may have.

The end of the narrative was naturally abrupt. The journey came to its felicitous close. [Cardinal John Henry] Newman, in his great *Apologia* [1914], tells us that, after he was received into the Church, there was no further "history of his religious opinions," for they knew no further change. Not that he thought less. It was scarce necessary to have told us that. But though of opinions there may be many changes to chronicle, of the Faith, once attained, there are none, only deepening, expanding, clarifying. "He whom the Eternal Word teaches," says Thomas à Kempis [see Kirvan 1995/ca 1530], "is delivered from many an opinion."

After a year of Catholic life one begins to have a perspective; and now, at the end of my fourth year in the Church, it is as if I had always been a Catholic. I have heard converts say that they tried to forget that they ever had not been Catholics. I feel no such disposition to turn my back on my spiritual origins. Since God did not have me "born a Catholic," the process by which He made me one is full of grateful interest to me, when I think of it, which, indeed, is less and less frequently, because of the increasing interest and satisfying variety of the inheritance into which I have entered.

Rich it is for us all in our degree—rich for the scholar, who draws upon the Church's inexhaustible storehouse of learning; rich for the artist, who, even if faithless, cannot afford to cut himself off from his Catholic sources; rich for the poor Sicilian peasant woman, reft of her hills, her vineyards, her olive orchards, or her little *paese* [land], where all her neighbors were her friends, many of them her kindred, now lost and bewildered in a squalid tenement district, with no greenness in sight except what she may succeed in making grow in a window box. When she enters, in winter, from the cold, dirty street, into the warmth and candle-glow of her patron saint's shrine, it must seem to her a paradise of comfort and beauty, though the dear saint's image be but one of hundreds turned out mechanically, and of no merit as art, but blessed; and made personal by love. She may choose her own patron, some of whose qualities she understands. Probably the choice will not be St. Thomas Aquinas, not St. Augustine, nor any of the scholar saints whose names grace the calendar; perhaps not the austere Apostle of the Gentiles [St. Paul], nor the Founder of western monasticism. Those great ones may be personally invoked by children of the Church of different taste and training. From one extreme to the other, intellectually, spiritually, and aesthetically, the great Mother provides food and healing, and it would ill beseem those to whom enough strong meat is given to cavil at babes receiving the milk of the Word in any form adapted to them. They are all children of the one Mother.

I often say at Mass the beautiful prayer in the office of Holy Saturday (after the second prophecy), to me the most beautiful and perfect of all the prayers for the Church:

> Oh God of unchangeable power and eternal life, look favorably on Thy whole Church, that wonderful and sacred mystery, and by the tranquil operation of Thy perpetual Providence, carry out the work of man's redemption. And may the whole world feel and see that things that were cast down are being raised up, and things that were grown old are being made new, and that all things are returning to perfection through Him from whom they took their origin, even Our Lord Jesus Christ.

When once this great unity has been realized and one's self as included within it (and how could such a conception come to one outside the Church Catholic), nothing remains except to strive to attain a more and more perfect personal actualization of it, by every means which the Church affords and for which one's capacity is fitted.

"Mine at last," Newman said, as he gazed upon the volumes of his beloved "Fathers" after his reception. And every one who has vainly tried to believe himself "a Catholic" or "Catholic" must often say to himself, when, with no effort, but with glad surrender, he feels himself wrapped about, swallowed up, happily, in that great union of the faithful of all ages, one of an infinitely extended family, infinitely diversified, yet supernaturally united, "Mine at last."

Notes

1. ["A Bypath Into The Great Roadway." *Catholic World* 119 (May 1924): 177-90. Reprinted Chicago: Ralph Fletcher.]
2. [There were huge celebrations across the country for the bicentennial of Parker's birth and the sesquicentennial of his death held in 1910. People in Chicago held several, including Addams as a speaker and organizer, but Starr did not participate in these events. See *Theodore Parker: Anniversaries of Birth and Death (August 24, 1810-May 10, 1860)*. 1911).]

3. [Stebner (1997, 207, n. 45) identified this minister as Collyer, who was the pastor of the Church of the Unity from 1859 to 1879 and then assumed the former pastorate of Theodore Parker in Boston.]

4. [Swing was Addams' pastor. He was originally the pastor of the Fourth Presbyterian Church of Chicago but was accused of heresy in 1874. He then founded an independent congregation called the Central Church of Chicago (Stebner 1997, 203, n. 40).]

5. The foundation of Hull House, in which I was privileged to accompany Miss Addams, took place in the autumn of 1889.

6. The arms of the author's maternal ancestors, the Allens of Chelmsford, Essex,- evidently those of a Crusader,-are: *Sable*; a cross potent, *Or*. Motto: Fortiter gerit Crucem. Crest: a demillion, Azure, holding in the two paws the rudder of a ship, *Or*.

7. ["Tenebrae" refers to the office of matins and lauds during Holy week when candles are gradually lit to symbolize the end of darkness and coming of light with the Resurrection.]

8. Rev. Daniel E. Hudson, C.S.C., editor of *Ave Maria* [of St. Mary's College], to which my aunt was for many years a contributor.

9. These are dealt with, partially and slightly, in some "Reasons, Pro and Con" which I wrote out later, at the suggestion of a friend, and for the purpose of clearing my own mind after I had begun seriously to face my situation with a view to finding the way out of it.

10. These groups hold the doctrine of the Real Presence (some of them of Transubstantiation), practice "reservation of the Blessed sacrament, invocation of the saints, the devotion of the Stations of the Cross, confession, fasting, Communion." So far as concerns articles of belief, with the exception of indulgences, the infallible authority of the Church and the Pope, and the immaculate Conception, I found little or nothing that was presented for the first time for my acceptance on being received into the Catholic Church. And I am told that many Anglicans now accept the dogma of the Immaculate Conception.

11. I smiled interiorly, then as now, at the assumption that the attraction toward the Catholic Church could ever have been, for me, in my own country, an aesthetic one; the almost uniform ugliness of American Catholic churches and their appointments, decorations, and articles of devotion being one of the trials which a Catholic of taste and education has to endure with what fortitude he may in this land. (Of course there are notable exceptions, such as the beautiful Dominican Church of St. Vincent Ferrer in New York.) And not less painful is the horror of operatic music, and modern religious tawdriness,—despite the injunctions of the last three Popes in regard to Gregorian. I recall saying, somewhat saucily, I fear, while still a Protestant, to a priest, "Don't you think, Father, that it is a little hard that there isn't a church in Chicago where one can hear a Mass such as the Pope and I like ?"

12. The work of the lumber companies. It would seem to be the interest of the worldliness to mar and destroy, as of out-of-the-worldness to preserve and restore.

13. ["A Bypath Into The Great Roadway." *Catholic World* 119 (June 1924): 358-73.]

14. [St. Athanasius (c. 296-373) was the Bishop of Alexandria and a prolific author. (Farmer 1987, 26-27).]

15. Those "weird little books" are a trifle less "weird" when considered from the standpoint of a necessarily somewhat standardized provision for all classes of minds. As I have frequently said to non-Catholics since I became a catholic, "you must remember that the Catholic Church isn't dealing solely with a little handful of "Intellectuals.""

16. [Of 1438, mentioned later.]
17. A Franciscan MS. of date 1438 in my possession, which Dr. Wager wrote out for me into plain Latin.
18. [St. Januarius (d. c305?) Bishop of Beevento and martyr. His blood is claimed to liquefy sometimes, and the last occasion occurred in 1978 (Farmer 1987, 223).]
19. I obviously used the word in the loose sense of something impossible or next to impossible.
20. On rereading this much later: How absurd to have had any hesitation! Of course the acceptance of the authority of the Church is the only way to become a Catholic. Still I was conscientious in my efforts to Aagree with" the church point by point.
21. Bishop Gunn of Natchez.
22. [We were unable to locate the reference to Handly's pamphlet but another one of this title was edited by John A. O'Brien, *The White Harvest: A Symposium on Methods of Convert Making*. London: Longmans, Green and Co., 1927.]
23. I refer to Father Handly's generous recognition, in the above pamphlet, of the virtues of separated Christians, and the truth they hold.
24. From Newman's "Prayer to be said by enquirers."
25. [Starr is probably referring to the major steel strike in Gary, Indiana in 1919.]
26. [Probably a religious pamphlet answering common questions raised by people considering converting to the Roman Catholic church.]
27. I had not, at that time, read-in fact, it had not then been published-Canon Dorlodot's [1923] volume, *Darwinism and Catholic Thought*, which embodies his conferences as representative from the University of Louvain at the Darwin Centenary at Cambridge. It would have smoothed my path very much.
28. [Many of Starr's relatives came from and lived in Deerfield Massachusetts.]

23

Reflections on the Breviary: Advent and Christmas[1]

The high places of the breviary[2] are, naturally, those of the Christian year. The marvellous dramatic sweep of the liturgical year has two climaxes, Christmas and Easter, peaks which tower above the rest, though there are many of lesser altitude, raised above the plain. These elevations are approached through valleys, —the broad, deep one of Lent, with its more and more intensified sorrow of Passion and Holy Weeks, ending in the tragic humiliation of Good Friday; and the lesser vale of penitential approach, Advent, ushering in the coming of Christ in the flesh. The early and mediaeval Church approached these two great festivals, these mountain peaks of devotion, as a matter of course through vales. The modern world craves the joys but rejects the sorrows. "The World" would have Christmas and Easter but will none of Advent and Lent. It is for Catholics to companion their Lord on the journey to Bethlehem and the Way of the Cross. The way is long and the flesh is weak, and devotion often flags. We need all the help we can have. Without the breviary and missal I wonder that it holds out. And even joy needs sustaining. An irrational joy—a spiritually inorganic joy, if one may so express it—how fleeting and unsatisfying it is. What is the world's Christmas? Gifts, rich food, smart apparel, gaiety, kindliness let us hope, but a kindliness and a joy with no supernatural basis. And of Easter in the world there is even less. Before the Catholic Easter was mine I dreaded it. I used to go through Holy Week with expectation (for I was long a Catholic at heart), and then experienced a painful drop—a sense of unreality. What had it all been and meant? Many years before I entered the harbor of the Visible Church, the office of the breviary was a regular part of my Christmas observance. The beginning of my attachment to the breviary office was largely due to a non-Catholic scholar.[3] In my High Anglican period, when I was fain to believe and call myself a Catholic, Dr. [Albert S.] Cook used to say to me, playfully, but how truthfully: "You will never be a very good Catholic until you know your breviary better." An authority in Old English, he had edited Cynewulf's *Christ*, with profuse notes, and an introduction interesting even to one who cannot read the text of the poem. *The Christ of Cynewulf* [Cook 1900] is divided into three parts: I. The Advent; II. The Ascension; [and] III. Doomsday. In his *Introduction* Dr. Cook, who "knew his breviary" thoroughly, makes copious reference to the office for Advent, with many excerpts from it, especially of the responsories and antiphons. He also refers frequently to [Pierre] Batiffol's *History of the Breviary* [1912] and Dom [Prosper] Guéranger's *Liturgical Year* [1868-1863], with quotations from them.

[Advent][4]

Before I owned an English translation of the breviary (the Marque of Bute's), I betook myself regularly, in Advent, to Cook's [1900] Introduction to *The Christ of Cynewulf* for the surpassingly beautiful antiphons and responsories: of the Advent office, with comments which he quotes from Batiffol [1912] and Guéranger [1868-1863]. I had never seen Batiffol's great *History of the Breviary* [Batiffol (1912)], nor read *The Liturgical Year* [Guéranger (1868-1863)], which later became for many years my Advent and Lenten guide. I am happy to express here my gratitude, and to suggest to others this beautiful Introduction to *The Christ of Cynewulf* (published by Ginn and Co.) as an inspiration to the further study of the breviary. In some cases it may be more easily accessible and less formidable than *The Liturgical Year* in 15 volumes, or Batiffol's great *History of the Breviary*, an exhaustive study, requiring time and sustained interest.

On pages 87 and 88 of the history are found the admirable selections from the responsories which Batiffol selects to summarize the spirit of the Advent offices. Cook avails himself of the arrangement and the comments, with "I borrow the language of Batiffol." He translates the Latin however, as Batiffol does not.

The first words of the Church, in the still midnight, of the new liturgical year are these:

"Come let us adore the King, our Lord, who is to come."

As this Sunday is often called the *Aspiciens a longe*, its character may be illustrated from the responsory.

Begins Batiffol:

"Take, for example, that admirable Respond for Advent Sunday, the *Aspiciens a longe,* where, assigning to Isaiah a part which recalls a celebrated scene in the Persae of Aeschylus, the liturgy causes the precentor to address to the listening choir these enigmatic words:

"I look afar off, and behold, I see the power of God coming, and a cloud covering the whole earth. Go ye forth to meet Him and say: Tell us whether Thou be He who shall rule over the people Israel.

"And the whole choir, blending in one wave of song the deep voices of the monks and the clear notes of its boy readers, repeats like a reverbertaing echo of the prophet's voice:

"I look afar off, and behold, I see the power of God coming, and a cloud covering the whole earth.

Precentor.

All ye children of the earth and sons of men, the rich and the poor together,

Choir.

Go ye forth to meet Him and say: Tell us whether Thou be He that shall rule over the people Israel.

Precentor.

Hear, O thou Shepherd of Israel, thou that leadest Joseph like a sheep,

Choir.

Tell us whether thou be he that shall rule over the people Israel.

But what need to scan the horizen in doubt? He whose coming is known, He is the Blessed One, and no triumph can be fair enough to welcome His Advent:

Precentor.

Lift up your heads, O ye gates, and be ye lift up, ye everlasting doors, and the King of glory shall come in.

Choir.

Who shall rule over the people Israel.

Precentor.

Glory be to the Father and to the Son and to the Holy Ghost. And then the whole of the opening text is repeated in chorus.

I look afar off etc."

Thus far Batiffol. Cook then gives the antiphons for Lauds and Vespers of the four Sundays of Advent, with comments on their distinct characters.

"The fourth Sunday is called Rorate, from the Introit [an early part of the Mass] . . . The thought is that of the desert, which needs the refreshment of the dew, and the personage in view is besides the Saviour, John the Baptist. The Introit is:

Drop down dew, ye heavens from above, and let the clouds rain the Righteous One; let the earth open and send forth a Saviour."

For the third and fourth Sundays the "Invitatory":

"O come, let us worship; the Lord is now at hand."

Matins of Christmas Eve begin with the grand "Invitatory":

"This day ye shall know that the Lord cometh: and in the morning, then ye shall see His glory."

After the hymn it is repeated, divided into verse and answer:

"*Verse*. This day ye shall know that the Lord cometh.
Answer. And in the morning, then ye shall see His glory.

Then the Gospel and a homily on it by St. Jerome, divided into lessons by most beautiful responsories:

First Responsory.

"Sanctify yourselves today and be ready: for on the morrow ye shall see the majesty of God upon you.
Verse. This day, ye shall know that the, Lord cometh, and in the morning, then ye shall see
Answer. The majesty of God upon you."

The lesson is then continued for a little further, but soon interrupted by another joyful responsory:

Second Responsory.

"Stand still, and ye shall see the help of the Lord with you. O Judah and Jerusalem, fear not. Tomorrow ye shall go out, and the Lord will be with you.
Verse. Sanctify yourselves, O ye children of Israel, and be ready.
Answer. Tomorrow ye shall go out, and the Lord will be with you."

The third responsory varies this theme with the introduction of a new one:

[Third Responsory.]

"On the morrow the sins of the world shall be washed away, and the Saviour of the world will be our King."

[Starr's Reflection on the Breviary During Advent]

The antiphons of Lauds [praises] repeat parts of these responsories with some changes and some additions. These, being the matins of Christmas Eve, have been said the night before, but I always make use of them for meditation and preparation before the Christmas matins and Mass, One falls asleep for a little while with the wonderful words weaving in and out through one's mind:

"Sanctify yourselves and be ready, for tomorrow you shall see the majesty of God . . . . . This day ye shall know that the Lord cometh . . . . .and in the morning ye shall see. . . ."

Is there any Christmas Eve preparation like that? Then, after a little sleep, if one is so fortunate as to be staying in a convent where there is to be midnight Mass preceded by Gregorian matins, one rises and goes to Christmas matins at a quarter after eleven.

[Christmas Matins][5]

And now Christmas matins. In the lessons we have those great prophetic utterances of Isaiah, which to many who do not read the prophets have been made familiar by the oratorio of The Messiah. The first lesson ends with:

"For unto us a Child is born, and unto us a Son is given and His name shall be called Wonderful, Counsellor, The Mighty God, The everlasting Father, The Prince of Peace."

The second [lesson] begins with the beautiful:

"Comfort ye, comfort ye, My people, saith your God. Speak ye comfortably to Jerusalem, and cry unto her that her warfare is accomplished, that her iniquity is pardoned: for she hath received of the Lord's hand double for all her sins."

That whole glorious passage follows.

If those words are thrilling sung in a concert hall sometime during the Christmas season, what are they to those who kneel before the altar of the Prince of Peace, waiting to welcome Him in the still midnight, on the festival of His Coming?

First Responsory.

"This is the day whereon the King of Heaven was pleased to be born of a Virgin, that He might bring back to heaven man who was lost. . . .

Verse. Glory be to God in the highest, etc.

Answer. There is joy among the hosts of angels, because eternal salvation hath appeared unto men. . . .

Second Responsory.

"This day is the true peace come down unto us from heaven. This day throughout the whole world the skies drop down sweetness.
Verse. This day is the day-break of our new redemption, of the restoring of the old, of everlasting joy.
Answer. This day throughout the whole world the skies drop down sweetness."

After the third lesson which begins with: "Awake, awake, put on thy strength, O Zion: put on thy beautiful garments, O Jerusalem: thou city of the Holy One!"—we have the beautiful colloquy with the shepherds:

Third Responsory.

"O ye shepherds, speak, and tell us what ye have seen; who is appeared in the earth? We saw the new-born Child, and angels singing praise to the Lord.
Verse. Speak; what have ye seen? And tell us of the Birth of Christ.
Answer. We saw the new-born Child, and angels singing praise to the Lord.
Verse. Glory be etc.
Answer. We saw the new-born Child. . . ."

The effect of these rhythmical repeats is cumulative in impressiveness. One begins to feel that one is a shepherd, and ready to say with conviction and joy: "We saw the new-born Child and angels singing praise to the Lord."

The remaining lessons are taken from homilies of the Fathers, very simple and sweet little sermons—the fourth, fifth and sixth lessons, by Pope St. Leo the Great, and the seventh by Pope St. Gregory the Great, on the Gospel of St. Luke, II. St. Leo begins:

"Dearly beloved brethren, 'Unto us is born this day a Saviour.' Let us rejoice. It would be unlawful to be sad today, for today is Life's Birthday; the Birthday of that Life, which, for us dying creatures, taketh away the sting of death, and bringeth the bright promise of the eternal gladness hereafter. . . (From the fifth:) When our Lord entered the field of battle against the devil, He did so with a great and wonderful fairness. Being Himself the Almighty He laid aside His uncreated Majesty to fight with our cruel enemy in our weak flesh. He brought against him the very shape, the very nature of our mortality, "yet without sin."[6]

[Starr's Reflections on the Breviary for Christmas Matins]

The practice of following, more or less closely, the breviary office, at least for the more important feasts, has brought me many rich experiences. Christmas must be rich in experience to any soul not barren or pitifully exiled from religious opportunity. One of the richest, for me, was a midnight Mass in a religious house, preceded by Gregorian matins which require about three quarters of an hour. I was following attentively the Christmas sermon of St.

Leo, which had reached the sixth lesson, when I became aware of a voice in the choir which proclaimed with wonderful sweetness and conviction, like a personal call to her own soul and to others:

> "Know, O Christian, how great thou art, who hast been made partaker of the divine nature, and fall not again by corrupt conversation into the beggarly elements above which thou art lifted. Remember Whose body it is whereof thou art a member, and Who is its Head. Remember that it is He that hath delivered thee from the power of darkness and hath translated thee into God's Light and God's kingdom."

From where I sat I could look into the choir, and I saw the face of the religious illumined with the greatness of that call to the Christian soul: "*Agnosce, O Christiane, dignitatem tuam*" [translated below]. I cannot say how sorry I was and am for those who were engaged in other devotions and had not heard the call. Always, wherever I may be, that lesson will hold it for me. "Know, O Christian soul thy dignity—how great thou art."

Like the missal, the Christmas office of the breviary begins with the simple, the human, the tender aspect of the Incarnation, the poverty of the manger and the attendance of shepherds (albeit by angelic announcement); and it ends with the augustness of the Everlasting Word. There is no disharmony in these juxtapositions. How much more harmonious with the Divine Glory is the austerity of poverty than luxury and the display of riches and power! We could not imagine our Lady wrapping the Holy Child in rich and costly fabrics, or bringing Him forth lodged in a luxurious hostelry or palace, amidst ranks of attendant servants in place of angels and the humble beasts.

Pope St. Gregory (seventh lesson) takes his text from the going up to Bethlehem. He begins, in his dear, simple way:

> "By God's mercy we are to say three Masses today, so there is not much time left for preaching, but the occasion of the Lord's Birthday itself obliges me to say a few words."

He then proceeds with a brief and simple instruction on the mystic significance of Bethlehem, the House of Bread, the birthplace of Him who is the Bread of Life.

The seventh responsory is our Lady, ending with the

> "*Answer*. This day hath He been pleased for the salvation of the world to be born of a Virgin."

St. Ambrose (eighth lesson) speaks symbolically of the shepherds:

> "Behold the beginning of the Church. Christ is born and the shepherds watch; shepherds to gather together; the scattered sheep of the gentiles, and to lead them into the fold of Christ, that they might no longer be a prey to the ravages of spiritual

wolves in the night of this world's darkness. And that shepherd is wide awake whom the Good Shepherd stirreth up. The flock, then is the people, the night is the world, and the shepherds are the priests. And perhaps he is a shepherd to whom it is said 'Be watchful and strengthen'. (Addressed to the Angel of the Church of Sardis) for God hath ordained as the shepherds of His flock not Bishops only, but also Angels."

The eighth responsory is of the Word made flesh, which gives the text for the homily of St. Augustine the theologian. Thus is completed the whole divine hymn of the Incarnation, every note having been struck and all harmonized. The Mass follows at midnight, sometimes all three Christmas Masses; and then lauds, beginning again in the antiphons of the psalms with the shepherds' motif, the Virgin Mother, the Angel's song of Glory to God and peace on earth. The last antiphon, gloriously blends all these strains into triumph:

"*Unto us this day a little Child is born, and His Name shall be called the Mighty God. Alleluia, Alleluia*."

Notes

1.   ["Reflections on the Breviary." *Orate Fratres* 2 (27 November 1927): 16-23. This article presents various passages found in the breviary, or prayerbook, that Starr presents as a scholar and as a person responding to the effect of these prayers. These prayers are said during the Mass and require answers, or "responses," from the congregation.]
2.   [This is the book containing the "Divine Office" or daily prayers required for priests to perform since 1611. Religious sisters are not necessarily bound to this duty. See *OED*. Starr read parts of the breviary regularly before entering the Roman Catholic church.]
3.   The late Dr. Albert Stanburrough Cook of Yale University, I have learned with sorrow of his death since writing these words.
4.   [This is the period of four weeks prior to Christmas that has special prayers anticipating the coming birth.]
5.   [Starr refers here to the morning Mass on Christmas. The breviary offers prayers for three Masses.]
6.   Nobody who knows the Dream of Gerontius can fail to recall the verses from the Fifth Choir of Angelicals:

O loving wisdom of our God!
When all was sin and shame,
A second Adam to the fight
And to the rescue came.

O wisest love! That flesh and blood
Which did in Adam fall,
Should strive afresh against the foe,
Should strive and should prevail.

24

Two Pilgrim Experiences[1]

[Abbey of] Whitby[2]

[St.] Caedmon, St. Hilda,[3] King David, the Lord Christ. So, on the face of a cross raised, not long since, by scholars to the memory of the first great singer of English sacred song, "hard by" the spot where he "fell asleep," the figures rise, one above another; at the base the humble swineherd and singer of the great song of Creation,[4] which passed through him almost unconsciously; above him the image of that woman and saint who held over both men and women a spiritual sway which has made her a living memory for centuries, who discerned the spirits, whether they were of God, knew them under the humblest guise and assigned the holy genius of Caedmon to its place. Over her, King David the type of sacred song, and over King David with his harp, the One Source of all religious genius, the inspiration and ruler of David and of St. Hilda, of Caedmon and of all saints. It is a modern cross and still too new, despite the winds which shortly mend all sharpness; but well conceived on the old models and far enough from the sad and solemn abbey ruin to save its newness from discord.

Alas for the abbey ruin, doomed, ere long, to perish, or worse than perish, like so many preserved and restored ruins.[5] Alas for a zealous pilgrim who wends his way to breathe some breath of the wild, lone coast where Abbess Hilda ruled or to feel for a brief time the solemn influence of the remains of that pile which rose over her followers. Led by the dream of Caedmon and Hilda the hapless pilgrim first finds—a fashionable seaside resort! "Patience—hard thing!"

The abbey looks small and unimpressive from the hotel, much cumbered by barrack-like structures near it and half hidden by a church directly in the way. One had thought of it and seen it in old engravings, grand and lone on its hilltop. This church, however, when one has ascended the hundred and ninety-nine steps leading up to it, proves to be in itself far from uninteresting. It was founded by Edwin, Hilda's uncle, on his baptism, and scholars say that there is good reason to believe that Christian worship on the spot has not been discontinued since his time.

The oldest part of the present structure is Norman, a beautiful Norman chapel containing the so-called altar of the church. This "altar" is "vested" still as in Reformation times, and would not be noticed as an altar at all had one not been notified to look for it. I attended public worship here on Sunday and was seated, fortunately, in front of the fine Norman arch separating the chapel from the later parts of the church. Directly across the arch some family of prominence ("In they came, those people of importance") has built for itself a gallery of white enameled wood, supported on twisted pillars and ornamented with rococo bands of fruit and flowers and angels' heads. Fortunately, the tip of the arch is spared and the Norman capitals, the balcony cutting off merely the space between. At right angles to the rococo gallery is another which makes the first seem rarely beautiful; the pillars of this second one being painted a mottled dirty yellow and brown. Even these, in their unpretentious ugliness, might rest the eye, should love of place inspire the building of yet another gallery in some present aggressive style.

The pews are of the high, walled-in variety and the pulpit in three stories, far more prominent and impressive than the altar. The clergyman was a canon of the English Church, and the service in keeping with the altar and pulpit.

But the Abbey; ah, the Abbey! Behind the church and churchyard and the barrack-like buildings, it is possible to see it with a view of the moors, stretching out limitlessly along the coast. Herds of cattle and flocks of sheep make it easy to figure Caedmon's hut almost anywhere; and when once inside the somber, doomed pile, or outside, with a chosen background of moors, it is easier to fancy that Hilda ruled over its inmates than to realize that she never saw this thirteenth century fabric.

Of what the good, substantial Yorkshire folk make of that inheritance of tradition, or what it has made of them, I found no hint as they sat in their walled pews or stood, groups of men in the gentle rain, chatting in shelter of the church angles on the Sunday afternoon A great tradition seems fading out of life, wearing away like the stones of the structure which enshrines it.

Iona[6]

To the shrines of a far greater tradition all this was but a preliminary pilgrimage. A greater saint than Hilda, a greater power, a far more elemental genius, nearer the source of all greatest gifts, kindled at this central shrine of Celtic Christianity the fire which spread over all Scotland and beyond it, from which, indeed, Hilda's own lamp was lit. "How great a man was the Irish monk called Colum the Dove; Columcille, the Dove of the Church." "In spiritual geography Iona is the Mecca of the Gael; to tell the story of Iona is to go back to God and to end in God."[7]

After many years of dreaming of Iona, the dream was "coming true." A proffered choice between Norway and Scotland caused no wavering; Scotland meant Iona, two weeks, at least, in which to trace the footsteps of Columba[8] as it had once been given me for two precious weeks to tread those of Francis at Assisi.[9]

One held it off a little, making the most of shrines less mystically hallowed; Cuthbert's, Bede's, Hilda's, outer courts, as it were, all leading the way to the holiest, the Mecca, not only of the Gael, but of all Christians of northern tradition. "And I shall find some peace there!" above all, in the Holy Isle, Peace. And then, suddenly, undreamed of, the dark cloud of war swept the whole horizon, and the pilgrim path seemed lost in confusion, uncertainty, even danger. But for me it lifted, partially for a little space; just long enough for one glimpse, the briefest, of my Mecca, on the last day accessible by ordinary means. Strict prudence would not have counseled even that. But there were other counselors; my own great desire, and the urgency of a friend, a poet painter, and life long lover of Iona and its lore. "No effort is too great for the shortest time. Once having seen Iona you will return."

One day, then, it was to be; my one day for Iona, not of the year like Pippa's day, but perhaps of a lifetime. But for those few hours the blessed little island lay in perfect light and ineffable color. Rain had fallen on it incessantly for weeks before; that day the first serene and clear one. There it lay in my intensified vision, its crosses moss-grown centuries deep, its sacred piles, abbey, cloisters, nunnery, tombs, its ruins, the restored and, happily, the unrestored, sheep grazing amongst them, and a young horse gamboling near the great St. Martin's cross. There it lay against a background of sea and sky and the neighboring shore of Mull, blue with another meaning for blue, as Iona itself was green and white and golden in a sense those words do not convey elsewhere. One recalls Dante's [1895] effort to record the supreme vision of Paradise, his acknowledgment of the failure even of memory and his final self-consolatory words, "But still trickles into my heart, the sweetness that was born of it." There it lies now, as it lay that day, the Holy Isle of Iona, by the mercy of God remote from battleships and too humble and poor to be worth the cost of destruction. I close my eyes sometimes in an ugly church or an ugly street, "as I stand by the roadside or on the pavement gray," I see it, "in the deep heart's core"; see it in a diminished and reflected way. But how describe it to any who have not seen it! And to those who have, what need? "There is one Iona," says Fiona Macleod, "a little Island of the West." There is another Iona of which I would speak. I do not say it lies open to all. It is as we come that we find— the Iona of sacred memories and prophecies. None can understand it who does not see it through its pagan light, its Christian light, its singular blending of paganism and romance and spiritual beauty.

"I am so glad," wrote my friend,

that you had a glimpse of Iona and that you felt it was worth all the fatigue and suffering it cost. There is some magic about Iona. Multitudes have experienced this joy; I think everybody does in greater or less degree who sets foot on its shore. Some other day—perhaps next year [Alas!] we will be all together there and I shall show you all the sacred spots. The sounding shore and the marble quarry and where Columba buried his coracle; and the cairns raised by the penitents; and the Pigeon's Cave and the Gothic Cave, and the Cave of the One Goblin, and the spot where St. Bride[10] most loved to sit and look out on the sea. "Victorious Bride loved not the vain shows of the world. Here she sat—a bird seat on a cliff." And the Hill of Angels, that was at one time a fairy hill; and was then the Druid's Hill of Fire; then a place for commune with heavenly beings. And it is a fairy hill again and in the twilight you can hear the mingled sounds of fairy harps and elfin bagpipes. But in the daytime, lambs graze on it and gambol about it.....Some day I am going to paint Columba on the Hill of Angels. But Columba will not take shape in my imagination. He was so full of contradictions; he was so stern and he was so sweet, so imperious and so humble. I have a kind of idea of him because I knew Father Allan of Eriskay, and Father Allan was like Columba in many ways, and lived in an almost identical place and under very much the same conditions. He always steered the boat. He had great personal strength and loved to work big rocks for building purposes, as Columba loved to carry the meal sacks. And he was a great traveler and knew what it was to be kept waiting at a ferry for eight or ten hours in the wind and rain. And when a soul needed his assistance he would put out to sea in any weather to reach him. And he was a king among his people and the smallest children loved him. And he was the terror of evil-doers and blew soap bubbles with the little folks."

The Duke of Argyll (may he rest in peace), even by his well-intentioned Protestant and patriotic generosity[11] could not efface the aura of Columba's soul from the island "of his heart and of his love." As one may still ". . . hear the roar by the side of the church of the surrounding sea,[12] "so one may still feel in this Gaelic bit of Eden, despite the worst that has happened in the restoration of the abbey, something one has nowhere else felt, different in kind and in degree, of the odor of sanctity, with the haunting witchery, the elemental poesy of a simple folk who lived so close to nature that the rocks, the sea and the creatures that dwell therein spoke to them an articulate speech.

And the very worst, as regards beauty, has not happened, even to the abbey, although for the altar, the Kirk of Scotland has substituted the pulpit.

Of royal lineage, Columba was banished from Ireland on account of blood shedding. There was a battle and death of his fellow men, due to him. And so he was punished and rightly; a heavy penance, to see his Ireland no more. The cause of his sin was greed. That we know about, ah yes! But can we imagine such greed, not of land nor of dominance in trade, but of beauty? All that coil that ended in the founding of Iona[13] was about a beautiful book that Columba must have and to which his right was contested. Love of beauty, love of art, love of poetry, self-will, vengeance; then contrition, obedience, a life of worship and of service, with a heart pressed close to the heart of nature. That was the stuff out of which was woven the fabric of this magic isle. Perhaps the mere respect for historic continuity, simple fidelity to tradition, may one day inspire a more true reproduction in some aspects (as it has already done in many) of the abbey as a monument.

How shall we dream of what future for Iona lies in the bosom of time; what fate other than to remain as she is until her precious stones crumble away, stones precious with genius and with memories. Of what will be ready, worthy to replace such things, who can form a reasonable hope? Columba himself foresaw his beloved island returned to its original pastures, and then remade and rehabilitated:

> In Iona of my heart, Iona of my love
> Instead of monks' voices shall be lowing of cattle
> But ere the world shall come to an end
> Iona shall be as it was.

A twilight melancholy creeps over the heart when one dares to think of the future of art and religion, in places such as Iona and Assisi, where nature, art and religion have made up life for simple folk. William Sharp (Fiona Macleod) who has written of Iona as only a Gael could, predicts the coming of the true historian of Iona and the book that shall be written. His prophecy falls soothingly on the war-weary heart. If we can but hold its final invocation as one to be fulfilled, not only for "this little lamp of Christ', but for, a lighted Christendom!

> What a book it will be . . . it will reveal to us what this little lamp of Christ was to pagan Europe; what incense of testimony it flung upon the winds; what saints and heroes went out of it; how the dust of kings and princes was brought there to mingle with its sands.... It will tell, too, how the nettle came to shed her snow above kings' heads, and the thistle to wave where bishops' mitres stood; how a simple people out of the hills and moors, remembering ancient wisdom or blindly cherishing forgotten symbols, sought here the fount of youth; and how, slowly, a long sleep fell upon the island, and only the grasses shaken in the wind, and the wind itself, and the broken shadows of dreams in the minds of the old, held the secret of Iona. And at the last— with what lift, with what joy—it will tell how once more the doves of hope and peace have passed over its white sands, this little holy land! This little holy land! Ah, white doves, come again! A thousand thousand wait.

Notes

1. [*Catholic World* 131 (September 1930): 680-84.]
2. [A Benedictine monastery was founded here in Yorkshire, England about 657. St. Hilda was the first abbess and St. Caedmon was a monk there. Caedmon is noted as the first poet to write in the English vernacular (Hudleston 1912).]
3. [St. Caedmon (d. 680) was a monk at Whitby whom St, Bede (673-735) claimed to be the author of the first writing in vernacular English (Farmer 1987, 67-68). St. Hilda (614-680) was the abbess of Whitby who was originally descended from a royal family and led a secular life for thirty-three years (Farmer 1987, 206-7).]

4.   [Caedmon is said to have dreamt the vision that resulted in his most famous poem "Hymn of Creation" (Crowne, 1908).]
5.   [The Abbey was attacked several times. Danes led the first attack about 680 and left it in ruins (Hudleston 1912).]
6.   [Iona remains a major pilgrimage site for Roman Catholics and Anglo Catholics. It is located on the island of Mull off the west coast of Scotland. It is said to be the burial ground of Scottish Kings for hundreds of years. It also is the site of several saints; most notably St. Columba, a famous abbey, and a Druid center.]
7.   Fiona Macleod.
8.   [St. Columba died in the sixth century and pilgrimages to honor him continue to this day on the Isle of Iona. Eliza Allen Starr also lectured on Columba. See McGovern (1935, 451).]
9.   [Franciscans and Benedictines often make pilgrimages to Iona in honor of the earlier visit of St. Francis. Perhaps Starr made another pilgrimage, however, following the path of Assisi elsewhere.]
10. [St. Bride is also known as St. Brigid of Ireland (d. 525). Her fame in Ireland is second only to St. Patrick (c.390-461?), where a cult devoted to her developed. She is claimed to have been ordained a bishop and is the patron of poets (Farmer 1987, 62-63).]
11. [The [8th] Duke of Argyll presented the Island of Iona with all its remains (that it should have lain in any man's gift) to the Kirk of Scotland.]
12. "Delightful would it be to me to be in Uchd Ailiun
On the pinnacles of a rock
That I might often see
The face of the ocean;
That I might see its heaving waves
Over the wide ocean
When they chant music to their Father
Upon the world's course
That I might see its level sparkling strand
It would be no cause of sorrow;
That I might bear the song of the wonderful birds
Source of happiness
That I might bear the thunder of the crowding waves
Upon the rocks
That I might bear the roar by the side of the church
Of the surrounding sea;

That I might see its noble flocks
Over the watery ocean."
Poem attributed to Columba.
13. Read over the story in Montalembert's *Monks of the West* [1861-1879].

Appendix A

A Chronology of Ellen Gates Starr's Life

19 March 1859	Born at Laona, Illinois, Unitarian religion
Fall 1877	Enters Rockford College and meets Jane Addams
1878-1879	Teaches in a country school in Mount Morris, Illinois
1879-1889	Teaches at Miss Kirkland's School for Girls, Chicago, Illinois
1884	Enters "low" Episcopal Church
1889	Enters "high" Episcopal Church
1888-1889	Travels to Europe and visits Toynbee Hall, meets with Arts and Crafts workers, especially C.R. Ashbee
1889	Co-founds Hull-House with Jane Addams
1890	Meets Mary Kenny
1891	Influences philanthropists leading to $5,000 donation to build the Butler Art Gallery
1891	Visits England and meets with more Arts and Crafts' workers, especially with T.C. Horsfall
1894	Founds Chicago Public School Art Society, first president
1896	Organizes textile unions, including the Dorcas League
1897	Organizes Easter Art Exhibit
1897	Co-founds CACS
1898-1899	Studies in England for 15 months with T.J. Cobdon-Sanderson
1899	Opens Hull-House Bookbindery
1901	Aunt Eliza Allen Starr dies
1902	Active in *International Socialist Review*
1903	Co-founds Illinois WTUL
1910	Member of the Strike Committee for the Garment Workers' Strike

1913	Active striker for Henrici Restaurant staff, leads to arrests
October, 1915	Active striker for the Garment Workers' Strike, leads to more arrests and notable trial, befriends Sidney Hillman and becomes Honorary life member of AGWA
1916	Runs unsuccessfully for alderman
March 1920	Converts to Roman Catholicism, leaves Hull-House and enters a convent
1920-1927	Occasional visits to Hull-House, lives at convent
1928	Paralyzed by a spinal operation, becomes a paraplegic; enters novitiate for Sisters of the Oblate
1930	Settles at the Convent of the Holy Child, Suffern, New York
21 May 1935	Jane Addams' dies
4 June 1935	Attends Jane Addams' Memorial
1935	Becomes an Oblate of the Third Order of St. Benedict
10 February 1940	Dies

Appendix B

Syllabus of the Tragedy of *King Lear* by Ellen Gates Starr, College Extension Course[1]

The tragedy of King Lear is a drama of retribution. "Whatsoever a man soweth that shall he also reap."

1. What is tragedy in the dramatic sense?
2. What is the nature of the wrong-doing in this play, and what determines the nature of the result to the wrong-doer?

There are interwoven in the tragedy of King Lear two separate stories of like character, and illustrating the same text. The result of Lear's long indulged arbitrariness and irascibility, and of Gloster's act of unchastity, in each case returns upon the offender and destroys him. Lear perished and Gloster perishes, each in consequence of his own act, the former through his sinfully indulged vanity and arbitrariness, the latter through the plots of his unlawful son.

Lear disclaims his guilt; he fails to recognize it until he sees it mirrored in its consequences. Gloster acknowledges his, but shirks the responsibilities of it and disowns the results, attributing his misfortunes to the sun, moon and stars.

By the same law of consequences Goneril, Regan, Cornwall and Edmund must also perish.

Kent survives the tragedy because he obeys the universal law and the law of his own being.

"When you act on the principle of revenge you not only violate a religious principle, but you destroy your own freedom; you are no longer a self-determined being; you are controlled by another person's act, and that an act you have yourself condemned"— Snider

Try to account for Shakespeare's not permitting Cordelia to survive.

Compare Shakespeare's theory of punishment with Dante's [1895] in *The Inferno*. For easily interpreted examples read Canto V, in which the carnal sinners, having been controlled in life by gusts of passion, are here tossed hither and thither without their volition. Also, Canto XIII., in which are the suicides. Having done violence to their own existence, they are allowed to cancel it and never again exist in the state of being which they have destroyed, but are condemned to the lower vegetable form of life, and appear here as gnarled trees.

Observe Shakespeare's landscape background. It is always vitally connected with the action of the drama. Though vividly pictorial, it never exists for its own sake, but, like every great landscape, is the setting for the human soul. In the third act the fearful tempest is manifestly the outward expression of Lear's internal state.

In the two cantos of Dante instanced above, the connection between the landscape background and the persons of the drama is so intimate as to blend and become indistinguishable.

Compare Greek myths, wood nymphs, river gods, etc.

Rolfe's [1908] edition of *King Lear* is recommended. For historical sources of the play and criticisms of commentators, see Introduction and Notes.

The Fool is omitted from the syllabus as being too subtle to "anatomize." A close study of this most beautiful character is urged.

Note

1.   [The printed syllabus is probably for both Hull-House courses around 1891-1892 and for the Summer School at Rockford Seminary, Rockford, Ill., July 1st to July 30th, 1891. Syllabus found on JAM.]

Bibliography

Archival Collections

Chicago, Illinois

University of Illinois at Chicago, University Library, Department of Special Collections, Jane Addams Memorial Collection
▫▫ Ellen Gates Starr Papers
▫▫ The Jane Addams papers, 1860 & 1960 [microform], Mary Lynn McCroe Bryan, editor

Northampton, Massachusetts

Ellen Gates Starr Papers, Sophia Smith Collection, Smith College
    "Art and Democracy." Typescript. Box 21, folder 273

Rockford, Illinois

Rockford College Archives
▫ Jane Addams Papers, Starr file

South Bend, Indiana

Rare Book Room, Cushwa Library, St. Mary's College
University of Notre Dame, Archives, Hezburgh Library
▫▫ Eliza Allen Starr Papers

Journals and Newspapers

Chautauqua, 1902-1910
Craftsman, 1898-1910
House Beautiful, 1902-1910
Hull-House Bulletin, 1896-1904
Hull-House Yearbook, 1907-1932
International Socialist Review, 1902-1904
Rockford Seminary Magazine, 1878-1920

Bibliography of Ellen Gates Starr

Starr, Ellen Gates. "Syllabus of the Tragedy of King Lear." Chicago: Hull House, 1891. Privately printed broadside.

_____. Untitled Speech. October 1892. Pp. 2-7. Privately printed pamphlet. (Rockford College Archives)

[_____.] *Chicago Public School Art Society*. Chicago: Privately printed, n.d.

_____. "Art and Labor." Pp. 165-79 in *Hull-House Maps and Papers*, by the Residents of Hull-House. New York: Crowell, 1895.

_____. "Art and Democracy." typescript. Smith 1895.

_____. *Report of Chicago Public School Art Society*. Chicago: Privately printed, March, 1896.

_____. "Settlements and the Church's Duty." *The Church Social Union* 28 (15 August 1896): 3-16. (Boston: Office of the Secretary, The Diocesan House).

_____. "Hull-House Bookbindery." *Commons* Whole Number 47 (30 June 1900): 5-6. ["A Note of Explanation" in *Hull-House Bulletin* 4 (May 1900)].

_____. "The Renaissance of Handicraft." *International Socialist Review* 2 (February 1902): 570-74.

_____. 1910 Testimony by Ellen Gates Starr of the Picket Committee. Pp. 31-32 in *The Clothing Workers of Chicago, 1910-1922*, edited by Leo Wolman with Eleanor Mack, H.K. Herwitz and Paul Wander. Chicago: Amalgamated Clothing Workers of America, 1922/1915.

_____. "Efforts to Standardize Chicago Restaurants—The Henrici Strike." *Survey* 32 (23 May 1914): 214-15.

_____. Petition to the Mayor on Behalf of the Garment Workers by Mary McDowell, Mrs. Medill McCormick, Ellen Gates Starr, and Sophonisba Breckinridge. P. 101 in *The Clothing Workers of Chicago, 1910-1922*, edited by Leo Wolman with Eleanor Mack, H.K. Herwitz and Paul Wander. Chicago: Amalgamated Clothing Workers of America, 1922/1915.

_____. Testimony by Ellen Gates Starr on her Arrest. *Chicago Tribune* (1916).

_____. [anon.] "Cheap Clothes and Nasty." *The New Republic* (1 January 1916): 217-9.

_____. "The Handicraft of Bookbinding [Article 1]." *Industrial Art Magazine* 3 (March 1915): 102-107.

_____. "The Chicago Clothing Strike." *The New Review* 4 (March 1916): 62-64.

_____. "The Handicraft of Bookbinding (Article II)." *Industrial Art Magazine* 4 (September 1916): 104-106.

_____. "Bookbinding (Third Article)." *Industrial Art Magazine* 4 (November 1916): 198-200.

_____. "Bookbinding (Article 4): Tooling and Finishing." *Industrial Art Magazine* 5 (March 1916): 97-103.

_____. "Reflections on the Recent Clothing Strike." Unpublished, n.d. [1916? 1917?]. Starr Papers, Smith College.

_____. "Why I am a Socialist." *Chicago Tribune: Daily Campaign Edition*, 1917. Box 2, Starr Papers, Socialism, Smith College.

_____. "Eliza Allen Starr." Unpublished, n.d. [1918?]. (Rare Book Room, Cushwawa Library, St. Mary's College).

_____. "A Bypath Into The Great Roadway." *Catholic World* 119 (May 1924): 177-90. Reprinted Chicago: Ralph Fletcher

_____. "A Bypath Into The Great Roadway." *Catholic World* 119 (June 1924): 358-73. Reprinted Chicago: Ralph Fletcher.

_____. "Reflections on the Breviary." *Orate Fratres* 2 (27 November 1927): 16-23.

_____. "Two Pilgrim Experiences." *Catholic World* 131 (September 1930): 680-84.

[Starr, Ellen Gates and Jane Addams.] *Hull-House: A Social Settlement*. Chicago: Hull-House, 1893. [Reprinted "Appendix." Pp. 205-30 in *Hull-House Maps and Papers*, by the Residents of Hull-House. New York: Crowell, 1895. Crowell, 1895.]

"One Dead, Three Hurt, in Strike Riots 'Angel of Strikers' Bears News of Killing to Hull House." *Chicago Tribune* 27 October 1915, 1, col. 8.

Starr's Exhibitions

The Chicago Arts and Crafts Society. Catalogue, Exhibit. Art Institute Chicago, March 23-April 15, 1898.

_____. Catalogue of the Second Exhibition. Art Institute Chicago, April-May, 1899.

General References

Adams, John Quincy. "The Relation of Art to Work." *Chautauquan* 38 (September 1903): 49-52.

Adams, Steven. *The Arts and Crafts Movement*. North Deighton, MA: JG Press, 1987.

Addams, Jane. "The Subjective Necessity of Social Settlements" and "Objective Value of a Social Settlement." Pp. 1-26 and pp. 27-56 respectively in *Philanthropy and Social Progress: Seven Essays by Miss Jane Addams, Robert A. Woods, Father J.O.S. Huntington, Professor Franklin Giddings, and Bernard Bosanquet*. Intro. by Henry C. Adams. New York: Crowell, 1893.

_____. "The Art Work Done at Hull-House." *Forum* 19 (July 1895a): 614-7.

_____. Hull House Maps and Papers. 1895b. 183-204

[_____]. *First Report of the Labor Museum, 1901-1902*. Chicago: Privately printed pamphlet, 1902a.

_____. *Democracy and Social Ethics*. New York: Macmillan, 1902b.

_____. "The Humanizing Tendency of Industrial Education." *Chautauquan* (May 1904): 266-720.

_____. "Work and Play as Factors in Education." *Chautauquan* 42 (November 1905): 251-55.

_____. *The Spirit of Youth and the City Streets*. New York: Macmillan, 1909.

_____. *Twenty Years at Hull-House*. New York: Macmillan, 1910.

_____. "A Modern Lear." *Survey* 29 (2 November 1912): 131-37.

_____. Memorial Address for Jenkin Lloyd Jones. *Unity* 82 (28 November 1918): 148-49.

_____. *The Second Twenty Years at Hull-House*. New York: Macmillan, 1930.

_____. *The Excellent Becomes the Permanent*. New York: Macmillan, 1932.

Amberg, Mary Agnes. *Madonna Center*. Chicago: Loyola University Press, 1976.

Anderson, Mary. *Woman at Work*. Minneapolis: University of Minnesota Press, 1951.

Andrews, Ethel. "Hull House." *Rockford Seminary Magazine* 20 (October 1892): 129-32.

Ashbee, Charles. *A Few Chapters in Workshop Re-Construction and Citizenship*. London: The Guild and School of Handicraft, 1894.

_____. *An Endeavor Towards the Teaching of John Ruskin and William Morris*. London: E. Arnold, 1901.

Batiffol, Pierre. *History of the Roman Breviary*. Translated by Atwell M.Y. Baylay. London: Longmans, Green, 1912

Benson, Robert Hugh. *Confessions of a Convert*. London: Longmans, Green, 1913.

Booth, Charles. *The Life and Labour of the People of London*, 9 vols. New York: Macmillan, 1892-1897. 8 additional vols. London: Macmillan, 1902. (The first volumes were originally published under the title *Labour and Life of the People: London*. London: Williams & Norgate, 1891).

Boris, Eileen. *Art and Labor: Ruskin, Morris, and the Craftsman Ideal in America*. Philadelphia, PA: Temple University Press, 1986.

Bosch, Jennifer Lynne. "Ellen Gates Starr, Hull House Labor Activist." Pp. 77-88 in *Culture, Gender, Race, and U.S. Labor History*, edited by Ronald C. Kent, Sara Markham, David R. Roediger, and Herbert Shapiro. Westport, CT: Greenwood Press, 1993.

Boswell, James. *Life of Samuel Johnson, 4 vols*, edited by Marshall Waingrow. New Haven, CT: Yale University Press, 1994/c. 1709-1765.

Bremond, Henri. *The Mystery of Newman*. 1907.

Browning, Robert. *The Statue and the Bust*. London: John Lane, 1900.

Bryan, Mary Lynn McCree and Allen F. Davis, eds. *One Hundred Years at Hull-House*. Bloomington: University of Indiana Press, 1990.

[Bryan] McCree, Mary Lynn. "The First Year of Hull-House, 1889-1890, in Letters by Jane Addams and Ellen Gates Starr." *Chicago History* 1, n.s. (Fall 1970): 101-14.

Bryne, Archibald. "Eliza Allen Starr." Pp. 350-51 in *Notable American Women*, Vol. 3, edited by Edward T. James. Cambridge, MA: Belknap Press of Harvard University Press, 1971.

Buhle, Mary Jo. *Women and American Socialism, 1870-1920*. Urbana: University of Illinois Press, 1981.

Butler, Alban. *Lives of Women Saints*, edited by the Right Rev. Mgr. Goddard. London: St. Anselm's Society, 1887.

Campbell, Matilda G. "Crafts in Elementary Schools." *Chautauquan* 38 (January 1904): 487-91.

Carlyle, Thomas. *Past and Present*. Introduction by Frederic Harrison. London: Ward, Lock, 1910.

Carson, Mina. *Social Settlement Folk*. Chicago: University of Chicago Press, 1990.

Catholic Church. *The Office of Holy Week*. Dublin: James Duffy, 1899.

"Chicago Arts and Crafts Society." *Commons* 3 (June 1898): 4.

"Chicago Arts and Crafts Society." *Hull-House Bulletin* 4 (Autumn 1900): 8.

Chicago Arts and Crafts Society. Catalogue, Exhibit. Art Institute Chicago, March 23-April 15, 1898.

Chicago Public School Art Society. Pamphlet. Chicago: Privately Published, 1910.

Chiellini, Monica. 1988. *Cimabue*, tr. Lisa Pelletti. New York: Harper & Row.

Cockerell, Douglas. *Bookbinding, and the Care of Books*. New York: D. Appleton, c. 1901.

Conway, Bertrand L. *The Question Box*. New York: The Paulist Press, 1929.

Cook, Albert S., ed. *The Christ of Cynewulf: A Poem in Three Parts: The Advent, the Ascension, and the Last Judgement*. Boston: Ginn & Company, Publishers. 1900.

Dante, Alighieri. *The Inferno*. Translated by Henry Francis Cary. New York: Cassell Publishing Co., 1895.

Darling, Sharon. *Chicago Metalsmiths*. Chicago: Historical Society, 1977.

_____. *Chicago Furniture*. New York: W.W. Norton, 1984.

Davis, Delia T. "Book-Making in the West." *Critic* 37 (September 1900): 239-41.

Deegan, Mary Jo. "Women in Sociology, 1890-1930." *Journal of the History of Sociology* 1 (Fall 1978): 11-34.

_____. "An American Dream: The Historical Connections Between Women, Humanism, and Sociology, 1890-1920." *Humanity and Society* 11 (August 1987): 353-65.

_____. *Jane Addams and the Men of the Chicago School, 1892-1920*. New Brunswick, NJ: Transaction Books, 1988.

_____, ed. *Women in Sociology: A Bio-Bibliographical Sourcebook*, intro. by Mary Jo Deegan. New York: Greenwood Press, 1991.

_____. "The Second Sex and the Chicago School: Women's Accounts, Knowledge, and Work, 1945-1960." Pp. 322-64 in *A Second Chicago School? The Development of a Postwar American Sociology*, edited by Gary Alan Fine. Chicago: University of Chicago Press, 1995.

_____. "'Dear Love, Dear Love': Feminist Pragmatism and the Chicago Female World of Love and Ritual." *Gender & Society* 10 (October 1996a): 590-607.

_____. "A Very Different Vision of Jane Addams and Emily Green Balch: A Comment." *Journal of Women's History* 8 (Summer 1996b): 121-125.

_____. "Gilman's Sociological Journey from *Herland* to *Ourland.*" Pp. 1-57 in *With Her in Ourland: Sequel to Herland* by Charlotte Perkins Gilman, edited by Mary Jo Deegan and Michael R. Hill and introduced by Mary Jo Deegan. Westport, CT: Greenwood Press, 1997.

_____. "Play from the Perspective of George Herbert Mead." Pp. xix-cxii in *Play, School, and Society*, by George Herbert Mead, edited and introduced by Mary Jo Deegan. New York: Peter Lang, 1999.

_____. "George Herbert Mead's First Book." Pp. xi-xliv in *Essays on Social Psychology*, by George Herbert Mead, edited and introduced by Mary Jo Deegan. New Brunswick, NJ: Transaction Publishers, 2001.

Deegan, Mary Jo and Christopher Podeschi. "The Ecofeminist Pragmatism of Charlotte Perkins Gilman: The Herland Sagas." *Environmental Ethics* 23 (Spring 2001): 19-36.

Deegan, Mary Jo and Linda Rynbrandt. "For God and Community." Pp. 1-25 in *Advances in Gender Research*, Vol. 4 (*Social Change for Women and Children*), edited by Vasilikie Demos and Marcia Texler Segal. Greenwich, CT: JAI Press, 2000.

Delaney, John J. *Dictionary of American Catholic Biography.* Graden City, NY: Doubleday, 1984.

Dewey, John. *School and Society.* Chicago: University of Chicago Press, 1899.

Dewey, John and James H. Tufts. *Ethics.* New York: Henry Holt, 1908.

Diliberto, Gioia. *A Useful Woman.* New York: Charles Scribner's Sons, 1999.

Dopp, Katherine Elizabeth. "The Place of Handicraft in Education." *Chautauquan* 38 (December 1903): 384-86.

Dorlodot, Canon. *Darwinism and Catholic Thought.* Translated by Ernest Messenger. New York: Benziger Brothers, 1923.

"The Dorcas Federal Labor Union," *Hull-House Bulletin* 3 (1 October 1897): 4.

The Episcopal Church. *The Book of Common Prayer: and Administration of the Sacraments, and other rites and ceremonies of the Church, according to the use of the Protestant Episcopal Church in the United States of America; together with the Psalter or Pslams of David.* New York: New York Bible and Common Prayer Book Society, 1845.

Farrell, John. *Beloved Lady.* Baltimore, MD: Johns Hopkins University Press, 1967.

Frank, Henriette Greenbaum and Amalie Hofer Jerome. *Annals of the Chicago Woman's Club.* Chicago: Chicago Woman's Club, 1916.

"Garment Strike Has Been Broken Say Employers." *Chicago Herald* (16 December 1915).

Garvey, Timothy J. *Public Sculptor: Lorado Taft and the Beautification of Chicago.* Urbana: University of Illinois Press, 1988.

Geddes, Patrick. *Patrick Geddes: Spokesman for Man and the Environment*, edited and introduced by Marshall Stalley. New Brunswick, NJ: Rutgers University Press, 1972.

Gilman, Charlotte Perkins. *The Dress of Women*, edited and introduced by Michael R. Hill and Mary Jo Deegan. Westport, CT: Greenwood Press, 2002

Goffman, Erving. *The Presentation of Self in Everyday Life*. Garden City, NY: Doubleday, 1959.

Goldman, Lawrence. "Ruskin, Oxford, and the British Labour Movement, 1880-1914." Pp. 57-86 in *Ruskin and the Dawn of the Modern*. Oxford, U.K.: Oxford University Press, 1999.

Guéranger, Prosper. *The Liturgical Year.* Dublin: Duffy. 1868-1883. Translated from the French by Laurence Shepherd.

Hall, J. Harman, Mrs. "The Beautifying of School Grounds." *Chautauquan* 38 (November 1903): 276-81.

Harris, Joel. "Ruskin and Social Reform." Pp. 7-33 in *Ruskin and the Dawn of the Modern*. Oxford, U.K.: Oxford University Press, 1999.

Hill, S.J., Michael Peter. *The Catholic's Ready Answer; A Popular Vindication of Christian Beliefs and Practices Against the Attacks of Modern Criticism.* New York: Benziger Brothers, 1915.

Horowitz, Helen. *Culture and the City.* Chicago: University of Chicago Press, 1989.

Hudleston, G. Roger. "Abbey of Whitby." *Catholic Encyclopedia*, Vol XV. New York: Appleton, 1912

"Hull-House Labor Museum." *Chautauquan* 38 (September 1903): 60-61.

Ickes, Harold, George H. Mead, and Irwin St. J. Tucker. *Brief History of the Clothing Strike in Chicago.* Pamphlet. 15 October 1915.

"Invitation Sent to Mayor and Members of City Council." (4 December 1915). Clipping.

James, William. *The Varieties of Religious Experience*; *A Study in Human Nature.* New York: Longmans, Green and Co., 1902.

Josephson, Matthew. *Sidney Hillman, Statesman of American Labor.* Garden City, N.Y.: Doubleday. 1952.

Kaplan, Wendy. "Spreading the Crafts." Pp. 298-314 in *"The Art That is Life,"* edited by Eileen Boris. Boston, MA: Museum of Fine Arts, 1987.

Kaufman, Edgar and Ben Raeburn, eds. *Frank Lloyd Wright: Writings and Buildings.* New York: Meridian Books, 1960/1901/c/1898.

Kelley, Florence. "The Sweating-System." Pp. 27-45 in *Hull-House Maps and Papers*, by the Residents of Hull-House. New York: Crowell, 1895.

Kelley, Florence and Almyra Stevens. "Wage-Earning Children." Pp. 49-76 in *Hull House Maps and Papers* by the Residents of Hull-House. New York: Crowell, 1895.

Kenney, Mary [O'Sullivan]. "Mary Kenney is Invited In." Pp. 21-23 in *One Hundred Years at Hull-House*, edited by Mary Lynn McCree Bryan and Allen F. Davis. Bloomington: University of Indiana Press, 1990.

Kenrick, Francis Patrick. *The Psalms, Books of Wisdom, and Canticle of Canticles.* Baltimore, MD: Lucas. 1857.

Korvan, John J. *True Serenity: Based on Thomas a Kempis' The Imitation of Christ.* Notre Dame, IN: Ave Maria Press, 1995/ca 1530.

Knox, R.A. *A Spiritual Æneid.* London: Longmans, Green, 1918.

Lathrop, Julia C. "The Cook County Charities." Pp. 143-61 in *Hull-House Maps and Papers,* by the Residents of Hull-House. New York: Crowell, 1895.

Levine, Daniel. *Jane Addams and the Liberal Tradition.* Madison, WI: State Historical Society of Wisconsin, 1971.

Linn, James Weber. *Jane Addams.* New York: Appleton-Century Crofts, 1935.

MacKay, Constance D'Arcy. *The Little Theatre in the United States.* New York: Henry Holt, 1917.

Marlatt, Abby. "Crafts in Secondary Schools." *Chautauquan* 38 (February 1904): 584-88.

Maturin, Basil William. *The Price of Unity.* London: Longmans, Green and Co., 1912.

McBride, Henry. "Crafts in Technical Schools." *Chautauquan* 39 (March 1904): 49-52.

McCauley, M. "Municipal Art in Chicago." *Craftsman* 9 (December 1905): 321-40.

McGovern, Rev. James J. *The Life and Letters of Eliza Allen Starr.* Chicago: Lakeside Press, 1935.

Mead, George Herbert. "The Working Hypothesis in Social Reform." *American Journal of Sociology* 5 (November 1899): 367-71.

_____. *Play, School, and Society,* edited and introduced by Mary Jo Deegan. New York: Peter Lang, 1999.

"Millet, Jean Francois" P. 898 in *Encyclopedia Britannica: Micropaedia, Volume VI.* Chicago: Encyclopedia Britannica, Inc., 1974.

"Miss Starr's Book-Bindery." *Hull-House Bulletin* (Autumn 1900): 9.

Montalembert, Charles Forbes, comte de. *The Monks of the West,* 7 vols. London: William Blackwood and Sons, 1861-1879.

Moody's Magazine. New York City: Moody Corporation, 1915.

Morris, William. *Art and Socialism; A Lecture Delivered January 23rd, 1884 before the Secular Society of Leicester.* London and Manchester; 1884.

_____. *A Note by William Morris on His Aims in Founding the Kelmscott Press.* Hammersmith, G.B.: Kelmscott Press, 1898.

_____. *A Dream of John Ball and A King's Lesson.* London: Longmans, Green, 1913.

Newman, Cardinal John Henry. *An Essay on the Development of Christian Doctrine.* London: Longman, Greens and Co., 1890.

_____. *Apologia Pro Vita Sua: Being a History of his Religious Opinions.* London: Longmans, Green and Co., 1914.

Nolan, H.J. "Kenrick, Archbishop Francis Patrick." Pp. 135-36 in *New Catholic Encyclopedia,* 8 vol. Washington, D.C.: Catholic University Press, 1967.

Nordhoff, Evelyn Hunter. "The Doves Bindery." *House Beautiful* 4 (June 1898): 21-28.

O'Brien, John A., ed. *The White Harvest: A Symposium on Methods of Convert Making.* London: Longmans, Green and Co., 1927.

Ν Preston, Emily. "Cobdon-Sanderson and the Doves Bindery." *The Craftsman* 2 (April 1902): 21-32.

Raupert, John Godfrey Ferdinand, ed. *Roads to Rome: Being Personal Records of Some of the More Recent Converts to the Catholic Faith*, introduced by Cardinal Vaughan. London: K. Paul Trench, Trubner, 1908.

Rice, Walter. "Miss Starr's Bookbinding." *House Beautiful* 12 (June 1902): 11-14.

Robinson, Robert V. and Ana-Maria Wahl. "Industrial Employment and Wages of Women, Men and Children in a 19th Century City: Indianapolis, 1850-1880." *American Sociological Review* 55 (December 1990): 912-928.

Rolfe, William James, ed. *Shakespeare's Tragedy of King Lear*. New York: American Book Company, 1908.

Ruskin, John. *Sesame and Lilies*, Rev. and Enlarged. New York: Thomas Y. Crowell, 1871.

_____. *Ruskin's Works, 13 vols*. New York: Clarke, Given, & Hooper, 1895.

Vol. 1: Stones of Venice, I & II, 1895/c. 1858.

Vol. 2: Stones of Venice, III, 1895/c. 1858.

Vol. 7: Laws of Fesole 1895/c. 1894.

_____. *Ruskin Today*, chosen and annotated by Kenneth Clark. London: John Murray, 1964.

Scudder, Vita. *On Journey*. New York: E.P. Dutton, 1937.

Sherman, Claire Richter. "Widening Horizons (1890-1930). Pp. 27-59 in *Women as Interpreters of the Visual Arts, 1820-1979*, edited by Claire Richter Sherman and Adele M. Holcomb. Westport, CT: Greenwood Press, 1981.

Sicherman, Barbara. *Alice Hamilton: A Life in Letters*. Cambridge, MA: Harvard University Press, 1984.

Sklar, Katharine. *Florence Kelley and the Nation's Work*. New Haven, CT: Yale University Press, 1995.

Starr, Eliza Allen . "[Women's Contribution to Catholic History.] " Pp. 79-82 in *The World's Columbian Catholic Congresses and Educational Exhibit*, Vols. 1-3. Chicago, IL: J.S. Hyland & Co., 1893.

Stebner, Eleanor J. *The Women of Hull House: A Study of Spirituality, Vocation, and Friendship*. Albany, NY: State University of New York Press, 1997.

"Stories of Violence of Police are Told" *Day Book* (7 December 1915): 1.

Synge, John Millington. "Riders to the Sea." *Samhaim* (September 1903).

Theodore Parker: Anniversaries of Birth and Death (August 24, 1810-May 10, 1860). Chicago: Unity Publishing, 1911.

Triggs, Oscar Lowell. "A School of Industrial Art." *Craftsman* 3 (January 1903): 215-23.

Twose, George M.R. "The Coffee-Room at Hull House." *House Beautiful* 7 (January 1900): 107-9.

Wahl, Ana-Maria. "Craft Traditions and the Preservation of Male Advantage: Indianapolis, 1850-1890." Masters Thesis, Indiana University, 1989.

Ward, Wilfred. *The Life and Times of Cardinal Wiseman*. London: Longmans, Green and Co., 1894.

_____. *Out of Due Time*; A Novel. London: Longmans, Green and Co., 1906.

Way, W. Irving. "Women and Bookbinding." *House Beautiful* 1 (February 1897): 57-63.

_____. "Women and Bookbinding Again." *House Beautiful* 3 (February 1898): 76-81.

Weber, Max. *The Protestant Ethic and the Spirit of Capitalism*, new intro. by Anthony Giddens, tr. by Talcott Parsons. New York: Charles Scribner's Sons, 1976/1920.

Wilson, Richard Guy. "Chicago and the International Arts and Crafts Movement." Pp. 209-27 in *Chicago Architecture 1872-1922*, ediited by John Zukowsky. Munich, Germany: Prestel-Verlag, 1987.

Wolman, Leo with Eleanor Mack, H.K. Herwitz and Paul Wander. *The Clothing Workers of Chicago, 1910-1922*, edited by Chicago: Amalgamated Clothing Workers of America, 1922/1915.

Wright, Frank Lloyd. "The Art and Craft of the Machine." Pp. 55-73 in *Frank Lloyd Wright: Writings and Buildings*, edited by Edgar Kaufmann and Ben Raeburn. New York: Meridian Books, 1960/1901/c. 1898.

_____. "The Art and Craft of the Machine." Pp. 85-88 in *Eighty Years at Hull-House*, edited by Allen F. Davis and Mary Lynn McCree. 1970/1953/1903.

_____. 1943. *Autobiography* New York: Duell, Sloan and Pearce.

Wyatt, Edith. "The Chicago Clothing Strike. *Harper's Bazaar* (15 December 1915): 556-8.

Zueblin, Charles. "The Chicago Ghetto." Pp. 91-114 in *Hull-House Maps and Papers*, by the Residents of Hull-House. New York: Crowell, 1895.

_____. "The World's First Sociological Laboratory." *American Journal of Sociology* 4 (March 1899): 577-92.

_____. *American Municipal Progress*. New York: Macmillan, 1902.

_____. *A Decade of Civic Development*. Chicago: University of Chicago Press, 1905.

Zueblin, Rho Fisk. "The Pre-Raphaelites: The Beginnings of the Arts and Crafts Movement." *Chautauquan* 36 (October 1902a): 57-61.

_____. "A Survey of the Arts and Crafts Movement in England." *Chautauquan* 36 (November 1902b): 167-73.

_____. "The Art Teachings of the Arts and Crafts Movement." *Chautauquan* 36 (December 1902c): 284-88.

_____. "Economics of the Arts and Crafts Movement." *Chautauquan* 36 (January 1903a): 409-14.

_____. "Continental Tendencies in the Arts and Crafts." *Chautauquan* 36 (February 1903b): 506-13.

_____. "The Production of Industrial Art in America, I." *Chautauquan* 36 (March 1903c): 622-7.

_____. "The Production of Industrial Art in America, II." *Chautauquan* 37 (April 1903d): 59-66.

_____. "The Education of the Producer and the Consumer." *Chautauquan* 37 (May 1903e): 177-82.

_____. "The Patronage of the Arts and Crafts." *Chautauquan* 37 (June 1903f): 266-72.

_____. "Public School Art Societies." *Chautauquan* 38 (October 1903g): 169-72.

_____. "Art Training for Citizenship." *Chautauquan* 39 (April 1904): 49-52.

Dissertation

Boonin-Vail, Martha Clara. *New Wine in Old Bottles: Anglo-Catholicism in the United States, 1840-1919*. Yale University. 1993.

Subject Index

Note: *Italicized* numbers indicate tables.

Abbey of Whitby, 209-210
AIC (Art Institute of Chicago), 3, 6, *13*, 21, 34 n. 10; and CACS, 21; and CPSAS, 18
Adult education, 14, 29-30; and college extension courses at Hull-House, 43-44, 157 n. 9. *See* Education
AFL (American Federation of Labor), 11, 129, 136, 141. *See* CFL
African Americans, 30. *See also* Rice, Harriet
AGWA (Amalgamated Garment Workers of America) 2, 11, 136; and the garment workers' strike of 1915, 129-43, 143 n. 3. *See also* Hillman, Sydney
Anarchism, 11
Anglo Catholic, 28, 34 n. 6, 210, and E.G.Starr, 169-98. *See also* Church of England; Episcopal Church
Apologia, 197
Architecture, and the Cathedral of Amiens, 41, 60, 76; and the Cathedral of Canterbury, 41; and the Cathedral of Rheims, 41, 62; and Lincoln Cathedral, 41; colonial, 64; Gothic, 62; Queen Anne, 64; Verona, of, 41, 66; Venice, of, 41, 66
Art, 29-30: and babies, 54; and Assyria, 59, 61; and democracy, 59-64; and war, 89; defined, 59; history of, 59-64; and labor 65-73; and public schools, 39-42, 45-46, 51, 65; and religious images, 196; and social class, 51; and socialism, 45; as painting, 60; as sculpture, 60; Gothic, 61-62; Greek art, 61; of the people, 66; Renaissance of Handicraft [essay] and, 83-87. *See* Art exhibits; Hull-House

Art and Progress, 26
Art exhibits, 78; at Hull-House, 43-46; of CPSAS, 18; of CACS at AIC, 21: Easter Art Exhibit, 18-19; Woman's Temple, 23
Arts and Crafts movement, 2, 4, 6, 11, 14, 16-26, *3 1*: Chautauqua movement and, 24; Renaissance of Handicraft [essay] and, 83-87
Automation, machine work, 86

BAAC (British Association of Arts and Crafts), 1-2, *4-7*, 17, 19, 23, 26, 83. *See* Ashbee, Charles; Cobdon-Sanderson, T.J.; Morris, William; Ruskin, John
Baptist, 34 n. 6
Beloved Lady, 33
Bakers' Journal, 123
Benedictine Order, 2, 16, 178-80, 188, 194, 214 n. 9; monastery of, 213 n. 2
Bookbinding, 1, 23, 24, 32, 79-8 1; and women, *22*; French, 106; Handicraft of [Article I, 89-93; Handicraft of [Article II], 95-98; Handicraft of [Article III], 99-103; Handicraft of [Article IV], 105-13; process of and terminology, 89-113

CACS (Chicago Arts and Crafts Society), 1-2, *12*, 14, 26, 34 ns. 12, 13; (AIC) and, 21; beginnings of, 18-19; Chautauqua movement and, 24; Frank Lloyd Wright and, 20-21, 26; *House Beautiful, The Craftsman*, and, 21, 22, 26. *See* Art exhibits. Hull-House
Chautauqua, 24. *See Chautauquan*

231

Name Index

Abbott, Edith, 32, 34, 130, 133 n. 4; and Sophonisba P. Breckinridge, 34 n. 8. *See* Breckinridge, Sophonisba P.

Abbott, Grace, 32

Abt, Jacob, 130

Adams, John Quincy, *25*

Addams, Jane, 1-11, *8, 13,* 15, 16, 24, 27-33, 58 n.1, 199 n. 4; and C. Ashbee, 5; and arts and crafts movement, 6, *25*; and BAAC, 6; and C.S. Barnett, 5; and CACS, 20, *22,* 35 n. 16; death of, 16-17; dress of, 10; and Henrici strike, 121; and Lincoln Statue, 41 n. 3; and T. Parker, 198 n. 2; and Pullman Strike, 41 n. 3; and Nobel Peace Prize, 1, 33; biography, 4; concepts of, 4-5; conversion experience, 4-5; intellectual and interpersonal influences in writings of, 31-32; Starr as professional colleague of, 30-31; *The Second Twenty Years at Hull-House,* 28, 35 n. 19; *Twenty Years at Hull-House,* xxii, 27-28. *See also* Hull-House; Starr, Ellen Gates and Jane Addams

Alden, Percy, Fabian, 49; lecture on "The London County Council," 49

Allen, Caleb, 159

Allen, Ethan, 118, 159

Allen, George, 160, 162, 169-70; conversion to Roman Catholicism, 160, 169

Allen, Lovina, 159

Ambrose, St., 207-208

Ames, Joseph, 160

American, Sadie, *22*

Anderson, Mary, *22,* 26; and the Children's Bureau, 26

Angelico, Fra, 40

Anthony, Susan B., "Woman's Suffrage", 49

Aquinas, St. Thomas, 198

Arnold, Charles C., 58 n. 1

Argyll, Duke of, 212, 214 n. 11

Ashbee, Charles, 1, 5, *8,* 23, 31; and AIC, 6; and BAAC, 5; CACS, 6, 23; and Hull-House, 6, 34 n. 12, 35 n. 16, 156 n. 4; and J. Ruskin, 5; and W. Morris, 5; and F.L. Wright, 34 n. 12

Athanasius, St. 181, 199 n. 14

Augustine, St., 198, 208

Baber, Zonia, 23

Baldwin, judge in Henrici Strike, 123

Balisdell, Mary, 2

Barnett, Samuel [Canon], 5, 31. *See* Toynbee Hall

Barnes, Clifford W. 58 n. 1

Barnum, Gertrude, 58 n.1

Bartlett, Caroline, *22*

Batiffol, Pierre, 202

Bebel, August, 193

Bede, St., 213 n. 3

Benedict, St., 178

Benedict, Enella, 58 n. 1

Benson, Robert Hugh [Father], 173, 175, 177, 188, 197

Boniface [Abbot], 178

Booth, Charles, 6, 15, 31; *The Life and Labour of the People of London,* 6, 11

Bosanquet, Bernard, *8*

Boswell, James, 159

Bowen, Louise deKoven (Mrs. Joseph T.), 32, 121

Bradley, Charles F., lecture on "Socrates," 50

Breckinridge. Sophonisba, 34, 125-127